PRACTICAL GUIDE TO QL GRAPHICS AND SOUND

WORKING WITH THE SINCLAIR QL

General Editor: Roy Atherton

The Sinclair QL and its suite of four programs has far more to offer than any other micro. The software – comprising word processing, spreadsheet, business graphics and database management – is both far more capable and infinitely more simple to use owing to the extraordinary power of the QL and its clear and well structured super-language, SuperBASIC. PSION have greatly enhanced the software since its original launch and these new developments are incorporated in this up-to-the-minute series.

The authors of this series, all experts in their field, are experienced teachers of the non-specialist. Consequently, the books are well paced and practical in approach, with many worked examples and exercises. In an imaginative, friendly way they will enable you to handle the QL's high capability programs with competence.

Good Programming with QL SuperBASIC *Roy Atherton*
Word Processing with QL Quill *David Dempster*
Managing Data with QL Archive *Albert Russell*
Practical Guide to QL Graphics and Sound *Alan Shinwell*
Calculating with QL Abacus *Malcolm Smith*

WORKING WITH THE SINCLAIR QL

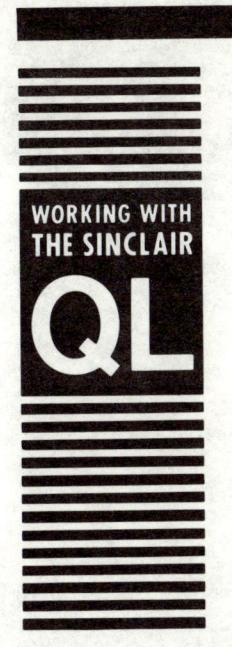

PRACTICAL GUIDE TO QL GRAPHICS AND SOUND

ALAN SHINWELL

LONGMAN
LONDON

Longman Group Limited
Longman House, Burnt Mill, Harlow
Essex CM20 2JE, England
Associated companies throughout the world

© Longman Group Limited 1985

All rights reserved; no part of this publication may be reproduced, stored in a retrieval system, or transmitted in any form or by any means, electronic, mechanical, photocopying, recording, or otherwise, without the prior written permission of the Publishers.

First published 1985

Sinclair is a registered trademark

British Library Cataloguing in Publication Data

Shinwell, Alan
   Practical guide to QL graphics and sound.—
   (Working with the Sinclair QL)
   1. Computer graphics   2. Sinclair QL
   (Computer)—Programming
   I. Title   II. Series
   001.64'43   T385

ISBN 0-582-29664-1

Library of Congress Cataloging in Publication Data

Shinwell, Alan, 1944–
   Practical guide to QL graphics and sound.

   Includes index.
   1. Computer graphics.   2. Sinclair QL (Computer)—
Programming.   I. Title.
T385.S44   1984   001.64'43   84-12238
ISBN 0-582-29664-1

Set in 9½/11pt Lasercomp Univers
Printed in Great Britain by The Bath Press, Avon

CONTENTS

Preface viii

How to use this book x

1. **First things first** 1
   Introduction 1
   Reset 1
   Microdrives 2
   Television or monitor? 3
   QL resolution 6
   Screen formats 8
   Presentation standards 12
   Your first graphics program 13

2. **Colour and contrast** 15
   Introduction 15
   Colour principles 15
   Mode selection 17
   Colour selection 17
   PAPER 18
   CLS 18
   INK 19
   BORDER 20
   The stipple effect 21
   FLASH 26
   STRIP 27
   OVER 28
   Stipple with other keywords 29
   RECOL 30

3. **Window watching 32**
   Introduction 32
   Pixel co-ordinates 32
   Window creation 33
   WINDOW 39
   BLOCK 39
   SCROLL 46
   PAN 49

4. **Points, lines and curves 52**
   Introduction 52
   Graphics co-ordinate system 52
   LINE 54
   SCALE 57
   POINT 65
   ARC 72
   CIRCLE 80
   ELLIPSE 84
   Relative co-ordinates 87
   FILL 91

5. **Character studies 101**
   Introduction 101
   Character size 101
   Character positioning 103
   UNDER 110
   Character movement 111
   Character generation 112

6. **Turn Turtle 121**
   Introduction 121
   Pen control 122
   Direction control 122
   Movement 123
   Direct command application 124
   Expanding turtle graphics 125
   QL turtle-talk 131
   Pattern generation 133

7. **EASEL: Basic concepts 136**
   Introduction 136
   EASEL outline 137
   EASEL back-up 139
   Loading EASEL 140
   Main display 142

Editing facilities 152
Graph data deletion 156
EASEL exit 156

8. **EASEL: More advanced facilities 158**
Introduction 158
Multiple graphs 158
Graph design 166
Graph storage and transfer 184

9. **A sound at the end 192**
Introduction 192
BEEPING 193
BEEP 193
Sound selection program 205

Appendix 1. RGB pin connections 210

Appendix 2. Binary numbers and all that 211

Appendix 3. Colour palette tables 215

Appendix 4. Sine curve generation 217

Solutions to problems 219

Index 227

PREFACE

A preface tends not to be read . . . prospective purchasers browse through the body of the book and many owners leap into the first chapter. However, now that you have started please read on.

The opportunity to write one of a new series of books on the Sinclair QL was something I accepted with great enthusiasm. Having spent many years producing technical training notes, which once briefly read were probably discarded, the thought of creating something more permanent for an innovative computer was very attractive.

I have endeavoured to structure the contents so that both the newcomer to graphics (and indeed to computing) and the more experienced reader will be able to work to their own depth. And there is plenty of choice. Containing over 160 program examples, the book is designed to involve the reader in discovering the facilities provided by QL graphics. Every program is a working program checked on a current production QL (Version AH), its listing then being transferred to a printer. It is that printed copy the reader will find in the book and so can use it with a high degree of confidence.

The objective has never been to show off fancy programming; few readers learn this way. So although some knowledge of SuperBASIC is assumed, most examples use deliberately simple programming techniques which should be easily understood. Armed with an appreciation of the techniques and principles described in the following chapters, the reader can feel confident of taking steps beyond the bounds of the book to develop his or her own creative skills to the full.

The preface would be incomplete without acknowledgements to Roy Atherton for giving me the opportunity to write the book, to David Dempster who first suggested it, and to Neil Hopkins for his generosity in allowing me access to his Kaga KP-910 printer on which all the programs and EASEL graphs were excellently printed.

Most of all I pay tribute to my wife Chris who not only meticulously typed the manuscript, tolerating as she did so the many amendments necessary to ensure all the content was compatible with current SuperBASIC, but also gave me continued support and encouragement throughout.

Alan Shinwell
Hampshire 1984.

HOW TO USE THIS BOOK

If you are a beginner to computer graphics you may appreciate a few ideas on how to obtain the best from this book. If more experienced, then roam through it as you wish.

CHAPTER 1

This is a very important chapter since it introduces a number of QL-related concepts such as microdrive usage, resolution, pixels and display modes. In particular it provides necessary information concerning the choice between a monitor and a television.

CHAPTERS 2 TO 6

Here you will find all the graphics keywords and principles explained with the continual aid of short programs which are an essential part of the description. Type in the programs, run them and try to work out what they are doing. Only in this way will you really understand the principles involved. At times you will find slightly more advanced techniques explained, which generally aim to help reduce the often tedious trial and error methods needed to fit a picture onto the screen. If you find these too complicated at a first reading, move on to the next keyword and when you feel more proficient and confident, return to re-examine them.

Mathematics can be largely avoided in programming, but where formulae have been used they have been presented to allow easy application by those with little inclination towards the subject.

CHAPTERS 7 AND 8

The software package EASEL has two chapters devoted to it. Again very practically oriented, the many sequences and facilities available are explored with examples for you to try.

CHAPTER 9

Last but not least you are shown how to add sound to your graphics, from musical notes to buzzes and zaps! In particular the longest program in the book gives you the ability to easily investigate all possible combinations of values used to create sound. It also demonstrates quite a number of the graphics facilities explained in the rest of the book.

PROBLEMS

At the end of most chapters you will find some problems to help you assess your progress. Re-read earlier material if you are unsure how to proceed, but if you become really stuck, look up the solution at the end of the book, then work out how your own attempt may be altered to produce the desired effect.

Finally, I sincerely hope you enjoy reading and using this book as much as I have enjoyed creating it.

For Mark Ross

CHAPTER 1
FIRST THINGS FIRST

INTRODUCTION

One of the excitements of graphics programming is finding out for yourself. The creative instinct lies within many of us and in programming it often surfaces very rapidly when stimulated by the abundance of visual effects available.

However, a sound basic knowledge of what *is* available will enable more rewarding work and avoid unnecessary disappointment, time-wasting and mistakes. It is intended to provide these essentials in the following chapters but, before flying headlong into QL graphics, we must consider a few important preliminaries first.

RESET

I am sure that you will want to experiment with many of the ideas and examples ahead. I am also quite sure you will make some mistakes! Do not forget that if you wish to clear everything out of the computer's memory so that you can start again, all you need to do is press and release the small RESET button located on the right-hand side panel of the QL. Do make sure that the microdrive cartridges are removed first.

PROGRAM INTERRUPTION

Sometimes you may want to stop a program that is going around in a continuous loop (deliberately or accidentally), or stop a program before it finishes. This can be achieved by holding down the CTRL key and pressing the SPACE bar. If no alteration is made to the program it may be restarted from where it stopped by typing: CONTINUE then pressing the ENTER key. Unlike RESET, this 'break' action only interrupts the program; it does not clear it out of memory.

Should you make any modifications to the program it will have to be restarted, from the beginning this time, by typing: RUN and pressing the ENTER key.

MICRODRIVES

If you are riding down a hill on a bicycle and suddenly have to stop, you certainly do not use the front brake only. If you did, then you would soon be investigating the quality of the road surface at close range. All devices involving movement require us to know the correct way of operating them. The microdrives are no exception. Disobey the rules and its 'one down, three to go'!

The microdrive and its cartridges are precision-engineered devices and must be looked after carefully. To prevent any unfortunate accidents, remember the following rules:

- **Do not** turn the QL on or off with cartridges in place.
- **Do not** attempt to remove a cartridge with the microdrive's corresponding red indicator light on.
- **Remove** all cartridges from the microdrives before pressing the RESET button.
- **Never** touch the tape with your fingers. Should a tape loop develop at the side or front (drive side) of the cartridge, gently ease it back into the cartridge using a non-metallic, dust-free item such as a plastic pen cap clip.
- **Never** move the QL when cartridges are installed.
- **Never** touch an installed cartridge when the microdrive is running.
- **Always** return the cartridges to their plastic sleeves when not in use.
- **Take care** when inserting or removing the cartridges. Do it slowly and carefully, and ensure that they are firmly installed within the microdrive before starting a read or write operation.
- **Do not** forget that when inserting a cartridge into a microdrive, the side with exposed tape must be to the left.

Tape

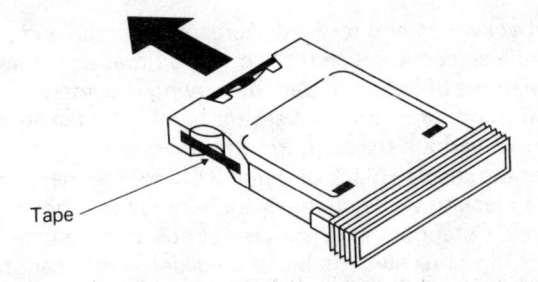

TELEVISION OR MONITOR?

Computer manufacturers are often criticised for misleading advertising, many deliberately relying on the technical ignorance of their customers. There is one particular area in which very little is said but it can make all the difference to the enjoyment of a new computer by its owner. This concerns the use of either a colour television or monitor with the computer. We all know what a television is, but what is a monitor?

Essentially a monitor is a television specially designed to reproduce information supplied by a direct cable connection from the transmitting device, in this instance from a computer. This is entirely different from most normal televisions which are *not* designed to accurately reproduce signals received from a computer. Why? It is all to do with something called **resolution**.

RESOLUTION

Let us consider the basic operation of a black and white television. A narrow beam of particles (**electrons**) are fired from a **gun** inside the tube at a special coating on the screen that emits light when hit by the electrons. The electron

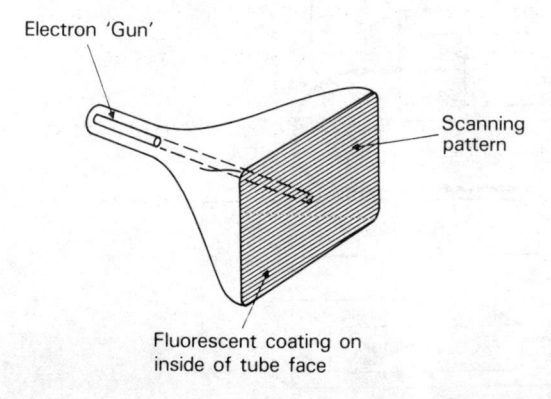

Electron 'Gun'

Scanning pattern

Fluorescent coating on inside of tube face

spot is moved very rapidly backwards and forwards across the screen and from top to bottom. The whole screen is covered twenty-five times a second. The picture is created as variations of light and dark by varying the intensity of the beam. It can either be off or on, or it can be at several levels of intensity in between to give black, white or various shades of grey at the screen.

A computer may only want to display black or white with no intermediate shades. Unfortunately, since black to white changes are infrequent in normal transmitted television pictures, a standard television is not designed to cater for such continuous rapid switching of its electron beam. The electronics cannot keep up and the required rapid switching between black and white takes longer, resulting in blurred edges at the black and white boundaries.

The more characters a computer attempts to display across the screen, the more rapid the switching must be and the higher the resolution of the television must be to reproduce it faithfully. Many computer owners have been disappointed when attempting to display eighty columns of characters across a normal television screen. The characters are too blurred to allow comfortable viewing.

MODULATION AND DEMODULATION

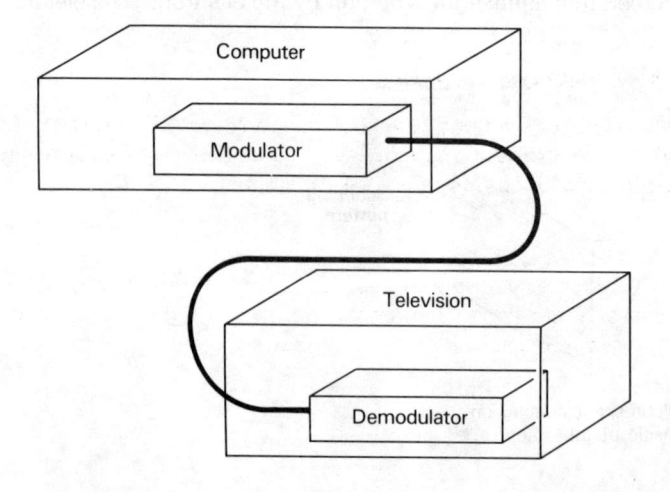

A further loss of definition occurs when a computer is coupled to a normal television via the aerial socket. When a transmitted signal received by the aerial is passed to the television it must be converted, through a device known as a **demodulator**, from its transmitted form to a form acceptable to the rest of the electronics. So the computer must trick the demodulator into thinking that its signal has also come from an aerial. To do this the signal is converted to the transmitted form by a device known as a **modulator**. When the computer's *modulated* signal is received by the television, it is *demodulated* back again. It is a bit like taking a photograph of a picture then asking an artist to paint a picture from the photograph. Definition losses inevitably occur.

Colour televisions are also subject to the same problems but in some areas they can be worse. For example, the switching speed limitation can result in not just blurred boundaries, but a miscellaneous mixture of colours at those boundaries. This is even more distracting. The problem is further compounded by limitations of the physical size of the 'dots' of colour-generating coating (*phosphor*). These are part of a more complex physical assembly at the front of the screen than is found in a black-and-white tube.

So what is the solution? There are two. Display fewer characters across the screen and allow the television to work within its capability, or use a television specially designed to switch at these higher speeds . . . a MONITOR.

MONITORS

There are monitors and monitors, some better than others. How do we choose? Generally, the better the resolution the higher the price. A reasonable means of assessing their capability is by comparing **bandwidths**. There is no need to go into technical details other than to say that bandwidth is normally specified in millions of cycles abbreviated to MHz (megahertz). The higher the number the better the resolution. But this only relates to the switching speed of the electronics. A colour tube of better quality than the average television is also necessary if 80 characters per line are to be clearly displayed.

Many monitors are advertised as being of low/medium/high resolution. Reputable suppliers will be able to give you the relevant bandwidths and the phosphor dot sizes. Generally the smaller the dot the better.

For the QL, any monitor with a bandwidth of 10 MHz or over should be quite acceptable. By comparison, a good quality television will only have a bandwidth of about 6 MHz. If in doubt about the quality of a monitor, see if you can have it demonstrated with your computer.

TELEVISON/MONITOR SIGNALS

At the rear of the QL you will find two sockets labelled RGB and UHF. These are the connectors for monitor and television respectively. The sockets are very different since they produce different types of signals.

UHF

The UHF socket provides a modulated signal suitable for feeding directly into the aerial socket of a television. Remember to turn down the volume control, as the QL does not provide a sound signal.

RGB

This stands for red, green, blue and is the socket which supplies the signals needed by a colour monitor. The socket also can supply a single black and white (composite monochrome) video signal. This can be used to drive a monochrome monitor or alternatively will produce a monochrome picture on some of the colour televisions which are now manufactured with a composite video input. This type of signal is fed into the television after the demodulator and is therefore of a slightly better quality than the conventional modulated aerial input.

However, the RGB signals feeding a colour monitor are the 'purest' signals to use and will produce excellent quality on a good monitor. We shall talk more about RGB in the next chapter, when we discuss colour generation on the QL.

For those who require the technical information to wire up suitable connectors, the table and diagrams in Appendix 1 should help.

The connector for the monitor will depend on the make chosen. While there is a generally accepted industry standard for the monochrome video, there is not one for the colour monitor. Sometimes a suitable connector is supplied with the monitor.

QL RESOLUTION

We have talked at length about television resolution, so now let us take a look at the resolution requirements of the QL. But first, resolution and computers are very rarely discussed without a mention of that delightful little word **pixel**. What is it?

PIXEL

A pixel is the name given to the smallest single area of illumination that can be displayed by a computer on a screen. As far as colour televisions or colour monitors are concerned, a pixel identifies the smallest area of pure colour that can be displayed. The greater the number of pixels in a given area then the better the quality of the picture, rather like the dots of a newspaper photograph.

Resolution is often defined as so many pixels across and down the screen. Naturally, the more pixels there are the higher the resolution of the television must be in order to display them as individual areas.

To return to resolution, the QL provides two selectable resolutions called MODE 8 and MODE 4.

- MODE 8 will give a resolution of 256 pixels across and 256 pixels down the screen.

- MODE 4 will give a resolution of 512 pixels across and 256 pixels down the screen.

Now, we mentioned earlier that bandwidth can help us to decide about the resolution of televisions and monitors. It is possible to relate pixels to bandwidth, about 60 pixels for each 1 MHz. So a television with a bandwidth of 6 MHz could only resolve about 300 pixels across the screen. This means that only MODE 8 is really suitable for viewing on a television. MODE 4 at 512 pixels across the screen would not be displayed so clearly.

If you feel you want to make full use of MODE 4, the high resolution mode, then a monitor provides the best solution.

SCREEN CHARACTERS

Characters on the screen are made from groups of pixels, therefore the more pixels across a screen, the more characters can be displayed. While it is possible to select different character sizes, the normal format will give:

MODE 8   40 characters per line

MODE 4   80 characters per line

One very useful facility provided within the four PSION software packages QUILL, ABACUS, ARCHIVE and EASEL allows you to select 40, 64 or 80 characters across the screen. You can therefore select the best resolution for the television or monitor you are using.

In all modes the normal format will allow a maximum of 25 rows of characters down the screen.

PIXEL SIZE

A pixel may be the smallest area of colour selectable by a particular computer, but just how small is it? If resolution is given as so many pixels across a screen, then the size of a pixel must depend on the size of the screen.

It is often not appreciated that a large television screen should be viewed from a correspondingly greater distance than when viewing a small screen. So although the physical size of a pixel will increase with increasing screen size, the relative size, when viewed from the correct distance, will remain approximately the same. When watching television programmes, a 12-inch screen should be viewed from about 1 metre, a 22-inch screen from about 2.5 metres. When using a television with a computer, you can reduce the distance by just over one-third to approximately 60 cm for a 12-inch, 160 cm for a 22-inch screen. If you sit too close you will effectively lose definition and, more seriously, you may strain your eyes.

TELEVISION PICTURE SIZE

It is appropriate at this stage to point out one discrepancy that exists between the output signal produced by the QL and the resultant picture size on the television screen. The QL output is slightly larger in that a portion of the top and left-hand side of the picture is not visible. You are not, however, aware of this since the QL automatically displays the default low-resolution screen area with a border around it. It does mean, however, that you cannot display a full 512 pixels across the screen if you try to work in MODE 4. Extra width, though still not the full 512 pixels, can be obtained by removing the border. This will be explained in Chapter 2.

SCREEN FORMATS

If you have already purchased a QL then you are sure to have tried it out before reading this far! You should by now be aware of the different screen layouts you can obtain after switching it on. Therefore this section is mainly directed at those who have not yet had access to a QL.

When a QL is connected to either a television or a monitor, turned on and the picture correctly tuned-in and adjusted, you will see a black screen with the following display:

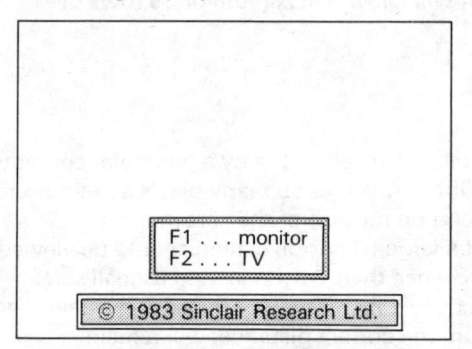

```
F1 . . . monitor
F2 . . . TV

© 1983 Sinclair Research Ltd.
```

The same picture will be obtained should you press the RESET button at any time.

You have a choice to make which at first sight is simply the answer to, 'Is the QL connected to a television or a monitor?' But the selection can be made independent of the display device fitted. There is no 'switch' inside the QL that will, for instance, disconnect the signal to a monitor if the F2 key is pressed. Having already talked about televisions and monitors it should be clear that selecting the monitor facility while feeding a television is not going to give particularly good definition. It is quite acceptable, though, to select F2, i.e. low resolution, for display on a monitor. There is a further advantage in this mode as we shall explain in a moment.

Having made the selection by pressing the F1 or F2 key, one of two possible displays will appear. But first we must introduce one important item common to both modes.

CURSOR

When the QL is able to accept your instructions, in other words when it is not busy executing a program, a small flashing rectangle will be displayed at the top left-hand side of the bottom section of the screen in either mode. This is the **cursor** and represents the position at which any information sent to that section of screen will begin. As each character is typed on the keyboard you will observe the cursor moving ahead of each new character. Pressing the ENTER key after typing an instruction will cause the cursor to re-position itself at the start of the next line. The cursor is always the clue to the state of the QL. When the cursor is not visible then the QL is busy, either running a program or perhaps stuck in either a deliberate or unintentional loop!

You will notice that the cursor is a different size in the two modes since it is related to the actual character size initially set by the QL. Just to emphasise the two modes, the cursor colour is also different. It is magenta in low-resolution mode and red in high-resolution mode.

MONITOR MODE (HIGH RESOLUTION)

On pressing the F1 key the screen will clear to display three areas of colour as indicated below:

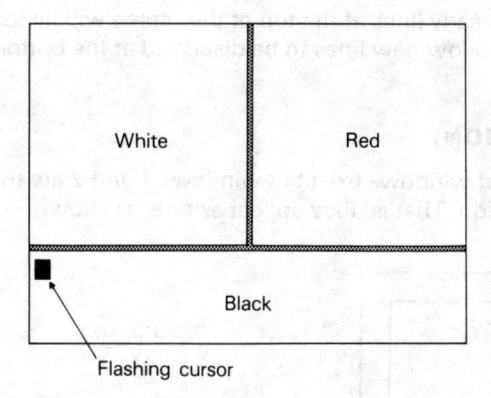

```
+---------------------+---------------------+
|                     |                     |
|                     |                     |
|       White         |        Red          |
|                     |                     |
|                     |                     |
+---------------------+---------------------+
|                                           |
|■                    Black                 |
|                                           |
+-------------------------------------------+
 ↖ Flashing cursor
```

The border colour between the areas appears grey but is actually a pixel-sized chequer-board pattern of black and white. This rather interesting effect will be explained in Chapter 2.

Each area on the screen is called a **window** and you will become much more familiar with this term in Chapter 3. It is sufficient to say that we are able to adjust the size and position of any window if required. This screen, and the one obtained in low resolution mode, is called a **default** screen. The word 'default' means any condition or value that is initially set up by the QL yet is capable of being altered at a later stage.

Each window has a purpose. We shall give each window a number for ease of reference:

Top left-hand (white) 2
Top right-hand (red) 1
Bottom (black) 0

Window 0 is used to display, in green, your instructions to the computer, either in program mode (each instruction preceded by a line number) or in direct command mode where the instruction is immediately obeyed on pressing ENTER. It also is used by the QL to display any error messages.

Window 1 is used for any program-generated display. For example, if we type in: PRINT "FRED" and press the ENTER key, then *FRED* will appear at the top left-hand side of the window, in white letters.

The use of window 2 will be revealed when the following is entered:

```
10 PRINT "HELLO"
20 PRINT "THIS IS MY PROGRAM"
```

Entering each instruction, now in program mode, will cause a copy of each, including the line number, to appear in red, starting at the top of the window. This is our program listing area. At any time when our program is not running, we are able to check all or selected parts of it by using the SuperBASIC keyword LIST. The lines (statements) selected will appear in window 2. If too many lines are selected then the early lines at the top of the screen will be lost as the listing scrolls upwards to allow new lines to be displayed at the bottom.

TV MODE (LOW RESOLUTION)

In this mode the same number of windows exist but windows 1 and 2 are the same size and in the same position. That is, they appear as one, as shown below:

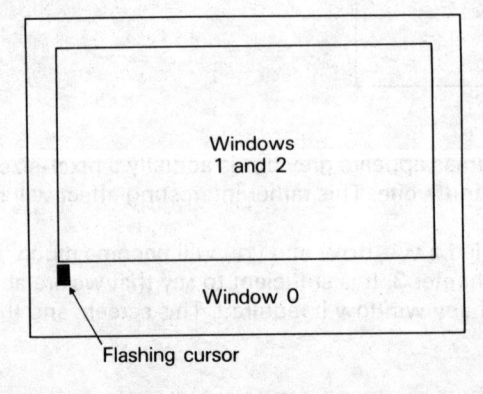

```
┌─────────────────────────────┐
│                             │
│                             │
│                             │
│         Windows             │
│         1 and 2             │
│                             │
│                             │
│ ▪                           │
│  \      Window 0            │
└───\─────────────────────────┘
     Flashing cursor
```

Since low-resolution mode uses larger characters, it is sensible to provide more space for your program display area and also for any listing that is required. Whether a program is running or a listing is requested, the QL will select the appropriate window to be displayed.

The windows are surrounded by a black border to take into account the inevitable loss of definition around the edges of most television screens. A further difference from the high-resolution mode is that when the very first instruction is entered into the QL, window 2 (for listing) appears with a blue background and white text. Running your program (if it invokes no colour changes) will cause the display window to appear with white information on a red background.

SCREEN/MODE COMBINATIONS

We have already mentioned that either mode can be used with a television or a monitor. This provides us with the following alternative selections.

Monitor & F2

When connected to a monitor the F2 key is selected to give the low-resolution default screen. By typing: MODE 4 (or MODE 512) the QL is now in high-resolution mode identified on the screen by the smaller red cursor. However, if a program has already been run in low-resolution mode, and a mode change made, the program is still intact in memory and can be run again. If no mode change (MODE 8) is specified in the program, then it will run with its graphics displayed in high resolution. The larger windows 1 and 2 are still present, and the default colours for window 1 are unchanged. The listing window, though, remains with a black background and white text.

This operation, then, has effectively doubled the width of the default-program area window and can be selected without the need to alter window sizes within a program.

Television & F1

When connected to a television, the F1 key is pressed to obtain a high-resolution display. Type in: MODE 8 (or MODE 256) and the high-resolution display format will remain but the QL is in low-resolution mode. True, windows 1 and 2 are smaller, but if you require two side-by-side this is an easy way to achieve them.

F1, F2 and microdrives

It is worth pointing out that after the F1 or F2 keys have been pressed, the red indicator associated with microdrive 1 will light for a short while. This is caused by the QL looking for a program to load immediately. It is important to remember that cartridges should not be placed in microdrive 1 before the F1 or F2 selection has been made, unless this initial loading is required.

WINDOW IDENTIFICATION

The final point in this section relates to window identification. As was said earlier, you will be shown how to alter windows in a later chapter. However, it is worth mentioning how windows are identified since this is necessary if we are to select them within our programs. They are identified by using what are termed **channel** numbers. The three windows we have been discussing possess default channel numbers of 0, 1 and 2. Our earlier referencing was quite deliberate, as you can now see. The QL will always treat these channel numbers and their associated windows (irrespective of size or position) in the same way as previously explained. Similarly, if we wish to use these channels in the same way (e.g. output our display to window channel number 1) then since they are default channels, we do not need to include their identification in our relevant instructions. Channel numbers and their selection will be discussed in Chapter 3.

PRESENTATION STANDARDS

Throughout the book you will be able to observe the various graphics facilities of the QL by typing in small programs. All the examples will be written to the same simple standard as follows:

1. All keywords and commands will be in capital or part-capital letters, but they do not need to be typed as capitals. The capitals indicate the minimum number of letters to be typed to represent the keyword or command required.
2. All identifiers and variables will be printed in small letters.
3. Any program or example for you to type will be displayed in a distinctive printer style.
4. The ENTER key will be symbolised by ENTER in the EASEL chapters 7 and 8.
5. Indenting will be used to increase readability.

PROGRAM NAMES

Many of the program examples in the following chapters will have an opening REMark statement to give each program an appropriate title. Should you wish to save any of them on a microdrive cartridge then the names could be used as file names. Conversely, if you are simply typing in the program with no intention of storing it, then the REMark line can be omitted.

Also, the MODE statement can be omitted if the QL is already set to the specified mode before running the program. Where a program omits a mode selection then it can be assumed to be optional. In this instance set up either mode as you wish, but do use the larger (MODE 8) type of program display window.

LINE NUMBERS

SuperBASIC provides us with an automatic line-numbering facility whereby typing AUTO will automatically display line numbers starting at 100 and incrementing in units of ten each time a statement is entered. This saves having to type them yourself and has been used for most of the programs in this book. Do remember to press CTRL and the SPACE bar to break out from the AUTO system when you have entered your last statement.

UNEXPLAINED KEYWORDS

There may be occasions when, for the sake of an interesting example program, we may include a SuperBASIC graphics keyword that has not yet been explained. Do not worry. Type the program, run it and make sure you understand the operation of the current facility being discussed. Any unexplained keywords will be made clear later on.

YOUR FIRST GRAPHICS PROGRAM

Just so that you can appreciate the size of a pixel on your television (or monitor), type the following program. Remember, do not worry about the keyword meanings at this stage.

```
100 REMark * pixel dots *
110 MODE 8
120 INK 2 : PAPER 7 : CLS
130 FOR across = 0 TO 165 STEP 2
140    POINT across,50
150 END FOR across
```

Type RUN and you should observe a central horizontal line of red dots, each a single pixel, on a white screen.

If you would like to see the same display, but in high resolution mode (MODE 4), edit your program by replacing line 110 with MODE 4.

The differences between the two displays will give you some idea of the resolution capability of your set.

Finally, remember to type NEW after each example program before you type in the next.

PROBLEMS

We cannot let you leave Chapter 1 without presenting a few questions for you to check your progress. Answers to these and to further problems are to be found on p. 219 onwards.

1. What happens to your program if you press the RESET button?
2. What key do you press to select MODE 8 on first switching on the QL?
3. Which part of the screen displays a list of your program instructions when in high-resolution mode?
4. Find the incorrect statement(s):
   a) A microdrive cartridge can only be removed when its associated red light is on.
   b) Always remove all cartridges before pressing RESET.
   c) Ensure that cartridges are rapidly inserted into their microdrives.
5. Does the modulation/demodulation process between a computer and a television:
   a) improve the picture quality?
   b) have no effect on the picture quality?
   c) degrade the picture quality?
6. Which socket at the rear of the QL do you use to connect to a monitor?
7. What is a pixel?
8. How many pixels are there across the screen in high-resolution mode?
9. How many normal-sized characters can the QL display across a screen in low-resolution mode?
10. Why must you not sit too close to a television when using a computer?

CHAPTER 2
COLOUR AND CONTRAST

MODE, PAPER, CLS, INK, BORDER, FLASH, STRIP, OVER, RECOL

INTRODUCTION

This and the following four chapters will be used to individually describe the various graphics facilities of the QL, excluding QL EASEL, which is treated separately.

It must be realised, of course, that it is not the intention of this book to teach you every aspect of SuperBASIC, but naturally all the graphics-related keywords will be fully explained. If you are not an experienced programmer do try all the example programs shown, as they are aimed specifically at helping you to understand the facility being described.

COLOUR PRINCIPLES

No, not a lot of theory, just an attempt to give you a simple appreciation of the principles of colour generation which will help your understanding of QL colour.

At some time in our lives we must all have mixed up different coloured paints and discovered that from red, yellow and blue we could make all other colours. These three are known as the primary colours since they cannot be created by mixing any other colours. However, if you mix coloured lights very different results are obtained. The primary colours in light rays are red, blue and green. If you shine white light through separate filters of these colours then a white image will be formed where they all overlap, while other colours (the secondary colours) will be found where just two overlap. The secondary colours are produced as follows:

    Red + Blue = Magenta
    Red + Green = Yellow
    Blue + Green = Cyan

You recall that the QL has an RGB output to feed a colour monitor. Well, the three colour signals (red, green and blue) end up controlling three separate 'guns', each producing an electron beam inside the monitor's tube. Each causes the illumination of a red, green or blue fluorescent spot on the screen. The spots are in groups of three and each will glow in its respective colour at a brightness depending upon the intensity of the electron beam. The spots are too small for us to see at normal viewing distances, our eyes seeing the resultant colour produced by the combination of the three primary colours in each group.

The UHF output to a standard television still transmits the same RGB information, but it is contained within a single signal which the television itself must split up into the red, green and blue components.

The QL, in supplying the RGB signals – whether to a monitor or a television – will switch them off or on with no intermediate intensities being available. This results in a range of primary and secondary colours only, plus white (all signals on) and black (all signals off). There is, though, a further modification to the QL colour range.

MODES AND COLOURS

One thing that must be made quite clear is that the two resolution modes of the QL do not have the same range of solid colour. By 'solid' we mean that all the pixels in a given coloured area will be of the same colour. It has become an accepted fact that generally on home and small business computers, the higher the resolution, the fewer the colours available. The mode/colour relationship is as follows:

MODE 8: Black   MODE 4: Black
        Blue   Red
        Red   Green
        Magenta   White
        Green
        Cyan
        Yellow
        White

You can now see the relevance of '8' and '4'.

The following program demonstrates the colour range in MODE 8. It can be used as a 'test card' to set the colour controls on your television to your own taste.

```
100 REMark * MODE 8 colour *
110 MODE 8 : PAPER 7 : CLS
120 LET increment = 0
130 FOR colour = 0 TO 7
140    BLOCK 256,25,0,increment,colour
150    LET increment = increment + 25
160 END FOR colour
```

The program should display eight horizontal bands of colour including white and black.

But the QL is rather more sophisticated than others in its high resolution mode, and even though the number of solid colours available has been reduced, the high resolution combined with a new 'stipple' feature allows more colours to be generated. We will look at this a little later.

MODE SELECTION

You can switch from one resolution to the other at any time in your program, and there are two very obvious ways of typing the instruction – so there is definitely no excuse for selecting the wrong mode!

MODE 8   low resolution
MODE 256   (8 colours, 256 pixels)

MODE 4   high resolution
MODE 512   (4 colours, 512 pixels)

When the MODE keyword is executed by the QL the entire screen will be cleared, allowing your program to start afresh in the new mode selected.

COLOUR SELECTION

The selection of colour is quite simple. Each colour has a number (a code) allocated to it. We combine the code with the keyword that requires a colour to be specified.

CODE	MODE 8	MODE 4
0	Black	Black
1	Blue	Black
2	Red	Red
3	Magenta	Red
4	Green	Green
5	Cyan	Green
6	Yellow	White
7	White	White

Note the duplication of code numbers in the high-resolution mode. Either number may be used.

We are now going to take a look at the keywords that use these codes. Many of the names used have been specially chosen to indicate their operation. Sinclair Spectrum users will already be familiar with some, such as PAPER, INK and BORDER.

PAPER

This keyword defines the colour to be used all over the current writing area. In this chapter you can assume we mean the whole screen. It is just like choosing coloured paper to write on. The keyword is followed by a colour code number or its variable name. For example:

PAPER 4

This will define the background colour as green (in both modes). In a program, we could have written:

LET colour = 6

We could then define the background by writing:

PAPER colour

This allows you to change the colour within, for example, a FOR . . . END FOR loop by setting the loop variable to *colour*.

We have deliberately used the word 'defines' and not 'produces' when explaining PAPER. If you typed PAPER 4 with no statement line number (i.e. a direct command), no difference would be seen. The keyword must be followed by another which has some control over the background. We shall be considering these later on, but the simplest to look at, at the moment, is the standard CLS (clear screen) keyword.

CLS

Used on its own, CLS will clear the screen to the colour defined by the most recent PAPER statement. To change a complete screen of colour we can therefore use: PAPER colour : CLS

```
100 REMark * paper colour *
110 MODE 8
120 FOR colour = 0 TO 7
130    PAPER colour : CLS
140    PAUSE 50
150 END FOR colour
```

The program will display, in turn, each of the eight screen colours.

CLS is more versatile than just being able to clear a whole screen. The keyword can be followed by a single number which defines a particular area on the screen relative to the current cursor position. This area will be cleared leaving the rest of the screen unchanged. The areas are defined like this:

Number	Area of screen cleared
0	Whole
1	From above cursor line to top
2	From below cursor line to bottom
3	Whole of cursor line
4	Right-hand end of cursor line including cursor

If we wish to clear the whole screen we do not need to write the zero, since the QL will automatically assume this on finding a CLS statement with no following value.

The next program demonstrates the effect of CLS when followed by various values:

```
100 REMark * clear screen *
110 MODE 8 : INK 0
120 PAPER 7 : CLS
130 FOR down = 1 TO 6 : PRINT
140 PRINT " CLEAR SCREEN BELOW TO NEW COLOUR"
150 PAUSE 100
160 PAPER 2 : CLS 2
170 FOR down = 1 TO 6 : PRINT
180 PRINT "CLEAR THIS LINE OF TEXT"
190 PAUSE 100 : CLS 3
200 PRINT "NEW COLOUR AFTER THIS:"
210 PAUSE 100
220 PAPER 5 : CLS 4
```

The PAUSE statements have been included to allow you time to see what happens. Delete lines 150 and 210 if you wish to see the normal CLS speed of operation.

INK

This keyword allows you to define the text colour to be used by any other keyword that outputs to the screen. For example, having defined INK, a following PRINT statement will cause its text to be printed in that colour. You should be careful about the colour combination selected for INK and PAPER. Choose the same colours and your text is invisible! This can be used for special effects. Choose the wrong contrast, and reading the text can be difficult. As a general rule when displaying text it is best to contrast a primary colour with a secondary one, rather than display two primary colours especially if using a television. The following program demonstrates this:

```
100 REMark * text and contrast *
110 MODE 8 : PAPER 7 : CLS
120 PAPER 1 : INK 4
130 PRINT "TWO PRIMARY COLOURS ONLY"
140 INK 6
150 PRINT "SECONDARY BACKGROUND, PRIMARY TEXT"
```

Note that this program gives a strip of background colour behind the text line, since it is the PRINT statement that uses the PAPER information. This gives you a simple and effective way of emphasising a line of text.

Just like PAPER, the INK keyword can be followed by either a colour code or a colour's variable name.

BORDER

Picture definition at the edges of television screens is sometimes not acceptable for graphics or text displays. One easy way to overcome this is to generate a coloured border all the way round the edge of the screen. BORDER does just that and by specifying an appropriate contrasting colour to the PAPER selected a much more pleasing result can be obtained. Both colour and width of border can be selected, though the width – in pixels – specifies the depth of the top and bottom edges, while the sides are twice this width. The two values can be numbers, variables or a mix of the two:

BORDER wide, colour   or   BORDER 25, colour

```
100 REMark * single border *
110 MODE 8 : PAPER 6 : CLS
120 BORDER 10,4
```

This would produce a single green border of 10 pixels deep top and bottom, and 20 pixels wide at each side on a yellow background.

Any output to the screen cannot be displayed in the border area, so your effective usable screen size is reduced. Further BORDER statements will be effective from the edges of the original screen size and will change part or all of a previously selected border colour.

```
100 REMark * multicolour border *
110 MODE 8 : PAPER 7 : CLS
120 FOR colour = 6 TO 1 STEP -1
130     BORDER colour*7, colour
140     PAUSE 50
150 END FOR colour
```

A multicoloured thick border will be displayed in stages. Note that we have used a numeric expression in the BORDER statement.

THE STIPPLE EFFECT

The examples shown so far have used MODE 8 resolution in order to demonstrate all eight solid colours available in conjunction with the keywords PAPER, INK and BORDER. The programs will still run if you replace MODE 8 by MODE 4, except that the colour range will be reduced. The keywords themselves will still work in the same way.

We mentioned earlier that we could produce more colours by means of a **stipple** facility. Let us now take a closer look at what is one of the more unusual graphics features of the QL.

You have already seen that the solid colours in either mode are generated by the QL's being able to turn on or off appropriate primary colour signals. As there are no intermediate intensities no other colours can be produced electronically. However, our eyes are apt to deceive us when looking at different colour points very close together. They will interpret, for example, two separate colours as one composite one.

To some extent the QL stipple effect makes use of this phenomenon, especially in high-resolution mode, and gives us a useful extension of the colour range. The effect mixes two selected colours in a fine stipple pattern.

Without wishing to dishearten anyone, it must be said that the stipple effect cannot be correctly reproduced on a television fed from the UHF socket of the QL. The set cannot technically process the effect accurately and an indeterminate display will be produced. Nevertheless, there is no reason at all why you should not experiment and see what effects it can produce on your own television! The example programs in this section, however, are designed to be run using a monitor.

Try this one to see the basic stipple effect:

```
100 MODE 4
110 PAPER 2,4 : CLS
```

We have actually used two colour codes in the PAPER statement, red and green, and even though we are in high-resolution mode, we now have a yellow screen!

STIPPLE CONTROL

The effect is created by controlling pixel colours in groups of four. In high-resolution mode the pixels are so close together that the colours visually 'mix' to produce an almost composite colour. The effect can, of course, be used in low-resolution mode, but since the pixels are larger the visual mix is not so prominent. Nevertheless, it will allow you to create a very wide range of stippled shades.

```
10 MODE 8
20 PAPER 1,4 : CLS
```

But stipple does not finish there. Apart from the 'chequer-board' stipple you have been viewing three other patterns are available. The following table gives all the possibilities, their associated codes and their pixel patterns (representing the pixels as squares for convenience):

Code	Name	Pattern
0	Single contrast pixel	M C / M M
1	Horizontal stripes	M M / C C
2	Vertical stripes	C M / C M
3	Chequer-board	C M / M C

M = main colour   C = contrast colour

So, you can produce not only colour shades but also horizontal or vertical stripes! The single contrast pixel pattern is also versatile in allowing two shades of a selected colour pair to be displayed just by reversing the colour code order.

PAPER 2, 4, 0 | R | G |
                | R | R |

PAPER 4, 2, 0 | G | R |
                | G | G |

R = RED   G = GREEN

The following examples display the range of shades produced using stipple codes 3 and 0 in MODE 8 and MODE 4.

```
100 REMark * high res stipple *
110 MODE 4 : CSIZE 2,0
120 PAPER 7 : CLS
130 DATA 208,224,248,242,234,220
140 DATA 16,32,56,50,42,28
150 DATA 18,36,63,52,47,31
160 FOR shades = 1 TO 18
170   READ value
180   PAPER value
190   REMark * print 20 spaces *
200   PRINT "                    "
```

```
210     PAUSE 20
220 END FOR shades
230 CLEAR
```

You can therefore use the stipple effect to extend the high-resolution colour range by eighteen.

Try this (chequer-board stipple only):

```
100 REMark * low res stipple *
110 MODE 8 : PAPER 7 : CLS
120 LET a = 1 : col = 2
130 LET stipple = 3
140 FOR main = 0 TO 6
150    FOR contrast = main TO 7
160       PAPER main ,contrast,stipple
170       AT a,col
180       REMark * 15 spaces *
190       PRINT "               "
200       LET a = a+1
210       IF a = 19 THEN a = 1 : LET col = 20
220    END FOR contrast
230 END FOR main
```

It is with stipple code 0 – the single contrast pixel pattern – that we can see a greater variation in shades for MODE 8. Remember you can generate two groups of shades by swapping the main and contrast colours. We can modify the previous program to show this effect by two successive changes:

First alter line 130 to:

```
130 LET stipple = 0
```

(of course, we could have just deleted line 130)

Then RUN the program. You will see one set of shades.
Now alter line 160 to:

```
160 PAPER contrast,main,stipple
```

Then RUN the program. You will see a second set of shades.

Now let us try horizontal and vertical stripes. Here are just a few of the combinations possible:

```
100 REMark * horizontal/vertical stipple *
110 MODE 8 : PAPER 7 : CLS
120 LET contrast = 7
130 FOR colour = 0 TO 3
140    FOR stipple = 1 TO 2
150       PAPER colour,contrast,stipple
160       CLS : PAUSE 25
170    END FOR stipple
180    LET contrast = contrast-1
190 END FOR colour
```

The program will display alternating horizontal and vertical striped colours in four combinations. Great for hypnosis!
But how do you select the effect or colour shade you want?

SELECTION

There are two methods. Either specify the individual main and contrast colour and stipple codes, or use a single code value which is equivalent to all three. Depending upon the program operation you require, one or other of these two methods can be selected. If you look back to the previous programs you will see that we did just that. The first program used a DATA/READ sequence to assign a single value to PAPER, while the second used a PAPER main, contrast, stipple statement.

STIPPLE DEFAULT

It should be pointed out here that when using the latter method it is not necessary to specify the stipple code if using the chequer-board pattern, i.e. code 3. This is the code automatically selected by the QL (the 'default' code) when it sees a two-number colour code.
Hence PAPER 2, 4, 3 is the same as PAPER 2, 4.

SINGLE VALUE CODE

To obtain the single value code you must understand a little more about the way the QL interprets the colour information that follows a keyword. For this you need an elementary knowledge of the binary number system and the exclusive-OR logical function. If you are not familiar with these Appendix 2 will supply you with a suitable introduction.

The QL converts all colour codes into a single 8-bit binary word. The word is divided up into three groups of bits appropriately labelled as shown:

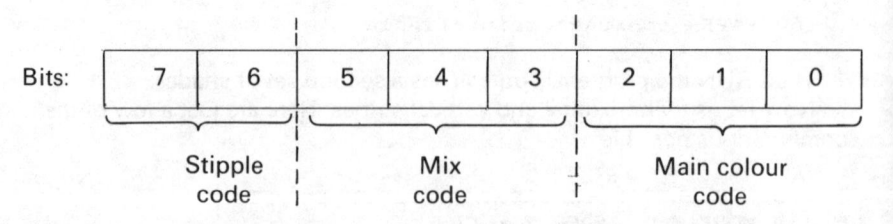

Bits:	7	6	5	4	3	2	1	0

Stipple code | Mix code | Main colour code

The main colour and stipple codes are the binary equivalents of the codes we already know. The 'mix' code is the exclusive-OR of the main colour code with the selected contrast-colour code. Note that the latter does not appear in the binary word. So if we stippled red and green, the mix code would be created like this:

	Red		Green
Decimal code:	2		4
Binary code:	010		100
Exclusive-OR		110	

If we wanted a stipple code 2 (vertical stripes) then our complete 8-bit binary value would be:

```
1 0 | 1 1 0 | 0 1 0
```

Stipple   Mix   Main colour (Red)

Converting this value into its decimal equivalent we have:

128 + 32 + 16 + 2 = 178

Hence PAPER 2, 4, 2 is equivalent to PAPER 178.

A HELPING HAND

As it is rather laborious working out the single value codes, Appendix 3 includes tables giving all the stipple mix combinations and codes.

In addition, the following programs will give you a visual indication of the actual colours available on your monitor (or television) together with their single value codes. Save these on your microdrive cartridge as colour palette reference programs for future use. Should you need to convert the single value code to its component parts, use the tables in Appendix 3.

High-resolution program

```
100 REMark * high res colour palette *
110 MODE 4 : WINDOW 512,256,0,0
120 PAPER 7 : INK 0 : CLS
130 DATA 208,220,224,234,242,248
140 DATA 16,28,32,42,50,56
150 DATA 18,31,36,47,52,63
160 FOR y = 16,87,158
170    FOR x = 35 TO 410 STEP 75
180       READ colour
190       BLOCK 60,60,x,y,colour
200       CURSOR x+20,y+11
210       PRINT colour
220    END FOR x
230 END FOR y
240 CSIZE 2,0 : INK 2
250 CURSOR 70,240
260 PRINT "HIGH RESOLUTION COLOUR PALETTE"
270 CLEAR
```

Low-resolution program

```
100 REMark * low res colour palette *
110 MODE 8 : WINDOW 512,256,0,0
120 PAPER 7 : INK 0 : CLS
130 DATA 200,208,216,224,232,240
140 DATA 248,217,209,233,225,249
150 DATA 241,202,242,250,226,234
160 DATA 251,243,235,227,204,217
170 DATA 220,221,213,206
180 LET shade = 8
190 FOR x = 55,135,215,295,375
200   LET n = 17 : y = 20
210   IF x = 375 THEN n = 16
220   FOR bar = 1 TO n
230     CURSOR x,y
240     IF shade > 63 THEN READ c :shade = c
250     STRIP shade
260     REMark * print 3 spaces *
270     PRINT "   ";
280     STRIP 7 : PRINT shade
290     LET shade = shade+1
300     LET y = y + 12
310   END FOR bar
320 END FOR x
330 CURSOR 70,230
340 CSIZE 3,0 : INK 2
350 PRINT "LOW RES COLOUR PALETTE"
360 CLEAR
```

FLASH

Let us now move on from stipple and look at the keyword FLASH. It will cause the INK colour of text to interchange at a slow flashing rate with the PAPER colour. It gives a neat way of calling attention to something on the screen. It does, however, only work in low-resolution mode. It has a single parameter, which may be a numeric expression if required. FLASH 1 will turn the flashing on, while FLASH 0 prevents its affecting any following text. Text in between the two statements will flash. For example:

```
100 REMark * quick flash *
110 MODE 8 : PAPER 7 : INK 2 : CLS
120 PRINT "JUST A";
130 FLASH 1
140 PRINT !"FLASH";
150 FLASH 0
160 PRINT !"IN THE PAN!"
```

Note that the flashing continues even though the program has stopped. It can only be stopped by either clearing the screen or pressing the RESET button.

STRIP

At times you may wish to highlight text with either a different colour or perhaps several colours. STRIP overcomes this problem and allows any colour (or stipple mix) to be specified as a background to a line of text. The keyword is followed by the colour codes or their variable name:

STRIP 6   yellow strip (MODE 8)
STRIP 2, 4, 2   red/green vertical striped strip

The STRIP effect extends for the length of the text along a line, it does not display from one side of the screen right across to the other.

```
100 REMark * strip *
110 MODE 8 : PAPER 7 : INK 0 : CLS
120 FOR colour = 1 TO 6
130    CURSOR 100,25*colour
140    STRIP colour
150    PRINT "THIS IS A STRIP SHOW !"
160 END FOR colour
```

You may have realised that we produced a similar effect earlier on in this chapter by using PAPER followed by a PRINT statement. Why two keywords doing the same thing? The reason is simply this. STRIP specifically identifies the action of producing a strip of colour behind the text, and more importantly, only affects a PRINT statement. PAPER, on the other hand, will affect a range of keywords (not all yet revealed) and it could well become confusing to have too many PAPER statements in a long program. Do, however, be careful in the use of STRIP and PAPER. If a PAPER statement follows a STRIP statement then the former will automatically set the STRIP colour to the new PAPER colour. For example:

```
100 REMark * strip 2 *
110 MODE 8 : PAPER 6 : INK 2 : CLS
120 STRIP 5
130 FOR LINES = 1 TO 5 : PRINT
140 PRINT "NORMAL STRIP"
150 PAUSE 100
160 PAPER 4 : CLS
170 PRINT "STRIP OVERRULED!"
```

Once a STRIP colour has been set that colour will be used either until a new STRIP is defined or, as in the previous example, a PAPER statement overrules it.

STRIP can provide you with a very neat way of producing coloured headings:

```
100 REMark * headings *
110 MODE 8 : PAPER 7 : INK 0 : CLS
120 FOR lines = 1 TO 6 : PRINT
130 STRIP 3
140 PRINT "NAME:" : PRINT
150 STRIP 4
160 PRINT "ADDRESS:"
170 FOR lines = 1 TO 6 : PRINT
180 STRIP 5
190 PRINT "TELEPHONE:"
```

OVER

The OVER keyword provides control over the relationship between background (PAPER), foreground (INK) and STRIP colours. Two of the three possible parameters, when selected, will affect all following PRINT statements until such time as the effect is cancelled. Chapter 3 will reveal another keyword, BLOCK, that one of the parameters also affects. The values used are 0, 1 and −1. We will look at each one separately.

OVER 1

Using this parameter allows the STRIP colour to become transparent and results in the INK colour appearing directly on top of the background colour or, as you will see in Chapter 5, on top of anything underneath it. It can be useful if you wish to remove the STRIP colour from behind selected words in a line of text. For example:

```
100 REMark * over 1 *
110 MODE 8 : PAPER 3 : INK 2 : CLS
120 STRIP 5
130 FOR lines = 1 TO 6 : PRINT
140 PRINT "OVER 1 CAN";
150 OVER 1
160 PRINT !"DELETE ";
170 OVER 0
180 PRINT "STRIP COLOUR"
```

Only the words *OVER 1 CAN* and *STRIP COLOUR* are displayed with the STRIP effect.

OVER −1

The most interesting of the three parameters, using −1, results in the STRIP colour being made transparent again, but the INK colour now becomes the exclusive-OR of the background colour and the INK colour. To simply demonstrate the effect the following program displays the use of all three OVER parameters.

```
100 REMark * all over *
110 MODE 8 : PAPER 7 : INK 6 : CLS
120 CSIZE 2,1 : STRIP 2
130 OVER 0
140 PRINT "OVER 0"
150 OVER 1
160 PRINT "OVER 1"
170 OVER -1
180 PRINT "OVER -1"
190 OVER 0
```

It is most important that line 190 is included to reset the OVER parameter back to zero. Otherwise the current parameter (in this instance −1) would continue to be active even if you deleted the program and typed in another.

The 'OVER −1' text is in blue INK − not yellow − since:

PAPER 7 (111) exclusive-OR'ed with INK 6 (110) gives 1 (001) = BLUE

STIPPLE WITH OTHER KEYWORDS

All the examples we have used to demonstrate the stipple effect have used the PAPER keyword. The single solid-colour code we first used when we introduced this keyword had been replaced by either a two- or three-number code or the single value code. Similarly the other keywords INK, BORDER and STRIP can also use the same range of colour codes. We are not restricted to just using PAPER for special stipple effects. For example:

```
100 REMark * multi-stipple *
110 MODE 4 : CSIZE 3,1
120 PAPER 50 : INK 2,0: CLS
130 BORDER 20,7,0,2
140 STRIP 4,0
150 CURSOR 10,128
160 PRINT "SEE WHAT WE MEAN !"
```

If any advice can be offered at this stage it would perhaps be: 'Do not over-do it!'

RECOL

The last keyword in this chapter allows us to allocate new colours to the colour values 0 to 7. We are effectively able to recolour each pixel. The effect is not fast and always operates progressively down the screen from the top.

Eight parameters must always be specified, the default values (i.e. having no effect) are:

RECOL 0, 1, 2, 3, 4, 5, 6, 7

We can change as many colours as we wish, for example:

RECOL 1, 1, 3, 4, 4, 5, 1, 7

This would change black to blue, red to magenta, magenta to green and yellow to blue – at the same time.

The keyword can be used in direct command mode, so to enable you to experiment type in the following program, run it, then type in RECOL statements, each followed by pressing the ENTER key.

```
100 REMark * recol test *
110 PAPER 2 : INK 6 : CLS
120 FILL 1
130 LINE 50,60 TO 90,60 TO 90,90 TO 50,90 TO 50,60
140 INK 4 : CIRCLE 25,30,20
150 FILL 0 : INK 3 : FILL 1
160 ELLIPSE 120,40,20,2,1 : FILL 0
```

Do not worry about all the 'unknown' keywords – they have been used just to give a little variety to the display. Note that MODE 8 should be selected first before running the program. Now try the following:

RECOL 0, 1, 2, 0, 4, 5, 6, 7

The magenta ellipse will turn black.

RECOL 3, 1, 2, 0, 4, 5, 6, 7

The ellipse will turn back to magenta. We deliberately left the magenta parameter at 0 to prove that all the parameters are acted upon at the same time. The picture did not contain any magenta when the statement was executed, so there was nothing to change to black.

RECOL 0, 1, 4, 3, 4, 5, 1, 7

This shows two colour changes with the effect that the circle has now disappeared. Unfortunately it cannot be retrieved! Changing green back to red will change all green pixels, as shown by the following:

RECOL 0, 1, 2, 3, 2, 5, 6, 7

RECOL can, of course, be used within a program and any or all of the parameters may be variables if desired. For instance:

```
100 REMark * colour change *
110 PAPER 2 : CLS
120 FOR c = 0 TO 7
130   RECOL c,c,c,c,c,c,c,c
140 END FOR c
```

Try altering the program as follows:

```
115 FILL 1 : CIRCLE 75,50,30 : FILL 0
130 RECOL c,c+1,c+2,c+3,c+4,c+5,c+6,c+7
```

So although the colour change is relatively slow, it can be quite effective.

PROBLEMS

In this chapter we have covered nine keywords. While it is instructive to type in and run the example programs to see the effect obtained, it is much more enjoyable being creative. Now is your chance! Try the following problems. Do make full use of this chapter and its related appendices; do not rely entirely on memory.

1. Display in sequence, as a plain background over the whole screen, the primary colours followed by the secondary colours in low-resolution mode. Enclose the screen within a green border of twenty pixels wide at the sides. Change each colour at approximately one-second intervals.
2. Create a screen display where the top half has a yellow message 'GREEN' on a green background, and the bottom half has a magenta message 'CYAN' on a cyan background.
3. Print the following message on the screen using red ink on a cyan background:

    THIS SHOWS FLASH STRIP AND OVER

    Make the words:

FLASH	flash
STRIP	appear on a black background
OVER	appear white on a cyan background

    Then after a pause, change black to blue, red to cyan, cyan to yellow and white to red.

CHAPTER 3
WINDOW WATCHING

WINDOW, BLOCK, SCROLL, PAN

INTRODUCTION

In Chapter 2 you become familiar with the capability of the QL to generate colour in both resolution modes. In this chapter we shall explore a group of keywords which allow more advanced creation and movement of coloured areas on the screen. Some of the new keywords were used in the previous chapter. When you understand how they operate, look back and work out how the earlier programs utilised them.

PIXEL CO-ORDINATES

Many computers are restricted to displaying information on a screen in character positions only, unless you select a separate graphics mode. The screen can be considered as a matrix of pigeon-holes into which information, each the size of a character, can be placed. This is often referred to as **block** graphics. It implies that the programmer can only move information around the screen in discrete character steps.

In both display modes the QL can select any pixel position on the screen and use that as a starting point from which display information can begin. To define any position on the screen, the QL uses a pixel co-ordinates system. This simply means that any point can be identified by two numbers representing the number of pixels across the screen and the number of pixels down from a specified reference point, or origin. The origin for the pixel co-ordinate system is in the top left-hand corner of the screen. (This assumes the whole of the screen is currently being used – more about this shortly.) All keywords using this system are known, collectively, as **pixel graphics** keywords.

All positions on the screen are referenced as if the QL were in high-resolution mode with 512 pixels across the screen (remember MODE 512?) and 256 pixels down.

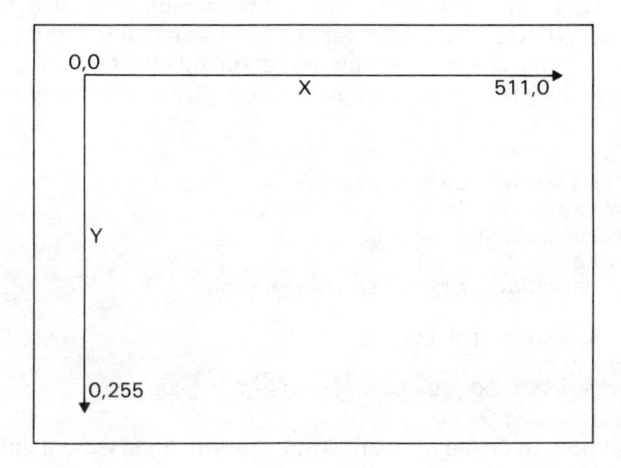

```
0,0
        X           511,0

Y


0,255
```

We can imagine the screen as a piece of graph paper with 512 divisions along the X-axis and 256 divisions down the Y-axis. Note that the co-ordinate ranges are:

X-axis: 0,0 TO 511,0 (Not 512,0 which would be 513 pixels across)

Y-axis: 0,0 TO 0,255

But supposing we wish to use this facility in MODE 8? Very conveniently for us the QL will always use the nearest pixel available for the particular mode selected, so that the positions on the screen are independent of the mode. In MODE 8 the exact correspondence with the pixel co-ordinate is lost, but the position is the same. We only need to consider one co-ordinate system. Hence the point 256,128 is always the centre of the screen in either mode.

WINDOW CREATION

Each example used so far to demonstrate the various keywords has been written on the assumption that the whole screen area was available for use by that program. This is the situation normally found on most computers. But the QL offers something rather more interesting that can open up a very wide range of applications.

It is possible to create, at any position on the screen, an area of defined size that can be made to act as if it were a separate, smaller screen in its own right. Any following text or graphic outputs or colour selections referenced to that window will be displayed within the window area, not on the rest of the screen.

The containment of display information within a window is perhaps the most useful effect provided by this facility. Text within the window will obey the normal screen rules of overflowing onto a following line and scrolling from bottom to top, one line at a time, when the bottom of the screen is reached. We have not introduced the WINDOW keyword yet but have included it in the following program to demonstrate the overflow and scrolling effects. Note that the program will run continuously. You will have to stop it by pressing any keyboard key.

```
100 REMark * line overflow/scrolling *
110 MODE 8 : PAPER 5 : CLS
120 WINDOW 150,100,50,50
130 PAPER 6 : CLS
140 PRINT "THIS DEMONSTRATES LINE OVERFLOW"
150 PAUSE 100
160 LET number = RND(1 TO 10)
170 PRINT !number;
180 IF INKEY$="" THEN GO TO 160
```

Before you find out how to create different windows, you must learn a little about the QL's method of handling 'channels'.

QL CHANNELS FOR GRAPHICS

When we use a keyword that will cause some form of display to appear on the screen, we are really programming the QL to perform an output transfer of that information to a peripheral device – the screen. The screen acts like an output device just as a microdrive acts like an input or output device. Similarly the QL keyboard is an input device. It is not an objective of this book to explain in detail the input/output (I/O) transfer requirements of the QL, but we shall be looking at those aspects which directly relate to graphics operations.

At any one time it is possible that several input and/or output devices may be connected to the QL. Every time an I/O operation is initiated by a keyword, the QL must know which device is to be used, even if it is the screen. So every device must have some means of identification. The identification consists of two parameters, a **channel number** and a **logical file name**. Let us explain these two terms first.

Channel number

Assume you are talking on the telephone to your local librarian. You wish to renew one book, reserve another and ask if a further one is available. To identify the three books you would give the librarian their titles, so that when telling her what you wish to have done with each, she will know what book you are talking about. You are identifying three unrelated actions over a single communications link.

Channel numbers allow the programmer to achieve the same effect. It is quite possible to have more than one channel number in use with, for example, a single microdrive while accessing different items of information. The channel number can range from zero to over two thousand and is selectable by you. There is no order of priority implied in the numerical value but it is sensible to allocate channels in ascending order. This allows you to keep an easy check on how many channels you are using.

Logical file name

Before you spoke to the librarian you must have dialled the library number. This is equivalent to the **logical file name** which identifies the source or destination of the information. For the word 'file' we can generally substitute 'device'.

All I/O transfers on the QL are to or from logical files whether referring to the screen, a microdrive or an external printer. Most devices on the QL have pre-defined logical file (device) names. Two are of importance for graphics use – CON and SCR.

CON (console) refers to the QL keyboard and screen as a combined input (keyboard) and output (screen) device. SCR refers to the screen alone as an output device. We shall discuss these device names a little more in a short while.

Access of logical files

After you first switch on the QL or press RESET, the QL will direct any statements such as PRINT or BORDER to the screen. The screen has automatically been allocated what is known as a 'default' channel number. This means that the channel number does not need to be included within any graphics statement destined for the screen. Should we wish to write statements to talk to a different device, we must include that device's appropriate channel number within the statements.

But we must also tell the QL which device (logical file name) is to be connected to that channel. We only need to do this at the beginning of the communication sequence. All following graphics statements then just need to have the appropriate channel number specified. In this way you can have several channels in operation in the same program, each selected when required purely by using the related channel number in the statements.

A logical file can be compared to a book. When we want to read from a book we first of all open it. Then, after reading what we wish to read, we close it. The same operations must be performed with logical files:

1. OPEN a channel to the file

2. use the file as required

3. CLOSE the channel

Note: In all the statements that we shall use to identify files, you will see the symbol '#'. It is a standard convention which means 'channel number'.

So before we write to or read from a device we must OPEN a channel to it, then on completion of the task we must CLOSE the channel. This is achieved by using the following keywords.

OPEN

The keyword opens a specified channel to a defined file-name on a particular device.

OPEN # 2, mdv1_test_program

This will open channel 2 to the file called *test program* on microdrive 1.

CLOSE

This keyword simply closes a channel when no further access to its file is required.

CLOSE # 4

This will close channel 4.

Graphics application

We have talked a lot about files and channels, but where or how do they affect our graphics with respect to the window facility mentioned earlier? The connection is found within the format for the two device names – CON and SCR.

CON/SCR

Both of these pre-defined device names require additional information. When either is used, a window area must be specified – in terms of an x, y starting co-ordinate for the top left-hand corner, and the window's size – all in pixels. The general form of the device name SCR is:

SCR_wxhaXxY

where: w = window width
h = window height
X = window x co-ordinate
Y = window y co-ordinate

The CON device name has an additional parameter, k, added on the end to define the length, in bytes, of the keyboard look-ahead buffer (normally set to 32). Hence:

CON_wxhaXxY_k

To open a channel to the screen we could therefore write:

OPEN # 5, SCR_100x150a10x20

In this example we are opening channel 5 to the screen and creating a window-size 100 pixels wide by 150 pixels deep. The top left-hand corner is at co-ordinates 10 pixels across by 20 pixels down. Note the use of the 'x' and 'a' meaning 'by' and 'at'. Either upper- or lower-case letters may be used when typing them.

If we wanted to create further windows then we just allocate further channel numbers, together with the required window position and size. We could, theoretically, create several hundred separate windows on the same screen!

So a window size and position is defined whenever a channel is opened to the screen (or console). Having opened a channel we simply add the channel number into the relevant statement wishing to output to that window. Of the graphics keywords considered so far all can have a channel number added:

PAPER	BORDER	CLS	INK	RECOL
STRIP	OVER	FLASH	STRIP	

To help you understand the use of channels with these keywords, here is a program to create three windows on the screen and produce various effects within each:

```
100 REMark * multi_channel *
110 MODE 8 : PAPER 7 : CLS
120 OPEN#4,scr_450x100a30x30
130 OPEN#5,scr_128x54a30x160
140 OPEN#6,scr_80x26a325x160
150 PAPER#4,6 : INK#4,1 : CLS#4
160 PAPER#5,3 : CLS#5
170 PAPER#6,4 : INK#6,0 : CLS#6
180 BORDER#4,5,2
190 BORDER#6,3,0
200 BORDER#5,2,7
210 PRINT#4,"THIS PROGRAM RECORDS A COUNT OF THE";
220 PRINT#4,! "NUMBER OF COLOURED STRIPS DISPLAYED"
230 PRINT#4
240 PRINT#4,"PRESS SPACE BAR TO STOP"
250 LET colour = 0 : count = 0
260 CSIZE#6,2,1
270 REPeat loop
280    STRIP#5,colour
290    LET count = count+1
300    REMark * print 10 spaces *
310    PRINT#5,"          "
320    LET colour = colour+1
330    IF colour = 7 THEN colour = 0
340    PRINT#6,count
350    IF INKEY$(25)= " " THEN EXIT loop
360 END REPeat loop
370 CLOSE#4 : CLOSE#5 : CLOSE#6
```

Your screen should contain three windows with text in the top one, scrolling colours in the left-hand one and an increasing count in the right-hand window, as shown below:

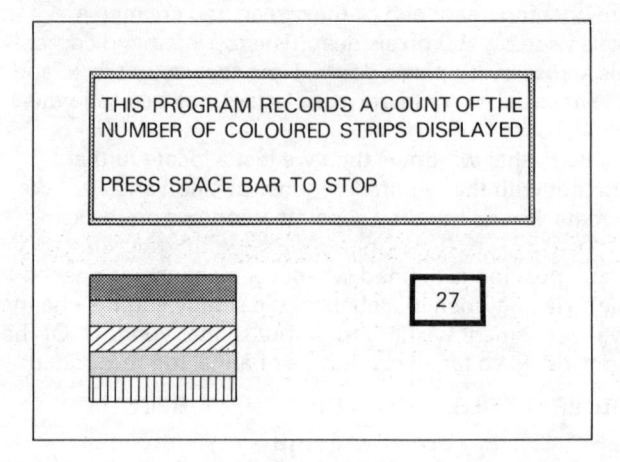

```
THIS PROGRAM RECORDS A COUNT OF THE
NUMBER OF COLOURED STRIPS DISPLAYED

PRESS SPACE BAR TO STOP
```

```
                              27
```

Some explanation of this program may assist your understanding. Line 110 colours the default screen background to blue. Lines 120 to 140 open three channels to the screen (arbitrarily chosen as numbers 4, 5 and 6). Lines 150, 160 and 170 colour their windows. Line 180 draws a red border around window 4. Line 190 draws a black border around window 6. Lines 210 to 240 print text in the top window. Line 280 sets up a STRIP colour statement to be used with a PRINT 'spaces' statement at line 300. This generates the coloured bars for window 5 within the REPeat loop. Line 260 sets the character size for window 6 (character size is explained in Ch. 5).

The loop alternately prints the strip colour in window 5, and prints the increasing count in window 6. Pressing the SPACE bar jumps the program out of the loop and closes all three channels.

RECOL channel use

The RECOL keyword deserves a special mention with respect to channel allocation. Using the keyword without a channel number recolours *all* channel windows on the screen, not just the default channel 1.

Unopened channels

You will see that at the end of the program examples using channels, we have always included a CLOSE statement. This is essentially tidy programming. But one thing you must remember is that should you attempt to use a channel that has not been previously opened, or has been already closed, your program will stop. Reset the QL and type in the following line in direct command mode:

PRINT # 4, "END"

Press the ENTER key and you will be presented with an error message, telling you the file is not open. You must always open a file before using it. Whether you type the OPEN statement before you run the program (i.e. in direct command mode) or include it as one of the first statements in your program it does not matter, but it must be done.

Conversely, it does not matter if you try to close a channel that is already closed. The statement is ignored.

WINDOW

Although you specify the size of a window when using the OPEN/SCR sequence, the WINDOW keyword allows you to alter the size of that window at any time later in your program. WINDOW is followed by five parameters. The first, optional, is the channel number of the window to be altered. If it is omitted, then the WINDOW statement will apply to the default channel. Of the remaining parameters, two give the size and two give the top left-hand co-ordinate of the window. All the parameters are specified in pixels, or variables representing pixel values. For example:

WINDOW 120, 80, 20, 40

This would alter the default channel window to size 120 pixels wide and 80 pixels high. The top left-hand co-ordinate would be 20 pixels across and 40 pixels down. We could write:

WINDOW wide, height, across, down

The four parameters must have been defined previously. Note we cannot use 'width' as a variable name since it is a keyword. The parameters may also be numeric expressions:

WINDOW wide, wide * 3, across, across * 4

Try the following:

```
100 MODE 8 : PAPER 2 : CLS
110 WINDOW 120,80,196,80
120 PAPER 7 : CLS
```

You will see a white rectangle in the centre of a red screen. Any attempt to put graphics information onto the screen will be restricted to within the new window's boundary. Add the following line and RUN the program again:

```
130 PRINT "TEXT NOW CONTAINED WITHIN THIS WINDOW"
```

Note how the text overflows onto the next line and does not encroach on the red screen area.

If we want to alter the size of a window other than the default window we must include the channel number. Hence:

WINDOW # 6, wide, height, 20, 10

For example:

```
100 REMark * channel window change *
110 MODE 8 : PAPER 5 : CLS
120 OPEN#7,scr_200x100a30x30
130 PAPER#7,4 : CLS#7
140 WINDOW#7,150,80,50,40
150 PAPER#7,6 : CLS#7
160 CLOSE#7
```

WINDOWS IN WINDOWS

Once a window has been changed to a new size and/or position you must remember that any information left in the space between the new window area and the previous one will remain visible. WINDOW does not automatically clear the previous window. Also the information cannot be cleared by using CLS since this only affects the newly defined window.

Unless achieving this effect deliberately it is good practice to clear the old window before you change its parameters. Preferably, also alter its colour to the background colour of the unused parts of the screen. In this way, when creating the new size, no remains of the previous window's contents are visible. The following program demonstrates this effect; PAUSE statements have been included to allow you to see the various stages of it more easily.

```
100 REMark * window cleaner *
110 MODE 8 : PAPER 7 : CLS
120 OPEN#4,scr_200x100a50x50
130 PAPER#4,4 : INK#4,0 : CLS#4
140 PRINT#4,"ORIGINAL WINDOW"
150 PAUSE 100
160 WINDOW#4,108,50,60,60
170 PAPER#4,5 : CLS#4
180 PRINT#4,"NOT VERY GOOD!"
190 PAUSE 100
200 WINDOW#4,200,100,50,50
210 PAPER#4,7 : CLS#4
220 WINDOW#4,108,50,60,60
230 PAPER#4,5 : CLS#4
240 PRINT#4,"THAT'S A LOT"\"BETTER"!
250 CLOSE#4
```

Line 200 was required to change the window size back to its original parameters, thus allowing line 210 to alter the PAPER colour and clear out the original text. As a SuperBASIC reminder, do not forget that the "\" in line 240 will force a new line after 'LOT'.

If a border had existed around the old window then it would have to be re-defined for the new window. The latter is always created without a border.

Of course, the effect of leaving display information from a previous window, after having re-defined the window, may be deliberate. For example, you may wish to create an offset border for your window. This cannot be achieved by using the BORDER keyword.

```
100 REMark * offset border *
110 MODE 8 : PAPER 6 : CLS
120 OPEN#5,scr_200x150a50x20
130 PAPER#5,0 : INK#5,7 : CLS#5
140 PRINT#5,"OFFSET BORDER"
150 WINDOW#5,150,90,60,70
160 PAPER#5,2 : CLS#5
170 CLOSE#5
```

A red window is set towards the bottom left-hand corner of a black square. The latter contains a title 'OFFSET BORDER'.

This type of display feature may be carried further:

```
100 REMark * chapter hierarchy *
110 MODE 8 : WINDOW 465,200,15,15
120 PAPER 7 : INK 0 : CLS
130 DATA "CHAPTER","PAGE","PARAGRAPH","SENTENCE","WORD"
140 LET wide = 200 : x = 15
150 FOR colour = 1 TO 5
160    READ title$
170    WINDOW wide,wide,x,x
180    PAPER colour : CLS
190    PRINT title$
200    LET wide = wide-30 : x = x+25
210 END FOR colour
220 CLEAR
```

This time we have altered the default channel's window. The display will give a three-dimensional effect to enhance the intended structure. The example does leave you with a rather small window, but that may be the desired effect.

TELEVISION DISPLAY CORRECTION

In Chapter 1 we mentioned that the QL provides a screen output signal that cannot be completely displayed on a television. The default window set up when the QL is switched on, or RESET, will reduce the effective size to allow for this discrepancy. Should it be required to restore full size you can do so just by redefining the window as we have seen earlier in this section.

You may already be feeling that the allocation and use of channel numbers seems to take up quite an amount of programming effort. If you are content to stay with the default window then, of course, you do not need to worry about channels. But it is necessary for more adventurous programs.

BLOCK

The WINDOW keyboard allows us to define an area on the screen that acts in itself like another screen. Often we may need to produce simply an area of colour at a specified position on the screen. The keyword BLOCK allows us to do this. We must specify the block's size and the co-ordinate for the top left-hand corner. All values are expressed in pixels or numeric expressions representing pixels. The colour of the block is also specified using any of the allowable colour-code formats. The co-ordinate used will always be relative to either of the following:

1. The default window
2. The window identified by a channel number.

The general format for the keyword is:

BLOCK channel number, width, height, x origin, y origin, colour

If you are not stating a channel number then it may be omitted. Hence, on the default screen (e.g. following a power-on or RESET action):

BLOCK 150, 30, 120, 110, 4

This will give a green-coloured block of size 150 pixels wide by 30 pixels high. The top left-hand corner will be positioned at co-ordinate 120 pixels across and 110 pixels down.

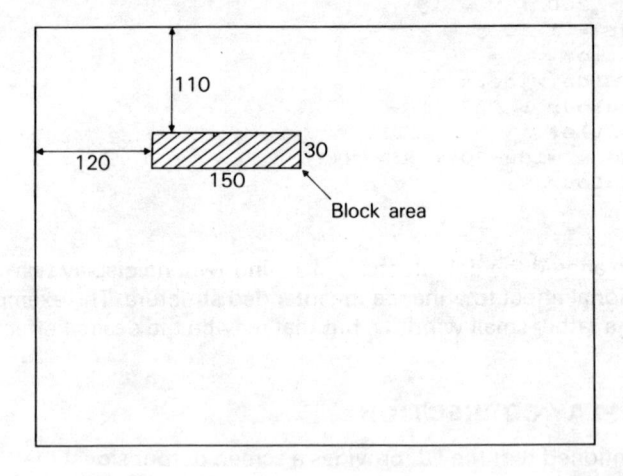

BLOCK # 6, 150, 30, 120, 110, 4

This would give the same size block, but positioned relative to the top left-hand corner (the origin 0,0) of the window defined as channel 6.

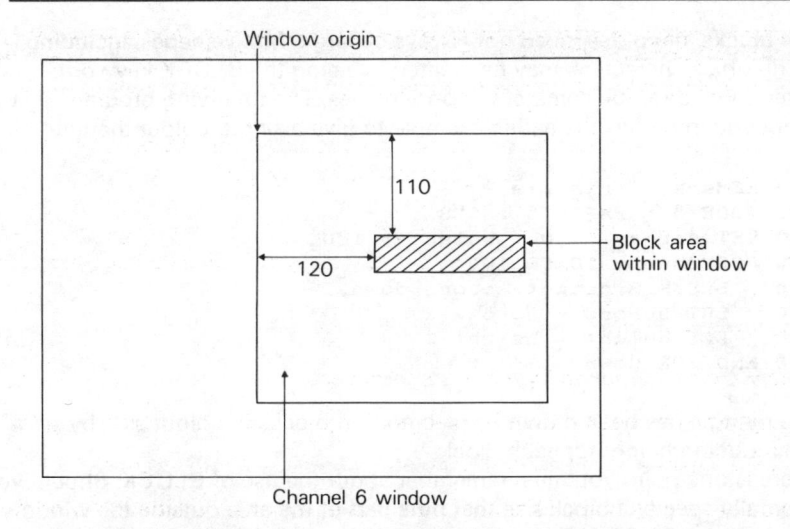

```
                    Window origin
                         │
                         ▼
          ┌──────────────────────────────────┐
          │                                  │
          │           ┌──────────┐           │
          │           │   110    │           │
          │           │    ▼     │           │
          │           │  ▓▓▓▓▓▓  │◄── Block area
          │      120  │──────────│      within window
          │     ◄────►│          │           │
          │           │          │           │
          │           │          │           │
          │           │          │           │
          │           └──────────┘           │
          │           ▲                      │
          │           │                      │
          └──────────────────────────────────┘
                Channel 6 window
```

A BLOCK statement is therefore similar to WINDOW, without the screen operating ability. The position of any following text or graphics on the screen is not affected. The main application of BLOCK revolves around the ability to freely create blocks of colour very rapidly. This first example program demonstrates creation of blocks on the default screen:

```
100 REMark * basic blocks *
110 MODE 8 : PAPER 7 : CLS
120 LET height = 180
130 FOR colour = 0 TO 6
140   BLOCK 50,height,40+colour*50,10+colour*11,colour
150   LET height = height - 22
160 END FOR colour
```

The program will create coloured blocks from left to right in descending height order.

The second example shows the same effect, but contained within a window.

```
100 REMark * window block *
110 MODE 8
120 OPEN#5,scr_300x116a30x30
130 PAPER#5,7 : CLS#5
140 BORDER#5,3,0
150 LET height = 110
160 FOR colour = 0 TO 6
170   BLOCK#5,40,height,colour*40,colour*7,colour
180   LET height = height - 14
190 END FOR colour
200 CLOSE#5
```

The blocks, of course, need not always be large. Many shapes, including block graphics characters, may be created by using the BLOCK keyword. Chapter 5 will describe some of the possibilities. The following program, just to tempt you, modifies the earlier example to give a single-colour triangle:

```
100 REMark * triangle *
110 MODE 8 : PAPER 6 : CLS
120 LET across = 50 : height = 180
130 FOR down = 10 TO 100
140     BLOCK 3,height,across,down,2
150     LET across = across+2
160     LET height = height-2
170 END FOR down
```

The triangle has been drawn by placing thin blocks of colour side by side with a reducing height for each block.

There is one point you must remember about the use of BLOCK. Should you accidentally specify a block size that puts part of the area outside the window being used, the BLOCK statement will *not* be implemented.

MULTIPLE BLOCK

All of our BLOCK examples so far have shown the production of separate, non-overlapping, coloured areas. When an overlap is produced the colour of the most recent BLOCK statement will cover any previous BLOCK colour. For example:

```
100 BLOCK 100,50,50,20,2
110 BLOCK 50,60,20,40,6
```

BLOCK WITH OVER

The operation of OVER has been described in Chapter 2, but only in connection with INK and PAPER. OVER −1 also affects BLOCK colours. If a BLOCK area overlays any text then OVER −1 will cause the BLOCK colour to be exclusive-ORed with the INK colour.

The BLOCK overlapping effect can become quite involved. If OVER −1 is active when BLOCK colours are overlaid, each successive colour is exclusive-ORed with the one underneath. To further complicate matters any BLOCK area that covers the background (PAPER) colour will be exclusive-ORed with that also! For example:

```
100 REMark * overlap *
110 MODE 8 : PAPER 7 : CLS
120 BLOCK 100,50,20,20,2
130 OVER -1
140 BLOCK 60,70,40,40,1
150 OVER 0
```

Instead of having a blue area overlapping a red area, the second BLOCK statement at line 140 has been split, by the exclusive-OR action, into two new colours – magenta and yellow.

Top colour: 010 XOR 001 = 011

Lower colour: 111 XOR 001 = 110

To see how involved this can become, try the following program. It will generate two windows with two identical sets of overlapping BLOCK areas. But the left-hand window will be using OVER −1.

```
100 REMark * block overlap *
110 MODE 8 : WINDOW 180,170,280,25
120 OPEN#6,scr_180x170a40x25
130 PAPER 7 : PAPER#6,7 : CLS : CLS#6
140 blocks 1
150 OVER#6, -1
160 blocks 6
170 OVER#6, 0 : CLOSE#6
180 DEFine PROCedure blocks (channel)
190   LET down = 25 : colour = 1
200   FOR side = 160 TO 70 STEP -30
210     BLOCK#channel,side,50,10,down,colour
220     LET down = down+25
230     LET colour = colour +1
240   END FOR side
250 END DEFine
```

We have been able to use a procedure to draw the two sets of BLOCK areas, the default window from reset or power on being channel 1. BLOCK parameters are always relative to their current window, so the two routines are identical apart from channel number.

By comparing the two displays, you can work out the various colour combinations produced by OVER −1.

THREE-DIMENSIONAL BLOCK

The position of a block of colour on the screen is referenced to a pixel co-ordinate, so if we cause that co-ordinate to move in both axes at once, each time creating a BLOCK, a three-dimensional figure will be generated. Thus:

```
100 REMark * 3-D block *
110 MODE 8 : PAPER 7 : CLS
120 FOR increment = 1 TO 20
130   BLOCK 50,80,20+increment,20+increment,0
140 END FOR increment
150 BLOCK 50,80,40,40,2
```

A shadow effect has been produced with a single red block being displayed at the end of the progressively moved black ones. The perspective of the block (or rather, the cuboid) can be altered by changing the increment value for one of the pixel co-ordinates. Change lines 130 and 150 to these statements:

```
130 block 50,80,20+increment*2,20+increment,0
150 BLOCK 50,80,60,40,2
```

Run the program again. The figure is elongated more to the right.

BLOCK AND FLASH

The interaction between a BLOCK area and flashing text, though a less complex point, is nevertheless worth mentioning. If a BLOCK area completely covers a flashing word, then it is hidden by the block's colour. However, if a flashing word is only partly covered, then the rest of the line on which the word occurred will flash and the partly visible original flashing word will have its character corrupted. An undesirable effect. The next example shows what we mean.

```
100 REMark * bad flash *
110 MODE 8 : PAPER 2 : INK 7 : CLS
120 PRINT "NOT A"
125 PAUSE 100
130 FLASH 1
140 PRINT "DESIRABLE";
150 FLASH 0
160 BLOCK 70,100,0,0,4
170 PRINT!"EFFECT"
```

BLOCK AND STRIP

One final point concerning BLOCK relates to its use with STRIP. Should your program generate a BLOCK coloured area where a STRIP text is being displayed, then the STRIP colour will overprint the BLOCK colour. You could see the effect by referring to Chapter 2, locating the program called *strip* and adding in:

```
170 BLOCK 30,240,180,10,1
```

SCROLL

When a screen, or window, is full of text further PRINT statements will cause the whole contents to scroll upwards, one line at a time. New text appears at the bottom while that at the top scrolls off the screen. If a program is running in a loop the scroll effect is so fast that the display becomes very difficult to read. For example:

```
100 REMark * fast scroll *
110 MODE 8 : PAPER 4 : INK 0 : CLS
120 LET number = 0
130 PRINT number
140 LET number = number+1
150 GO TO 130
```

You will have to use the CTRL/SPACE break routine to stop it!

Scrolling of the display, if under the programmer's control, can be very useful and we achieve this control on the QL using the SCROLL keyword.

SCROLL can cause the current window to scroll not just upwards, but also downwards. We may be using a contrasting PAPER colour for the window background and the selected colour will be scrolled in from the top or bottom as appropriate to 'fill-up' the scrolled 'space'. When using SCROLL we also include a parameter giving the distance we wish the display to scroll, expressed in pixels. To scroll the contents of a display *downwards* by 100 pixels we would write:

SCROLL 100

To scroll the contents *upwards* by the same distance we use a minus sign to indicate the direction:

SCROLL −100

The parameter could be a numeric expression such as:

SCROLL 4 * height + 20

If the expression yielded a negative result then the scroll action would be upwards.

Here is an example of a simple scroll action:

```
100 REMark * simple scroll *
110 MODE 8 : PAPER 1 : CLS
120 WINDOW 256,128,128,64
130 PAPER 6 : INK 0 : CLS
140 PRINT "SIMPLE SCROLL"
150 SCROLL 10
160 FOR row = 1 TO 10
170   AT 0,0
180   PRINT row
190   SCROLL 10
200 END FOR row
```

We used the SCROLL keyword twice, first to move down the title, then within the loop to successively scroll down by 10 pixels between each PRINT statement. Perhaps a useful way of printing something in reverse order?

The scrolling action was still fast and if we wanted to read the display while it was moving, the action must be slowed down. We can achieve this by scrolling in smaller increments.

```
100 REMark * slow scroll *
110 MODE 8 : PAPER 7 : INK 2 : CLS
120 DATA "ONE","WORD","AFTER","THE","NEXT"
130 FOR t = 0 TO 28 STEP 7
140   READ word$
150   PRINT TO t ;! word$
160   FOR roll = 1 TO 20
170     SCROLL 1
190   END FOR roll
200 END FOR t
210 CLEAR
```

The individual words will appear at approximately two-second intervals and scroll smoothly down the screen to give a diagonal display.

PART SCROLLING

You may recall that in Chapter 2 we said that the CLS keyword allows a partial clearing of the screen dependent upon the cursor position. A similar action is possible with SCROLL by using a second parameter as listed here:

Parameter	Scrolling
0	Whole screen
1	From above cursor line to top
2	From below cursor line to bottom

The zero parameter is the default setting so we do not need to write it when scrolling the whole screen. Part scrolling can be quite interesting. Here is a slightly longer program to demonstrate it:

```
100 REMark * part scroll *
110 MODE 8 : PAPER 7 : INK 6 : CLS
120 LET colour = 0
130 FOR number = 1 TO 50
140   LET x = RND(5 TO 50)
150   LET y = RND(5 TO 50)
160   BLOCK x,y,x*7,y*3,colour
170   LET colour = colour+1
180   IF colour = 7 THEN colour = 0
190 END FOR number
200 CURSOR 0,100
210 STRIP 1
220 PRINT "READY,STEADY...";
230 PAUSE 100
```

```
240 PRINT "GO!"
250 SCROLL -80,1
260 SCROLL 80,2
270 CLS 4
```

Lines 130 to 190 created fifty random blocks of colour. By positioning the cursor half-way down the screen (more about CURSOR in Chapter 5) we were able to scroll the display above and below the printed line. The text was not affected. Note the use of CLS 4.

PAN

Apart from being able to scroll the screen contents upwards or downwards, the QL gives us the ability to pan to the left or right just like panning a video- or cine-camera. Like the scrolling operation the current PAPER colour moves in to fill the cleared area. The distance moved is specified in pixels and this can also be a numeric expression. Panning to the *left* requires a *positive* value, to the *right* a *negative* value.

PAN 150

This will pan the window 150 pixels to the left. Again like SCROLL, if a numeric expression is used, the polarity of the result (plus or minus) will control the direction of panning.

You must remember that if you pan a camera to the left the display in the viewfinder moves to the right and vice versa. Panning to the left on our screen will progressively create a cleared area from the left, thus giving the impression of movement on the screen to the right. You can see this effect with the next program:

```
100 REMark * pan left *
110 MODE 8 : PAPER 3 : CLS
120 BLOCK 50,180,10,10,5
130 BLOCK 50,180,90,10,1
140 PAUSE 100
150 FOR times = 1 TO 40
160   PAN 3
170 END FOR times
```

The operation is, in fact, a modified scrolling action. Increase the parameter for PAN to 10 and you will see what is meant.

PART PANNING

PAN can also include a second parameter to select a partial panning action on the current window.

Parameter	Panning area
0	Whole screen (default)
3	Whole of the cursor line
4	Right end of cursor line from and including cursor position

Again we do not need to write the zero parameter when panning the whole screen.

Using parameter value 3 we can create a moving text line:

```
100 REMark * panning text *
110 MODE 8 : PAPER 4 : INK 6 : CLS
120 BLOCK 300,30,65,50,2
130 BLOCK 300,30,65,150,2
140 PAPER 1 : CLS 3
150 LET text$ = "   ***JUST LIKE PICADILLY***"
160 FOR character = 1 TO 28
170   CURSOR 436,110
180   PRINT text$(character)
190   FOR times = 1 TO 8
200     PAN -1,3
210   PAUSE 2
220   END FOR times
230 END FOR character
```

Lines 170 and 180 print successive characters extracted from the string at the same position on the screen. Overprinting is avoided by moving each character to the left (panning right). The two BLOCK statements were included to prove that only the text line was affected by the panning. Note that we used a partial clearing of the screen (CLS 3) to give the blue text-strip right across the screen.

The next program demonstrates the use of PAN with parameter value 4:

```
100 REMark * letter eater *
110 MODE 8 : PAPER 6 : INK 0
120 BORDER 20,2 : CLS
130 AT 8,0
140 PRINT "TEXT GOBBLER";
150 AT 8,4 : PAUSE 50
160 FOR times = 1 TO 8
170 PAN -12,4 : PAUSE 2
180 END FOR times
```

The text 'GOBBLER' should disappear down a hole!

PROBLEMS

This chapter has seen the introduction of four graphics keywords and the way in which channels and windows are interrelated. Here are a few exercises for you to try.

1. Write a program that repeatedly displays randomly coloured and positioned 20 × 20 blocks in groups of fifty at a time. The blocks must not come within 5 pixels of the window boundary of 460 × 200. Use stipple mode 3.

2. Write a program to perform the following:

   a) Clear the whole screen area to yellow.
   b) Reduce the channel 1 window to 200 × 100 centrally placed on the screen and colour it black.
   c) Create a second window next to it on the right, of size 80 × 100 coloured red.
   d) Place a green block 50 × 20 central in the black window and a white block the same size central in the red window.

3. Display your name at the top of a window 260 × 100 and program for it to move slowly down to the bottom of the window then make it disappear out of the right-hand side.

CHAPTER 4
POINTS, LINES AND CURVES

LINE, SCALE, POINT, ARC, CIRCLE, ELLIPSE, POINT_R, LINE_R, ARC_R, CIRCLE_R, ELLIPSE_R, FILL

INTRODUCTION

So far we have looked at ways in which we can manipulate colours, areas of colour and windows around the screen. Now we will move on to investigate methods of producing display effects that are equivalent to drawing lines on paper. This is what we really mean when we use the word graphics (Greek: *graphé* writing).

By looking at the keyword list at the start of this chapter you will have an idea of the range of graphics facilities available. Again we shall occasionally be using some keywords that have yet to be explained in order to assist demonstration of those being discussed. They will all, however, be dealt with in this chapter.

GRAPHICS CO-ORDINATE SYSTEM

Many of our previous keywords used the pixel co-ordinate system to reference their position on the screen within a window. However, the pixels change in shape depending upon the resolution selected; MODE 512 and MODE 256 should by now be self-explanatory. The pixel count down the screen does not, of course change, so any shape drawn with direct reference to pixel position would change its proportion. While it is true that the QL corrects for this, a fixed pixel reference range is always used when changing modes (e.g. X-axis 0 to 511).

Since so much of graphics drawing involves precise position and size, the limitation of the pixel range is too restrictive. So the QL provides us with a completely new reference system for the 'drawing' type of keywords we shall be covering in this chapter. It is called the **graphics co-ordinate** system where all dimensions are related to an arbitrary **scale**, selectable by you, that is accurate in either mode. The keywords using this system are known as **scale graphics** keywords. Having created a figure it is possible to alter the scale factor and display the same figure, true in all proportions, either larger or smaller. For example:

```
100 REMark * shrink *
110 MODE 256 : WINDOW 400,200,20,20
120 PAPER 5 : INK 0 : CLS
130 FOR range = 50 TO 500 STEP 50
140    SCALE range,0,0
150    LINE 10,10 TO 60,10 TO 60,40 TO 10,40 TO 10,10
160    PAUSE 25
170 END FOR range
```

The rectangle will reduce in size yet maintain its original proportions.

Within the QL there is an ultimate conversion into related pixel positions but that, fortunately, is not our concern! Although a figure drawn in one mode will have the same proportions in the other mode, a low-resolution figure will naturally be 'chunkier' since the pixels are larger. All the examples in this chapter can be run in either mode. Apart from obvious colour differences the 'chunkier' low-resolution effect will be the only distinction.

To make quite sure we appreciate that we are using a different system, the QL references the origin (0,0) of the graphics co-ordinate system at the bottom left-hand corner of the default (or current) window. This allows standard **cartesian co-ordinate** terminology to be used. For those who may not be too familiar with graphic expressions, the word 'cartesian' refers to the method of identifying any point on a graph by means of its position relative to the **X** (horizontal) axis and the **Y** (vertical) axis. It is very similar to our pixel co-ordinate system in this respect. In the illustration below, the point marked 'A' is identified as having co-ordinates (70,40), the X-axis value always being written first.

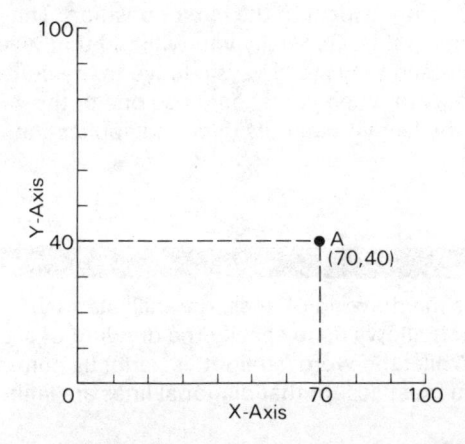

Drawing graphics on the screen is rather like using a pen on paper except that the graphics cursor is our pen. To draw on the screen we move the cursor around by using graphics keywords that control it.

RELATIVE AND ABSOLUTE

There are two terms that you will be meeting as you progress through this chapter which relate to co-ordinates. They are relative and absolute. So let us start by defining these for you in the graphics context in which they will be used. The figure shows two points A and B at the ends of a line, within a window whose bottom left-hand graphics co-ordinates are (0,0).

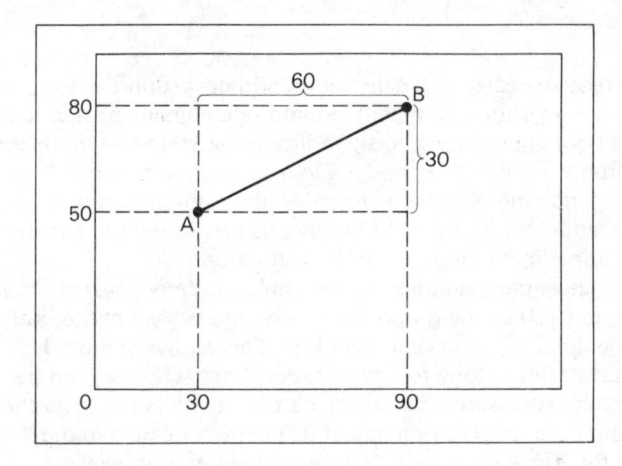

Absolute co-ordinates are those which always have values referenced to the origin (0,0). So point A has absolute co-ordinates (90,80). However, assume that we have placed the cursor at point A. Then point B would also have **relative** co-ordinates (60,30) with respect to the cursor position. The bracketed values should help to explain this. Generally you will find that when relative co-ordinates are being discussed they are always relative to the current position of the cursor. The decision as to when you should use one or the other depends, as you will see, on the keyword and its intended application.

LINE

Since so much of graphics involves the drawing of lines, we shall start by introducing the LINE keyword first. It allows us to specify the drawing of a straight line between two points. Whilst the word 'straight' is perfectly correct for horizontal and vertical lines, you must accept that diagonal lines are limited in their straightness by the ultimate resolution of the pixels used to draw them. They therefore approximate to straight lines in a series of small steps whose size is, of course, affected by the resolution mode used to display them and the angle at which they are drawn.

We can use the keyword in two ways, either by specifying both points or by specifying the end point of a line only. The standard notation for defining graphics keyword parameters is such that co-ordinates (x,y) are written as:

point

The co-ordinates themselves may be either numbers or numeric expressions. Here is the definition for the LINE keyword:

LINE [#n,] [point] TO point * [TO point] *

The square brackets indicate that their contents are optional. The * symbols enclose items that may be repeated. Let us translate this symbolic definition into some examples. To start with we shall ignore the channel number parameter, having fully dealt with this aspect in Chapter 3. If we wish to draw a line between two points we can say, for example:

LINE 10,20 TO 50,90

(10,20) are the starting co-ordinates and (50,90) are the ending co-ordinates. The following figure shows line A to be this example. If we then wanted to continue the line to (40,10) by drawing line B we just extend the statement:

LINE 10,20 TO 50,90 TO 40,10

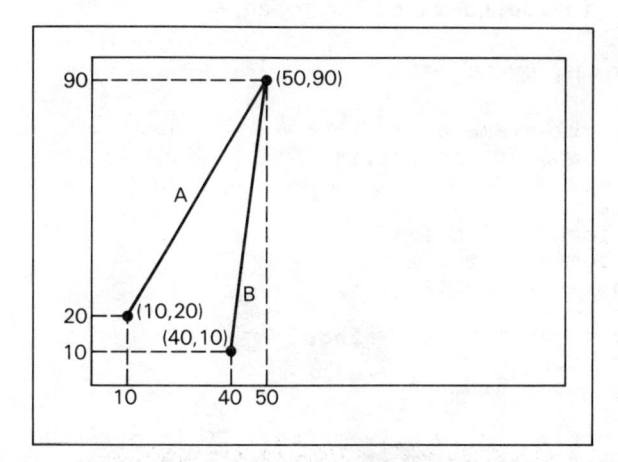

The reason why we can extend the statement in this manner is that the graphics cursor remains at the last specified co-ordinate. So further lines are added by following each previous co-ordinate with:

TO point

Add a fourth co-ordinate:

LINE 10,20 TO 50,90 TO 40,10 TO 10,20

This will draw a triangle.

Now, we initially specified the start of our line A (10,20) but if we knew that the cursor was already at that point, all we needed to write for line A was:

LINE TO 50,90

So omitting the first 'point' in the symbolic definition will generate a line from the current graphics cursor position to the next specified point. In all the above variations, 'TO' can be replaced by a comma but use of 'TO' does help to break up the figures into more easily recognisable co-ordinate pairs. This is especially so in long strings of co-ordinates or where numeric expressions are being used.

A further variation is possible:

LINE x,y

This has no 'TO'. It will cause the current cursor position to be moved to new co-ordinates (x,y) *without* drawing a line. Note that all the co-ordinates are absolute in that they always are referenced to the graphics origin.

Here is a simple example to show how easy it is to draw lines:

```
100 REMark * lines *
110 MODE 4 : WINDOW 465,200,15,15
120 PAPER 4 : INK 2 : CLS
130 LINE 60,10 TO 100,50 TO 60,90 TO 20,50 TO 60,10
```

If that one was too easy, try the next:

```
100 REMark * multi-diamonds *
110 MODE 8 : WINDOW 465,200,15,15
120 PAPER 7 : CLS
130 REPeat loop
140    LET x = 10*RND(1 TO 12)
150    LET y = 10*RND(1 TO 12)
160    LET offset = 10*RND(2 TO 5)
170    diamond
180    IF INKEY$<> "" THEN EXIT loop
190 END REPeat loop
200 DEFine PROCedure diamond
210    INK RND(6)
220    LINE (x-offset),y TO x,(y+offset) TO (x+offset),y
230    LINE TO x,(y-offset) TO (x-offset),y
240 END DEFine
```

In this example the LINE keyword uses numeric expressions to derive the line co-ordinates from the centre co-ordinates of the diamond. The parameters for *x,y* and *offset* are randomly produced within the REPEAT loop. Only one LINE statement, but lots of diamonds!

SCALE

Now we can look at one of the more important graphics keywords. When we talk about **scale** we are often referring to the way we represent the size of something by means of other related dimensions. A look at any of the older types of wooden rule will probably reveal a number of different scales: eighths, tenths, centimetres, millimetres, different values which can all be made equal to a 'foot'. Scales are useful for controlling the reduction or enlargement of drawings since, when converting from one scale to another, proportion will be retained. The scale we select depends entirely on the application. Many divisions in a given length enable a higher accuracy of measurement to be obtained than when compared with fewer divisions for the same length. Use of scale in QL graphics will tend to be a matter of what is most convenient.

The first program in this chapter achieved its effect solely by altering the scale of the window. So let us look at the keyword SCALE and its associated parameters:

SCALE # 4, 200, 0,0

Apart from the channel which the SCALE will affect, we have actually specified two parameters: 200 and (0,0). These two parameters must always be supplied. We shall ignore the channel number in our subsequent use of the keyword.

SCALE FACTOR

The first parameter is known as the scale factor. Any vertical line drawn the full height of the current window will have a length of 200 **units**. If we draw a line half the height of the window, it will be 100 units long. The actual value of the 'unit' is irrelevant, since it will depend not only on the size of the window but also on the size of the screen on which the picture is being displayed.

If we set up a particular scale factor for a window and then alter the size of that window the scale factor will still be the same, but if the window is made larger the 'unit' will become larger in proportion.

```
100 REMark * window change *
110 MODE 8 : WINDOW 400,200,20,20
120 PAPER 6 : INK 0 : CLS
130 SCALE 100,0,0
140 LET down = 175
150 FOR across = 375 TO 225 STEP -25
160    WINDOW across,down,20,20
170    LET down = down-25
180    LINE 10,10 TO 90,10 TO 90,90 TO 10,90 TO 10,10
190    PAUSE 20 : CLS
200 END FOR across
```

By leaving the background colour the same the extent of each window is not visible. Note that CLS is used in each loop to remove the previous window's figure. This prevents any lines that may be in the area between the old window and the new from being displayed.

If we draw a line 50 units long, then change the scale factor from 200 to 100, the line will expand to twice its original length.

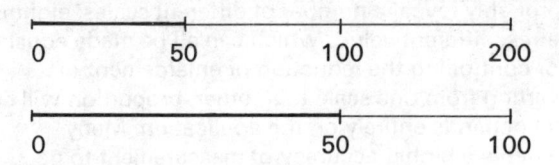

```
├─────────────┼─────────────┼─────────────┤
0            50           100           200
├─────────────────────────┼─────────────┤
0                        50           100
```

So far we have only talked about vertical lines on the display since the scale factor is defined with respect to the vertical; but of course the scale factor equally affects all lines. The maximum number of units in the horizontal axis, though, for any particular scale factor is controlled by the width of the window. It is perfectly possible, therefore, to produce a graphics drawing at a particular scale and, if it is either too large or too small, alter the scale factor appropriately to create the size you want. Simply remember that reducing the scale factor increases the size and vice versa.

WINDOW/SCALE FACTOR RELATIONSHIP

When planning the layout of your display you may well want to know 'how many pixels wide must a window be to give an X-axis of so many units?' Since pixels are not square a direct relationship between pixels and scale factor is not immediately obtainable. To save you from delving into the maths required, the following formulae can be used as a reasonable approximation:

1. Window width for a given number of X-axis units:

$$\text{Width} = \frac{\text{number of units} * \text{window height} * 1.36}{\text{scale factor}}$$

2. Number of X-axis units for a given window width:

$$\text{Number of units} = \frac{\text{window width} * \text{scale factor}}{\text{window height} * 1.36}$$

As an example, a window of 400 × 200 would, for a scale factor of 100, allow an X-axis of approximately 147 units. Remember that the height of a window will always contain units equal in number to the scale factor value.

GRAPHICS ORIGIN

The second parameter in the SCALE keyword represents the value of the co-ordinates we wish to assign to the graphics origin. When the QL is switched on the scale factor is automatically set to 100 and the graphics origin to (0,0) — so the last statement in line 130 of the previous program is not really necessary, unless the scale has been altered by an earlier program. If we assume that you wished to create a graph within a window, then you would want to draw X- and Y-axis lines. If the axes are drawn with the graphics origin as their crossing point, you would not be able to display anything to the left of the Y-axis or below the X-axis.

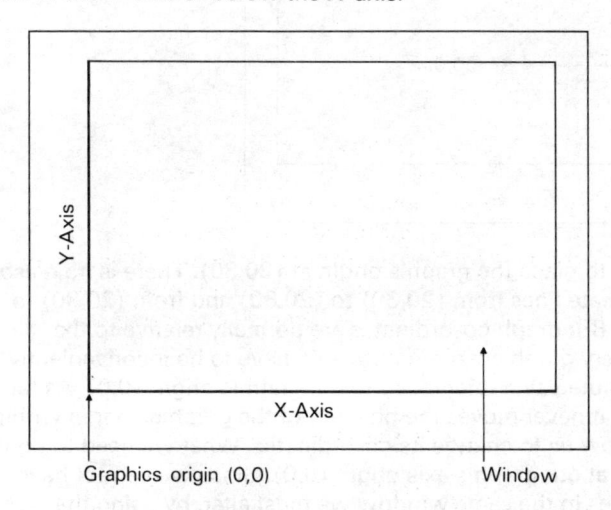

[Figure: window with Y-Axis and X-Axis drawn from Graphics origin (0,0); Window labelled]

This may be inconvenient, so if necessary we are able to move the origin using SCALE. The following two figures show an example of how this is achieved.

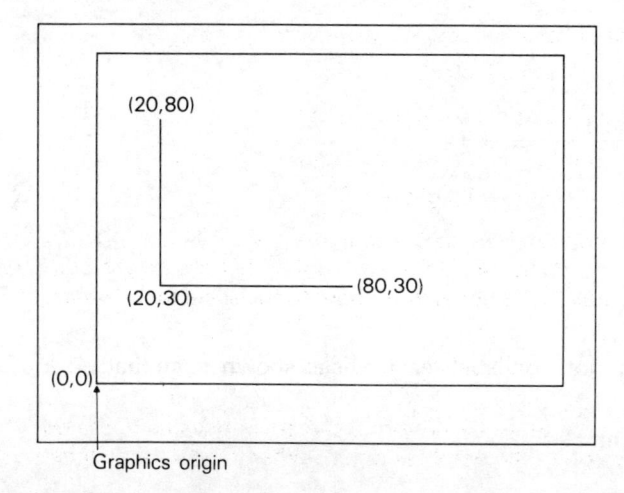

[Figure: window showing points (20,80), (20,30), (80,30), and (0,0) marked as Graphics origin]

```
                    (0,60)
                      │
                      │
         +20  (0,0)   │
        ◄────►├───────┼──────────── (60,0)
                      │+30
                      │
(-20,-30)             │
```

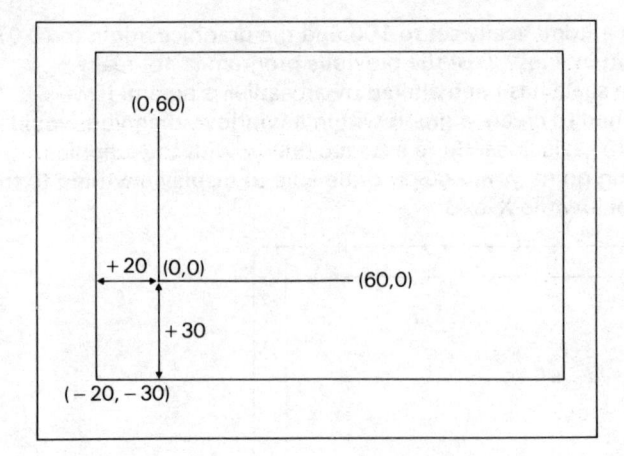

Suppose we wish to place the graph's origin at (20,30). There is no reason why we could not create lines from (20,30) to (20,80) and from (20,30) to (80,30) for the axes. But graph co-ordinates are normally relative to the graph's origin. So every graph co-ordinate would have to be inconveniently converted to an absolute value referenced to the graphic origin (0,0). As far as the QL is concerned, it never moves the position of the graphics origin within a window but does allow us to change its co-ordinates. What we need to do is call the co-ordinates at our graph's axis origin (0,0). Since we cannot have two (0,0) co-ordinates in the same window we must alter, by using the SCALE keyword, the graphic origin co-ordinates. But to what value?

Again, for those of you who may not be too familiar with graphs, our two axes are only part of the standard graph axis system, shown below:

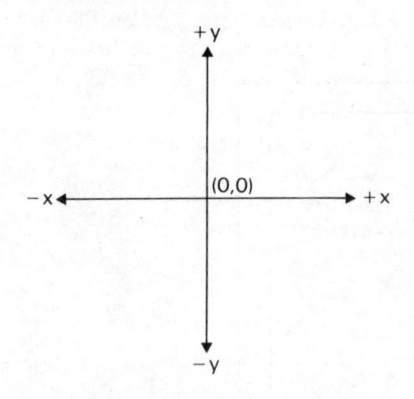

```
              +y
              ▲
              │
              │
     -x ◄─────┼─────► +x
           (0,0)
              │
              │
              ▼
             -y
```

A standard method of notation labels each axis as shown, such that:

up   = +y   left = -x
down = -y   right = +x

Our graph is represented by the top right-hand section, or **quadrant**, with axes +x and +y. With this type of graph we tend to ignore the 'plus' signs. Since the origin is at the centre of the axes any co-ordinates to the left will have a 'minus' x value, and any co-ordinates down will have a 'minus' y value. Relating this diagram to our original graph opposite you should be able to see that with co-ordinates (0,0) at the graph's origin, the original origin is 20 units left in the X-axis and 30 units down in the Y-axis, i.e. at co-ordinates (−20, −30). So we can write:

SCALE 100, −20, −30

This will achieve the necessary origin movement.

We can now simply state the graph co-ordinates relative to the graph's origin, the computer automatically compensating for the offset. The following program shows the effect of applying this change of origin:

```
100 REMark * origin change *
110 MODE 8 : WINDOW 465,200,15,15
120 PAPER 7 : INK 2 : CLS
130 LINE 0,0 TO 60,0
140 LINE 0,0 TO 0,60
150 PAUSE 50
160 SCALE 100,-20,-30
170 INK 1
180 LINE 0,0 TO 60,0
190 LINE 0,0 TO 0,60
200 SCALE 100,0,0
```

There are two things to note. First, it was not necessary to use SCALE 100, 0, 0 at the start of the program as we wanted the default scale factor of 100 to be used. Second, the first axes drawn along the left-hand and bottom edges of the window are not affected by the SCALE parameters at line 160. In other words, if a diagram is to be moved (or scaled) it must be drawn by the program after redefining the SCALE parameters; there is no retrospective action. Note that at the end of the program we have restored the original origin.

As a general rule the new origin co-ordinates for SCALE will be equal, and opposite in sign, to the original co-ordinates of the intended origin before the move takes place.

INVISIBLE ORIGIN

A further point to appreciate is that a (0,0) origin need not be visible in the window; it can be off the edge! If you should specify any co-ordinates where the value of one or both parameters is greater than the maximum that can be accommodated in the window, the QL will still accept them. But you will not be able to see the point referenced by those co-ordinates. So why should we wish to do it? It allows us to create a figure larger than the current window and then move the origin to selectively display parts of it. The effect has many applications. It can be used to simulate the scanning of a large scene through the window of a moving vehicle, or generate simple animation effects. We have included next a longer program that demonstrates in simple sequences how the origin and scale factor changes can be made to interact visually.

The program creates a simple scene of line shapes, zooms in on part of the scene progressively changing the scale factor, then moves diagonally across the scene at the same scale by changing the origin. This is followed by a random selection of parts of the scene, then a zoom out to finally view the whole scene again.

```
100 REMark * TITLE: origin move *
110 MODE 8 : WINDOW 400,205,40,20
120 PAPER 6 : INK 0 : CLS
130 OPEN#5,scr_400x10a40x225
140 PAPER#5,4 : INK#5,1 : CLS#5
150 REMark * basic display *
160 SCALE 300,0,0
170 display_screen
180 PAUSE 100 : CLS
190 REMark * reducing scale *
200 FOR scale_factor = 250 TO 100 STEP -10
210     SCALE scale_factor,0,0
220     display_screen
230     info scale_factor,0,0
240     PAUSE 20 : CLS
250 END FOR scale_factor
260 REMark * diagonal move *
270 FOR x = 0 TO 200 STEP 10
280     SCALE 100,x,x
290     display_screen
300     info scale_factor,x,x
310     PAUSE 20 : CLS
320 END FOR x
330 REMark * random origin *
340 FOR times = 1 TO 10
350     LET x = RND(200)
360     LET y = RND(200)
370     SCALE 100,x,y
380     display_screen
390     info scale_factor,x,y
400     PAUSE 50 : CLS
410 END FOR times
420 REMark * increasing scale *
430 FOR scale_factor = 100 TO 300 STEP 10
440     SCALE scale_factor,0,0 : CLS
450     display_screen
460     info scale_factor,0,0
470     PAUSE 20
480 END FOR scale_factor
490 DEFine PROCedure display_screen
500     LINE 40,230 TO 80,280
510     LINE 90,130 TO 160,30 TO 140,200 TO 120,140 TO 90,130
520     LINE 50,40 TO 70,60 TO 50,80 TO 30,60 TO 50,40
530     LINE 210,90 TO 260,40
```

```
540     LINE 200,240 TO 280,220
550     LINE 190,160 TO 390,230 TO 300,70
560     LINE TO 280,140 TO 190,160
570 END DEFine
580 DEFine PROCedure info(scale_factor,x_origin,y_origin)
590     CLS#5
600     PRINT#5,"SCALE FACTOR:";scale_factor;
610     PRINT#5,!"  ORIGIN:";x_origin;",";y_origin
620 END DEFine
```

The program could have been made more compact by using a procedure for the SCALE loops, but in the interests of providing a clearer program for you this has been omitted.

FIGURE CENTRING

The very first program in this chapter displayed a box progressively reducing in size and also progressively moving towards the bottom left-hand corner of the window. This occurred because the origin remained at (0,0) so the actual distance between the centre of the box and the origin reduced at each stage of the loop.

In reducing (or increasing) the size of a figure you may want to keep the figure in the same position on the screen. To prevent movement of the figure in any axis while its size alters, we need first of all to identify the central co-ordinates around which the rest of the figure will either reduce or expand. These would generally be the geometrical centre of the figure, but in a non-symmetrical design a trial and error method may have to be used.

Then we must find a way to re-define the graphics origin so that the central co-ordinates always remain in the same screen position. Each time the scale factor is altered the central co-ordinates must change in proportion. The following figures show the principle.

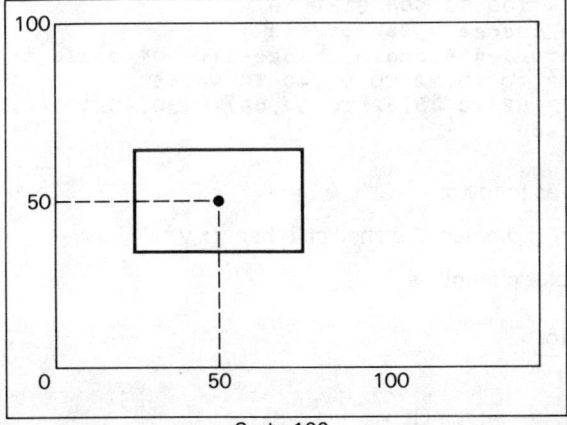

Scale 100

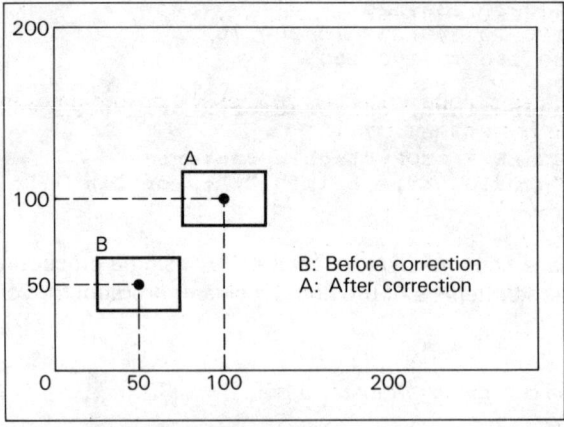

```
                    ┌─────────────────────────────────┐
                 200│                                 │
                    │                                 │
                    │                                 │
                    │            A                    │
                 100│        ┌───────┐                │
                    │        │   ●   │                │
                    │     B  │       │                │
                    │   ┌────┼──┐    │   B: Before correction
                  50│   │  ● │  │    │   A: After correction
                    │   └────┼──┘    │                │
                    │        └───────┘                │
                    │                                 │
                   0└───┴────┴───────┴────────┴───────┘
                        50   100              200
                              Scale 200
```

If the scale factor is doubled then the co-ordinates are doubled. By knowing the change in scale factor the same change can be applied to the co-ordinates. The required change in graphics origin is then equal (but opposite in sign) to the difference between the old centre co-ordinates and the new ones.

If reduction of a figure is carried out to its ultimate conclusion you will end up with a single point on the screen. The co-ordinates of this 'vanishing' point can be anywhere on the screen, but only the centre point of the figure will cause reduction without axis movement. Try the following program which demonstrates a shrinking figure that maintains its screen position. The simple rules necessary to create the effect will then be explained.

```
100 REMark * shrinking octagon *
110 MODE 8 : WINDOW 350,200,60,30
120 PAPER 3 : INK 1 : CLS
130 LET old = 100
140 FOR factor = 100 TO 500 STEP 50
150   LET scale_change = factor/old
160   SCALE factor,-60*(scale_change-1),-50*(scale_change-1)
170   LINE 48,22 TO 73,22 TO 90,40 TO 90,65
180   LINE TO 73,82 TO 48,82 TO 30,65 TO 30,40 TO 48,22
190 END FOR factor
```

The full sequence is as follows:

1. Define the central co-ordinates. We shall call them (x,y).

2. Express the scale factor change as:

    $$\frac{\text{original scale factor}}{\text{new scale factor}}$$

    We shall call this 'S', but let the QL work it out!

3. The new co-ordinates relative to the new scale factor are:

   (S * x, S * y)

4. The central co-ordinates change, necessary to keep the co-ordinates in the same screen position (*new* minus *old*), is:

   for the X-axis: S * x − x
   for the Y-axis: S * y − y

   which is the same as x(S − 1) and y(S − 1).

5. The SCALE origin co-ordinates are now these values but with opposite sign.

   If you know what the actual values of x and y are, then simply invert the sign. For example, if the central co-ordinates were (20, − 50) then the SCALE keyword would become:

   SCALE factor, − 20*(S − 1), 50*(S − 1)

   The above formula for the SCALE origin is all you need to remember, apart from the meaning of S. The program should now be self-explanatory, but do note that the *old* scale factor was defined before the program entered the reduction cycle loop. This ensured it was always a constant value, i.e. the original scale factor in the subsequent calculations for S.

   Should you be writing a more complex program where you are altering the size of several figures using a standard procedure, you may not know the actual values for x and y. In this case just invert the sign by, for example:

   LET x = − x*(S − 1)
   LET y = − y*(S − 1)

   Your SCALE keyword becomes:

   SCALE factor, x, y

   x and *y* represent the new co-ordinates.

Just to make sure that you have understood the way in which SCALE may be used to affect scale factor and origin position, try problem 1 at the end of this chapter before you go on to look at the other graphics keywords.

POINT

Now let us go on a little further and take a look at the keyword POINT. Apart from the usual optional channel number parameter, it has parameters in (x,y) co-ordinates form to define where a single point is to be placed using the current INK colour. Its basic form is:

   POINT[#n,] point * [TO point]*

For example:

POINT # 6, 10, 20

This will place a single point at co-ordinates (10,20) in the window defined as channel 6.

Since a point is specified in scale co-ordinates, the QL must switch on the nearest pixel to it.

The resolution mode selected does, of course, affect the size of the point as the next example shows:

```
100 MODE 4 : INK 2
110 PAPER 7 : CLS
120 POINT 50,50
```

Now change line 100 to:

```
100 MODE 8 : INK 2
```

Run the program again. Which mode you use will generally be a compromise between the colour range and the resolution required.

As for the LINE keyword the co-ordinates may be extended so that we could have:

POINT 10,20 TO 30,40 TO 80,100 TO 90,60

The following program generates random POINT co-ordinates in different colours:

```
100 REMark * random points *
110 MODE 8 : WINDOW 465,200,15,15
120 PAPER 7 : CLS
130 FOR points = 1 TO 200
140   INK RND(6)
150   POINT RND(1 TO 170), RND(1 TO 100)
160 END FOR points
```

A 'rocket-eye' view is obtained with the next program:

```
100 REMark * going up *
110 MODE 8 : WINDOW 420,200,45,20
120 PAPER 217 : INK 7 : CLS
130 REPeat up
135   AT 0,0 : PAPER 0 : CLS 1
140   POINT RND(1 TO 38),100 TO RND(39 TO 77),100
150   POINT TO RND(78 TO 116),100 TO RND(117 TO 154),100
160   SCROLL 1
170   IF INKEY$ <>"" THEN EXIT up
180 END REPeat up
```

POINT AND SCALE

Although we are dealing with scale graphics keywords, POINT – as we have said – plots pixel-related points. This means that if you want to distinguish individual points from one another, you cannot use a scale factor that implies a higher resolution than that possible in pixel graphics. Points closer together than the pixels will naturally appear as one. For example:

```
100 REMark * scale points *
110 MODE 4 : PAPER 7 : INK 0 : CLS
120 SCALE 1200,0,0
130 POINT 250,200 TO 251,200 TO 250,201 TO 251,201
140 INK 2 : POINT 300,200
```

Both black and red points will appear the same size despite line 130 specifying four separate points.

If we want to avoid duplicating points then we must look at the pixel/scale factor relationship a little closer. And the relationship varies depending upon the screen resolution used.

Effect of high resolution

If you imagine a square on the screen of 100 × 100 units, then in high resolution mode the X-axis will contain 1.5 times the number of pixels that are in the Y-axis. If we arrange the scale factor to give a one-to-one relationship between units and pixels in the X-axis, then successive points plotted in the Y-axis would result in duplication of some of them. (100 pixels in the X-axis but 66 pixels only in the Y-axis).

To help you understand the effect, if you are using a monitor, the next example will draw two sets of successive points. One set in the X-axis is given a staggered arrangement so that individual points may be seen, since with one unit per pixel successive points would display a straight continuous line. The Y-axis points are plotted diagonally. The overlaps on the diagonal demonstrate the duplication of points that has occurred.

```
100 REMark * x-axis resolution *
110 WINDOW 300,221,100,20
120 MODE 4 : PAPER 7 : INK 2 : CLS
130 SCALE 300,0,0
140 LET y = 15
150 FOR x = 1 TO 300
160   IF y = 15 THEN
170     LET y = y - 10
180   ELSE
190     LET y = y + 10
200   END IF
210   POINT x,y
220 END FOR x
230 LET x = 0
240 FOR y = 0 TO 300
```

```
250     POINT x,y
260     LET x = x + 1
270 END FOR y
280 INK 4
290 POINT 300,300
```

Lines 160 to 200 achieve the stagger of points in the X-axis. We have included a green pixel at the end of the diagonal to indicate the co-incidence of line and window corner. Now we shall change the program and allow the Y-axis to have a one-to-one relationship between units and pixels and see the effect on the X-axis points.

```
100 REMark * y-axis resolution *
110 WINDOW 313,230,100,20
120 MODE 4 : PAPER 7 : INK 2 : CLS
130 SCALE 230,0,0
140 FOR x = 1 TO 230
150     POINT x,5
160 END FOR x
170 LET x = 0
180 FOR y = 0 TO 230
190     POINT x,y
200     LET x = x + 1
210 END FOR y
220 INK 4
230 POINT 230,230
```

This time the diagonal points are in a straight line but the X-axis points, which we have not staggered, have gaps between some of them. We can summarize the effects:

- With maximum resolution in the X-axis (one unit per pixel), sequential points in the Y-axis will show duplication.
- With maximum resolution in the Y-axis, sequential points in the X-axis will show gaps.

Since the pixels are rectangular it is impossible to achieve maximum resolution in both axes at once. Again, the method you choose depends upon your application. You will generally find, however, that it is more acceptable to have duplication rather than gaps. The latter would, of course, break-up continuous lines as you will have seen on the diagonal of the last program.

Maximum resolution formula

Fine, you may say, but how do we determine the scale factor required for a particular maximum resolution? The solution lies within the formula we have already used to find the relationship between X-axis units and window size. Rearranging it we can say:

$$\text{Scale factor} = \frac{\text{X-axis units} * \text{window height} * 1.36}{\text{window width}}$$

For maximum resolution:

X-axis units = window width

Therefore we can simplify the formula to:

scale factor = window height * 1.36

So a window 400 by 200 would require a scale factor of 272 to give maximum resolution in the X-axis. The formula does not involve the window width, therefore *any* width will always be subject to having the maximum resolution.

In the example programs the manipulation of the standard formula was carried a little further. You may have noticed that the WINDOW statements in lines 110 changed their parameters for the two programs. This was deliberate, in order to produce a square window for each program. The width of the window in the first example had to be 300 to give maximum resolution with an X-axis length of 300 units. The scale factor was also set at 300 to give 300 units in the Y-axis. Re-arranging our formula again we have:

$$\text{Window height} = \frac{\text{window width} * \text{scale factor}}{\text{X-axis units} * 1.36}$$

which gives a value of 221 pixels.

The formula can be similarly re-arranged to find the required window width for maximum resolution in the Y-axis.

Effect of low resolution

The resolution mode selected on the QL does not appear to affect the formulae we have been using, since WINDOW parameters are always treated as if high-resolution mode is selected. The QL automatically adjusts to the nearest pixel when in low-resolution mode. But if we are attempting to place points close together without landing on the same pixel in low-resolution mode, we must allow for the larger pixel size.

We have, essentially, only half the resolution in the X-axis that we have in high-resolution mode. All we need to do is calculate the X-axis maximum resolution as if using high resolution, then separate each point by a minimum of two units. If we were, for example, drawing a series of points using a FOR ... END FOR loop we could simply write:

FOR x_axis = 0 TO 200 STEP 2

This will, of course, increment in units of two. If generating random points, you could modify the function like this:

LET x = RND(10 TO 50) * 2

This would give even unit numbers. Or:

LET x = RND(10 TO 50) * 2 − 1

This would give odd unit numbers.

To round off this section, for those readers using a television here is an example of maximum resolution X-axis plotting in low-resolution mode to show the effect of incrementing in units of one or two:

```
100 REMark * low resolution *
110 WINDOW 300,221,40,20
120 MODE 8 : PAPER 5 : INK 2 : CLS
130 SCALE 300,0,0
140 plots 255,1
150 plots 35,2
160 DEFine PROCedure plots (y_start,increment)
170   LET y = y_start
180   FOR x = 0 TO 300 STEP increment
190     IF y = y_start THEN
200       LET y = y - 20
210     ELSE
220       LET y = y + 20
230     END IF
240     POINT x,y
250   END FOR x
260 END DEFine
```

The program is very similar to the first one introduced in this section, except that a procedure has been used to draw the two sets of X-axis points. The effects created should be self-explanatory.

But before we leave this program one further point can be demonstrated. Add the following statement to the end of line 190 (after 'THEN')

GO TO 240

Run the program again. This time only single lines will be drawn, but note how much faster the second line is and yet there are no gaps. Using steps of one unit wastes time and is unnecessary since a full line can be drawn using the maximum resolution 'step of 2' principle.

If lines, arcs, circles or even areas of colour are being produced using graphics keywords, then in the process of the QL finding the nearest pixel to each scale point, gaps will occasionally occur in the resulting display. This must either be tolerated or a greater degree of overlap programmed at the expense of drawing time. In some instances the gaps can create quite interesting effects (as the 'rainbow' arc example later will show). Many of the remaining programs in this chapter will use the maximum resolution principle to help you become familiar with it, but do experiment to find the result you prefer.

DRAWING CURVES

The LINE statement can be used to compose a curve of a number of straight lines, but this is naturally only an approximation. Since the shortest LINE can consist of just two points – the start and the end of the line – it is sensible to use the POINT keyword to draw curves. In this way reasonable approximations can be produced. Also the closer the points, the more continuous the curve appears. We can therefore make good use of the maximum resolution effects just discussed. The next program will draw a reasonable sine wave:

```
100 REMark *sinewave *
110 MODE 4 : WINDOW 510,240,0,0
120 PAPER 7 : INK 4 : CLS
130 SCALE 326,-20,-155
140 LINE 0,-150 TO 0,150
150 LINE -20,0 TO 450,0
160 INK 2
170 FOR x = 0 TO 450
180   POINT x,INT(SIN(x*PI/225)*150+.5)
190 END FOR x
```

Line 130 uses the SCALE statement to offset the X-axis to the centre of the screen, thus allowing both positive and negative values of y to be plotted. The rather involved expression in line 180 is used to calculate the y co-ordinates for the curve. For those wishing to know how it was derived, Appendix 4 gives an explanation. The scale factor is also set to give maximum resolution in the X-axis and so produce an acceptable curve.

If maximum resolution in the X-axis is exceeded (more scale units than pixels) then a ragged curve will be produced, though a more continuous line will be created. If we make the Y-axis scaling value (150) a variable (*height*) we can create a family of curves like this:

```
100 REMark * sine wave family *
110 MODE 8:WINDOW 510,240,0,0
120 PAPER 0:INK 7:CLS
130 SCALE 326,-20,-155
140 LINE 0,-150 TO 0,150
150 LINE -20,0 TO 450,0
160 FOR height = 150 TO 25 STEP -25
170   INK height/25+1
180   FOR x=0 TO 450 STEP 2
190     POINT x,INT(SIN(x*PI/225)*height+.5)
200   END FOR x
210 END FOR height
```

POINT AND SHAPES

The keyword can also be used to create small shapes. By forming each within a procedure the latter can be called whenever the shape is required. The following example displays random star-like shapes.

```
100 REMark * stars *
110 MODE 8 : WINDOW 512,256,0,0
120 PAPER 1 : INK 7 : CLS
130 BORDER 15,6
140 SCALE 348,0,0
150 FOR number = 1 TO 50
160   LET x = RND(36 TO 446)
170   LET y = RND(22 TO 310)
180   star x,y
190 END FOR number
200 DEFine PROCedure star(x,y)
210   POINT x,y-2 TO x, y-1 TO x,y+1 TO x,y+2 TO x-2,y-1
220   POINT TO x-2,y TO x-2,y+1 TO x+2,y-1 TO x+2,y
230   POINT TO x+2,y+1 TO x-4,y TO x+4,y
240 END DEFine
```

The star shape was made up as shown below:

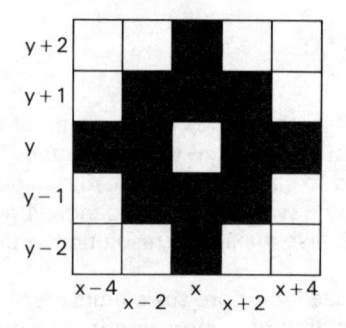

```
y+2
y+1
y
y-1
y-2
     x-4    x    x+4
        x-2   x+2
```

But something is wrong. Some of the stars look correct, but others are very different. Despite our attention to detail with respect to scale factor and maximum resolution rules, we have been defeated by the QL's 'approximate' conversion of graphics co-ordinates into pixel positions, giving too random an effect. Many factors control the end result and quite a lot of experimenting must be expected before achieving the desired effect using the POINT keyword in this way.

ARC

The next keyword to consider enables the QL to draw an arc between two co-ordinates in the current INK colour. To achieve control over the curvature of the arc, we must also include the subtended angle (θ in the figure) expressed in radians.

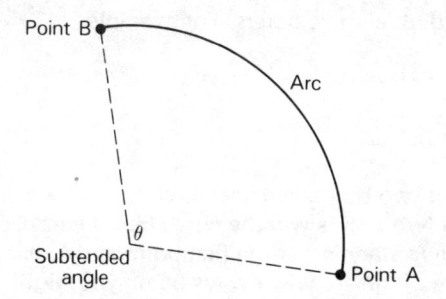

As a gentle reminder, a radian is the angle subtended at the centre of a circle by an arc equal in length to the radius. (For those who may have forgotten school trigonometry, the radius is the distance from the centre of a circle to any point on its circumference.)
This means that:

$$\frac{\text{Length of arc}}{\text{Radius of circle}} = \text{number of radians subtended at the centre.}$$

All we need to know for radian/degree conversion is:

1 radian = $180/\pi$ degrees (approximately 57°)
1 degree = $\pi/180$ radians

We can also make use of the QL SuperBASIC function:

RAD(n)

This will return the value of *n* degrees in radians.
The statement format is, in general terms:

ARC[#n,] * [point] TO point, angle *

The channel number is optional as usual, and the whole expression may be repeated to enable the drawing of more than one arc with a single keyword. Each set of parameters is separated from the next by a comma. If the first *point* is omitted, then the first arc co-ordinates will be those of the current cursor position. Here are some possible variations:

ARC # 4, 10,20 TO 90,100, 1

This will draw an arc in the window of channel 4 between co-ordinates (10,20) and (90,100) with a subtended angle of one radian.

ARC TO 50,80, 2

This will draw an arc from the current cursor position to co-ordinates (50,80) with a subtended angle of two radians.

ARC 10,20 TO 80,100, 1, 80,20 TO 100,10, 1.5

This will draw two arcs.

Numeric expressions may be used for all parameters. For example:

ARC x, y TO x+10, y+8, angle

ARC POSITION

Returning to the drawing of an arc, if two points are specified then on which side of an imaginary line joining the two points will the curve lie? The easiest way to remember the rule is to imagine standing at the first point and looking towards the second point. The curve of the arc will always be on your right. Putting it another way, the curve is always drawn anti-clockwise from the first point. The following simple example should sort out any remaining problem with the rule.

```
100 ARC 10,20 TO 130,80,1
110 PAUSE 100
120 ARC 130,80 TO 10,20,1
```

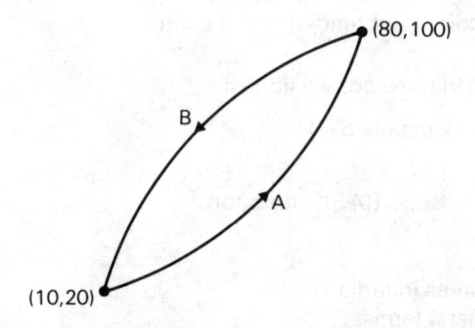

To draw curve A we must start at point (10,20), since looking towards point (80,100) the curve will be to the right. To draw curve B we must start at point (80,100).

ARC SELECTION

An arc is, of course, part of the circumference of a circle, so referring to the figure below, you can see that there are two possible arcs that can be drawn for every pair of co-ordinates.

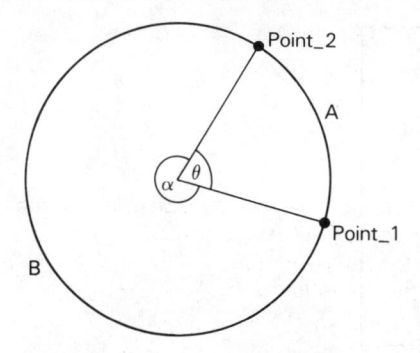

ARC point_1, TO point_2, θ

This will draw curve A.

ARC point_2, TO point_1, α

This will draw curve B. Note the order in which the points were written in the second ARC statement. Also note that you do not have to work out the two angles separately. Since 2π radians is equal to 360°, a full circle, then knowing one, the other is found from the formula:

$\alpha = 2\pi - \theta$

Wherever possible let the computer do the calculation! To demonstrate the effect of selecting both arcs try the following program:

```
100 REMark * double arcs *
110 MODE 8 : SCALE 200,0,0
120 PAPER 6 : INK 4 : CLS
130 ARC 40,100 TO 120,100,2,120,100 TO 40,100,2
140 INK 2 : PAUSE 100
150 ARC 40,100 TO 120,100,2*PI-2,120,100 TO 40,100,2*PI-2
```

Two interlocking circles are produced with the smaller arcs in green. Note how we write the angle expression using the SuperBASIC function PI.

ANGLE RANGE

Looking back, it would appear that the range of angles we can use (in radians) should be from greater than 0 to less than 2π. We normally write this as:

0 < angle < 2π

Obviously, the nearer the angle is to 0 then the slighter the curve of the arc; it almost approaches a straight line. At the other end of the range, the nearer to 2π the angle becomes the closer the arc is to being a circle. It is not possible to have angles of 0 or 2π. The following figures show typical examples of what you could see when using angles near these limits with large radii.

Small angle

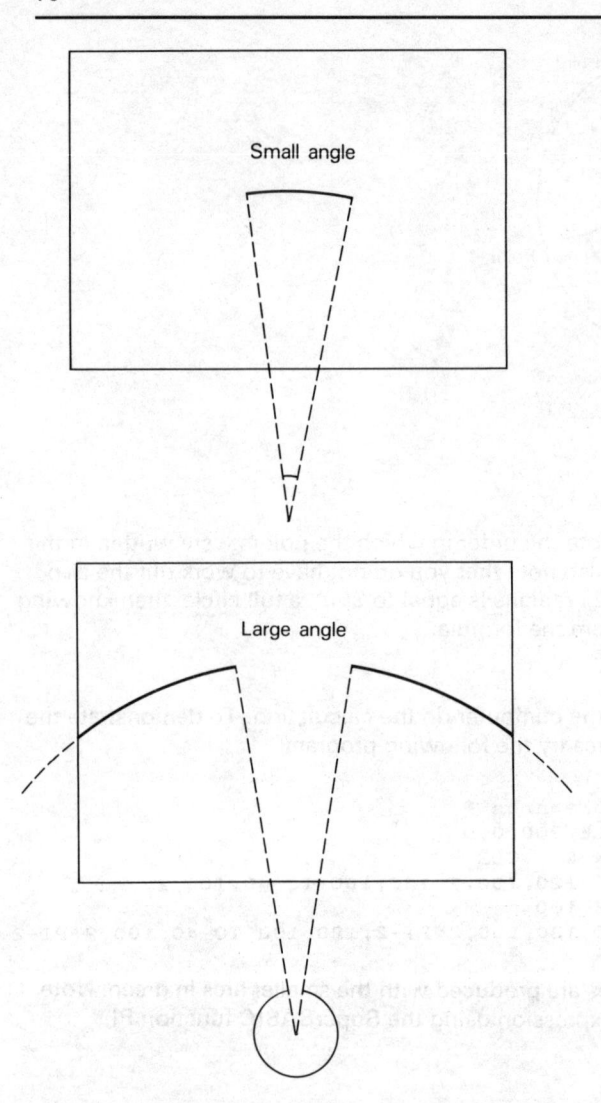

Large angle

However, the QL specification for the angle is given as:

$-2\pi <$ angle $< 2\pi$

What is the significance of the negative angle? It allows you to specify an arc where the curve will be produced *clockwise* from the first point to the second. In other words, the reverse of our earlier rule. It can make arc programming easier. For example, suppose we wanted to draw a series of arcs from left to right, such as are shown below:

```
     A       B        C       D
 (10,50)  (40,50)  (70,50) (100,50)
```

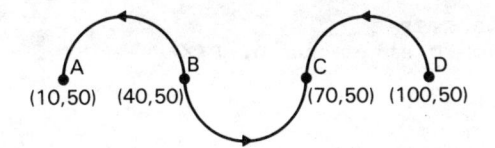

Without the 'minus angle' facility, the arcs would have to be drawn on the screen in the order:

B TO A, B TO C, D TO C

Try the next example:

```
100 REMark * arc sequence *
110 MODE 8 : WINDOW 465,200,15,15
120 PAPER 4 : INK 2 : CLS
125 PAUSE 50
130 ARC 40,50 TO 10,50,1.5
140 ARC 40,50 TO 70,50,1.5
150 ARC 100,50 TO 70,50,1.5
```

By using the minus angle for the end arcs, we can write the program more easily. Add the following lines and run the program again:

```
160 PAUSE 100 : INK 0
170 ARC 10,60 TO 40,60,-1.5 TO 70,60,1.5 TO 100,60,-1.5
```

It also has a further use, as will be seen a little later in this chapter.

CONCENTRIC ARCS

By using a fixed angle, but varying the co-ordinates in equal increments, a series of concentric arcs may be produced:

```
100 REMark * concentric arcs *
110 MODE 8 : WINDOW 465,200,15,15
120 PAPER 7 : INK 1 : CLS
130 FOR num = 0 TO 60 STEP 10
140    ARC 90+num,10+num TO 70-num,10+num,PI/2
150 END FOR num
```

The 'PI/2' expression gives an angle of 90 degrees. Concentric arcs are drawn in increasing size up from the bottom of the screen. You can create an interesting rainbow effect quite simply by:

```
100 REMark * QL rainbow *
110 MODE 8 : WINDOW 200,153,156,62
120 SCALE 200,0,0 :PAPER 0 : CLS
130 LET start = 200
140 FOR colour = 1 TO 6
150    INK colour
```

```
160     FOR num = 0 TO 20 STEP 2
170       ARC 0,start-num TO start-num,0,-PI/2
180     END FOR num
190     LET start = start - 20
200 END FOR colour
```

The expressions used for y and x in line 170 allow the co-ordinates to be decremented by 20 units each time around the colour loop to create bands of colour. Note also that line 160 is using an increment of two. We have deliberately chosen maximum resolution in the X-axis to show the 'gap' effect, and so only need to increment in units of two since we are in MODE 8.

FIXED CO-ORDINATES, VARIABLE ANGLE

By fixing the start and end points of the arc, but this time varying the angle, arcs of differing length are produced. For example:

```
100 REMark * variable angle *
110 MODE 4 : PAPER 0 : INK 7 : CLS
120 FOR angle = .5 TO 6 STEP .5
130   ARC 90,5 TO 60,5,angle
140 END FOR angle
```

Varying the angle in 0.5 radian steps (approximately 28.5°) gives twelve separate arcs. Try the same example with MODE 8 and notice the resolution difference.

Here is a more light-hearted example generating arcs of random size, position and colour:

```
100 REMark * random arcs *
110 MODE 8 : PAPER 7 : CLS
120 SCALE 150,0,0
130 REPeat arcs
140   INK RND(1 TO 6)
150   ARC RND(90),RND(90) TO RND(90),RND(90),RND(.5 TO 6)
160   IF INKEY$ <>"" THEN EXIT arcs
170 END REPeat arcs
```

ARC SIZE

There may be instances when you want to produce an arc of a particular size and must therefore know the subtended angle value accurately. There is no intention of taking you through lots of trigonometry to show how various formulae can be produced to achieve this. Instead, there are two formulae ([1] and [2]) below to help you. Both are written in a form that allows you to include them directly into your programs by appropriately changing the example parameter names. The figure shows the parameters used.

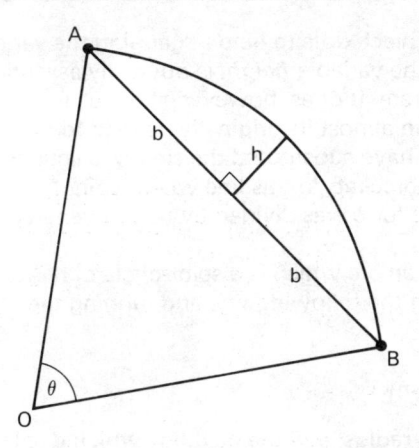

Point A represents (x_end, y_end)
Point B represents (x_start, y_start)
θ is the subtended angle in radians
h is the height of the arc
b is half the straight-line distance A to B

The straight-line distance between points A and B is given by:

$$2b = \text{SQRT}((y\_end - y\_start)^2 + (x\_end - x\_start)^2) \qquad [1]$$

Half this distance (b) is used in the following formula to find the subtended angle:

$$\theta(\text{in radians}) = 2 * \text{ASIN}(2*b*h/(b^2 + h^2)) \qquad [2]$$

To demonstrate use of these formulae the next example draws a dome of height 50 units on top of a rectangle. The values have been specially chosen to enable you to visually check the result. The green diagonal line from the top of the arc to the left-hand edge of the rectangle is bisected by the right-hand red line of the rectangle.

```
100 REMark * calculated arc *
110 MODE 4 : WINDOW 400,200,20,20
120 SCALE 200,0,0
130 PAPER 7 : INK 0 : CLS
140 FOR y = 20 TO 160 STEP 10
150   FOR x = 40 TO 200 STEP 10
160     POINT x,y
170   END FOR x
180 END FOR y
190 INK 2
200 LINE 120,20 TO 160,50 TO 100,130 TO 60,100 TO 120,20
210 INK 4 : LET height = 50
220 LINE 90,60 TO 170,120
230 LET b = (SQRT((130-50)^2+(100-160)^2))/2
240 LET angle = 2*ASIN(2*b*height/(b^2+height^2))
250 ARC 160,50 TO 100,130,angle
```

Lines 140 to 180 produce a grid of black dots to help in gauging the various sizes. On line 210 the assignment for the variable *height* is not really essential since it has only one value in the program. It does, however, allow us to demonstrate use of the angle formula in almost its originally defined form. Similarly, on line 230, we could easily have substituted the simply-calculated values of the co-ordinates. Watch the brackets in this line when typing!

Do note that at line 230 the formula for *b* was divided by two to generate the half straight-line value.

The program has, in fact, produced an arc which is a semi-circle of radius 50 units. This can be proved by adding the following line and running the program again:

    260 ARC 100,130 TO 160,50,angle

If anyone should query the 50 units radius, add the next line which displays a right-angled triangle whose sides have the 'standard' measurements of 30, 40 and 50 units each.

    270 LINE 120,20 TO 160,20 TO 160,50

So, apart from trigonometric exercises, the ARC keyword has many possible applications. But the arc, as we have already said, is part of a circle, so let us now go on further to see how we produce circles and their 'cousins', ellipses.

CIRCLE

Before delving into the generation of circles, we must make one point clear. For circles and ellipses there are two keywords called CIRCLE and ELLIPSE. Nothing would seem unusual about that except that *either* keyword, with the appropriate parameters, may be used to create either type of figure. To avoid confusion, in our descriptions we shall use CIRCLE and ELLIPSE only for their literally corresponding figure.

To draw circles then we shall use the keyword CIRCLE which has the following standard format:

CIRCLE[#n,]point, radius * [;point, radius] *

The channel number is optional and the other parameters may be repeated to produce several circles with one keyword. Note that a semicolon is used as a separator instead of the usual comma. Although we have met several other graphics keywords where repetition may occur, we will take the opportunity here to advise that the facility should not be overworked. Too many repeated parameters will make your program awkward to read and possibly difficult to fault-find.

All the parameters for CIRCLE can be numeric expressions if required. The x,y parameters denote the centre co-ordinates of the circle, with reference to the graphics origin. The radius is specified in scale graphics units. So, for example, we can draw a circle of centre co-ordinates (90,100) and radius of 60 units with the following:

CIRCLE 90, 100, 60

To draw circles is therefore quite straightforward and we do not need to worry about awkward trigonometric formulae. One other very satisfying aspect of this keyword is that it does produce circles, not ovals as can be the case with some other computers.

```
100 REMark * concentric circles *
110 MODE 4 : PAPER 3 : INK 5 : CLS
120 FOR radius = 35 TO 5 STEP -5
130     CIRCLE 40,60,radius
140 END FOR radius
```

Circles are always drawn in the current INK colour.

```
100 REMark * rainbow circles *
110 MODE 8 : PAPER 0 : CLS
120 FOR colour = 1 TO 7
130     INK colour
140     CIRCLE 40,60,35
150     PAUSE 50 : CLS
160 END FOR colour
```

All the colours are used to draw the same size circle, each circle being cleared from the screen at approximately one-second intervals.

Using random number expressions for each CIRCLE parameter allows us to demonstrate how simple it is to rapidly produce circles in all colours and sizes.

```
100 REMark * random circles *
110 MODE 8 : WINDOW 470,220,20,20
120 PAPER 7 : CLS
130 FOR loop = 1 TO 80
140     INK RND(6)
150     CIRCLE RND(25 TO 132),RND(25 TO 75), 5*RND(1 TO 5)
160 END FOR loop
```

The random number ranges for x,y co-ordinates have been chosen to enable all the circles to be visible in full within the window area. Remember the formula:

$$\text{Number of X-axis units} = \frac{\text{window width} * \text{scale factor}}{\text{window height} * 1.36}$$

(Refer to 'Window/scale factor relationship' (p. 58).)

For our example the scale factor was the default value of 100, so there will be about 157 units available in the X-axis. The maximum radius will be 25, therefore we simply reduce the maximum values for x and y co-ordinates by 25 and similarly increase the minimum values by 25. This keeps every random circle within the window.

RINGS

All the examples have been drawing single pixel-width circles but sometimes filled-in circles or annular circles are required. We shall be discussing filling techniques later in this chapter but here is one method of producing rings.

```
100 REMark * annulus *
110 MODE 4 : WINDOW 256,230,128,0
120 PAPER 0 : INK 7 : CLS
130 SCALE 313,0,0
140 FOR radius = 70 TO 110
150   CIRCLE 128,150,radius
160 END FOR radius
```

The program is actually drawing concentric circles again, the radius being incremented in sufficiently small units. If the increment were too large we would have produced only concentric circles with gaps in between. Our formula for maximum resolution in the X-axis has been used.

Scale factor = window height * 1.36

So for the window height of 230 we obtain a scale factor of 313.
Here is an example of producing rings in low resolution mode:

```
100 REMark * olympic *
110 MODE 8 : WINDOW 500,240,10,10
120 PAPER 7 : CLS : SCALE 326,0,0
130 DATA 250,150,100,150,400,150,325,90,175,90
140 FOR colour = 0 TO 2,4,6
150   INK colour
160   READ x : READ y
170   FOR radius = 50 TO 60 STEP .5
180     CIRCLE x,y,radius
190   END FOR radius
200 END FOR colour
210 CLEAR
```

Note that this time we have used a STEP interval of 0.5 to fill the rings more completely.

POLAR CO-ORDINATES

Before moving on from the CIRCLE keyword, we would like to introduce a little trigonometry that can be very useful for locating points on a circle. We have already seen that the cartesian co-ordinate system allows us to fix the position of a point in terms of its x and y distances from a graphic origin. The

polar co-ordinate system fixes a point by knowing its direction and its distance from an origin. When applied to a circle, it enables any point on a circle's circumference to be expressed in terms of the radius and the angle that the radius makes with the X-axis to meet the point. The figure shows the parameters involved.

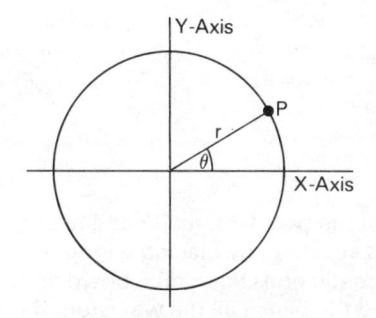

In cartesian co-ordinates point P would be x,y. In polar co-ordinates point P is expressed as r,θ, the two systems being related by:

x = r * COS(angle)
y = r * SIN(angle)

where (angle) is θ in radians.

The following examples demonstrate how polar co-ordinates can be easily applied, the first creating an elementary clock-face outline.

```
100 REMark * basic clock *
110 MODE 4 : PAPER 0 : INK 2 : CLS
120 CIRCLE 45,50,30 : INK 7
130 CIRCLE 45,50,2
140 FOR angle = 0 TO 11*PI/6 STEP PI/6
150   CIRCLE 45+30*COS(angle),50+30*SIN(angle),1
160 END FOR angle
```

The cartesian co-ordinates for CIRCLE have been replaced by their polar co-ordinates equivalents.

Our last example is a multicoloured circle:

```
100 REMark * multicolour disc *
110 MODE 8 : WINDOW 465,200,15,15
120 PAPER 0 : INK 7 : CLS
130 CIRCLE 75,50,45
140 REPeat loop
150   LET angle = RAD(RND(360))
160   INK RND(6)
170   LINE 75,50 TO 75+45*COS(angle),50+45*SIN(angle)
190   IF INKEY$ <>"" THEN EXIT loop
200 END REPeat loop
```

ELLIPSE

An ellipse can best be described, in non-geometrical terms, as a squashed circle. A typical ellipse is shown below:

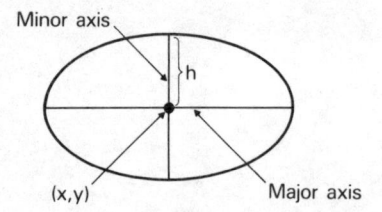

The shape is controlled by the lengths of the two axes, major and minor. I am sure that many will have drawn ellipses at school by placing a loop of string around two drawing pins about 10 centimetres apart on a board and holding the string taut with a pencil, moved the pencil all the way around the pins. The horizontal axis on which the pins were placed is known as the **major** axis. The vertical axis is called the **minor** axis.

To enable the QL to draw ellipses we must supply more parameters than we used for CIRCLE. Let us take a look at the basic format first.

ELLIPSE[#n,]point, height, eccentricity, rotation, * [; point, height, eccentricity, rotation] *

The channel number is again optional, and the remaining parameters may be repeated to produce several ellipses. Note that just like CIRCLE, a semicolon is used between ellipse parameter groups. All the parameters may be numeric expressions.

Values *x* and *y* are the scale graphics co-ordinates for the ellipse centre. But what do the rest mean? We shall look at them individually.

HEIGHT

When creating an ellipse we first of all assume it has one axis parallel to the graphics X-axis. It does not matter whether it is the major or minor axis. Imagine the ellipse above turned on its end so that the major axis is vertical.

We define the height parameter as being half the vertical axis. This has been labelled as 'h' in the diagram. Height therefore identifies the size of one axis. The other is obtained by the QL from the next parameter in the statement, **eccentricity**.

ECCENTRICITY

The true geometrical definition of ellipse eccentricity is a little awkward but in QL terms it has a simpler definition:

$$\text{Eccentricity} = \frac{\text{horizontal axis length}}{\text{vertical axis length}}$$

Since we have already related 'height' to the vertical axis, we can substitute it in the formula to give:

$$\text{Eccentricity} = \frac{\text{horizontal axis length}}{2 * \text{height}}$$

This allows us to use the formula directly in the ELLIPSE statement if required, as we shall be doing in a little while.

So if we want to draw an ellipse with a vertical axis of 20 units and a horizontal axis of 80 units, the eccentricity parameter will be 4. Conversely, if the axes were 80 units vertically and 20 units horizontally, then the eccentricity would be 0.25.

ROTATION

Now on to the final parameter. It was earlier that when creating an ellipse we first assume it has one axis parallel to the X-axis. In this way we can correctly derive the height and eccentricity parameters. But the ellipse may also be rotated through any angle about its centre point as shown below:

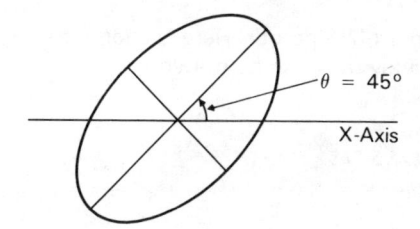

$\theta = 45°$
X-Axis

The ellipse has been rotated by 45 degrees (a little less than one radian) anti-clockwise from the X-axis. Note the references we must use: always anti-clockwise from the X-axis and expressed in radians. The rotation parameter must always be included, so the standard ellipse opposite will have a rotation parameter of zero.

EXAMPLES

To help you become familiar with the various parameters, here is a selection of ellipses to try. Type each statement separately then press ENTER. The ellipse will be displayed on whichever default screen is currently selected. Set the QL to MODE 4 first. Unless you wish to compare successive ellipses, type CLS before moving on to the next ellipse.

ELLIPSE 45, 50, 20, 2, 0
ELLIPSE 45, 50, 15, 2, 0
ELLIPSE 45, 50, 20, 0.5, 0
ELLIPSE 45, 50, 20, 2, 1
ELLIPSE 45, 50, 20, 2, PI/2
ELLIPSE 45, 50, 20, 2, RAD(120)
ELLIPSE 45, 50, 30 ; 45, 50, 20, 2, 0

No – the last example is not wrong. Remember that when circles were introduced earlier it was stated that both keywords, CIRCLE and ELLIPSE, could use the same parameters. Here the shortened form of the ELLIPSE statement (45, 50, 30) has been used to define a circle of radius 30 units. It is followed by the semicolon separator and then the full parameter form for an ellipse. We could, of course, have produced a circle this way:

ELLIPSE 45, 50, 20, 1, 0

This is because a circle is an ellipse with an eccentricity of one. Because the ellipse is a symmetrical figure it is possible to generate the same shape from different sets of parameters. For example:

ELLIPSE 45, 50, 20, 2, PI/2

This is the same as:

ELLIPSE 45, 50, 40, 0.5, 0

Ellipses are always drawn in the current INK colour. Here is a random selection which demonstrates how quickly they can be drawn.

```
100 REMark * random ellipses *
110 MODE 8 : WINDOW 465,200,15,15
120 PAPER 7 : CLS
130 REPeat loop
140   INK RND(6)
150   LET x = RND(10 TO 120)
160   LET y = RND(10 TO 80)
170   ELLIPSE x,y,RND(10 TO 40),RND(.1 TO 5),RND(2*PI)
180   IF INKEY$ <>"" THEN EXIT loop
190 END REPeat loop
```

The angle of rotation may be altered to give a static display:

```
100 REMark *static ellipse *
110 MODE 4 : PAPER 4 : INK 7 : CLS
120 FOR angle = 0,PI/4,PI/2,PI*3/4
130   ELLIPSE 75,50,20,2,angle
140 END FOR angle
```

It may also be altered to give a dynamic display:

```
100 REMark * rotating ellipse *
110 MODE 4 : PAPER 4 : INK 0 : CLS
120 REPeat rotation
130   FOR angle = 0 TO 2*PI STEP PI/16
140     ELLIPSE 75,50,20,2,angle
150     PAUSE 5 : CLS
160     IF KEYROW(1)= 64 THEN EXIT rotation
170   END FOR angle
180 END REPeat rotation
```

The height too, may be dynamically altered to give rotation about one axis:

```
100 REMark * axis rotation *
110 MODE 8 : PAPER 0 : INK 2 : CLS
120 REPeat rotate
130   FOR height = -19 TO 21 STEP 2
140     ELLIPSE 75,50,ABS(height),80/(2*ABS(height)),1
150     CLS
160     IF KEYROW(1)= 64 THEN EXIT rotate
170   END FOR height
180 END REPeat rotate
```

In line 140 the eccentricity parameter could have been simplified to '40/ABS(height)', but has been left as shown to demonstrate use of the formula explained earlier in this section.

The only parameters we have not altered so far are the x,y co-ordinates for the ellipse centre. Try this one:

```
100 REMark * rotating centre *
110 MODE 4 : PAPER 4 : INK 2 : CLS
120 FOR angle = 0 TO 2*PI STEP PI/16
130   ELLIPSE 75+20*COS(angle),50+20*SIN(angle),20,2,0
140 END FOR angle
```

The x,y co-ordinates have been expressed in the form of polar co-ordinates of a circle of radius 20 units.

Before you go any further, try problems 2 to 5 at the end of the chapter to check that you have understood the topics covered so far.

RELATIVE CO-ORDINATES

Earlier on in this chapter the difference between absolute and relative co-ordinates was explained. All the graphics keywords discussed so far have been using absolute co-ordinates referenced to the graphics origin. What has been deliberately kept hidden is the fact that all can use relative co-ordinates, i.e. relative to the current cursor position. To give both versions with each keyword at the same time would have been confusing.

To distinguish between absolute and relative co-ordinate forms, we add to the keyword:

_R

For example POINT becomes:

POINT_R

Similarly for all the others:

LINE_R
ARC_R
CIRCLE_R
ELLIPSE_R

The choice of which to use is really arbitrary since any program can generally use either form. The relative form, however, does have the ability to make certain aspects of programming neater and easier. This is especially so where a particular shape is to be reproduced at several places on the screen. It can also increase the speed of a program. Let us take a look at some examples of using relative co-ordinates for each keyword.

POINT_R

Suppose we wanted to draw a set of points A,B,C,D in a straight line as shown in the figure below.

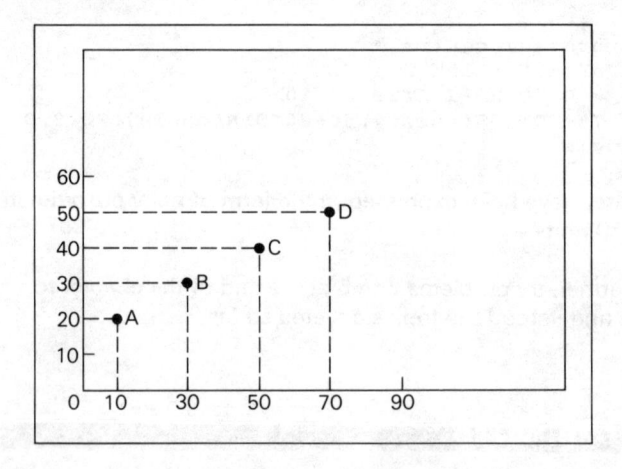

Using absolute co-ordinates we could write:

POINT 10,20 TO 30,30 TO 50,40 TO 70,50

Alternatively:

```
For number = 0 TO 3
POINT number * 20 + 10, number * 10 + 20
END FOR number
```

This would be more sensible for a large number of points. It needed, of course, a numeric expression to be derived by us and to be evaluated by the QL each time around the loop. Using relative co-ordinates we achieve the same result with:

```
POINT 10, 20
FOR number = 1 TO 3
POINT_R 20, 10
END FOR number
```

The first POINT statement places the cursor at the first point with absolute co-ordinates (10,20). The POINT_R statement will place a point at 20 units to the right from the cursor's x co-ordinate (10) and 10 units up from its y co-ordinate (20). The cursor's co-ordinates then become (30,30). Second time around the loop the same x and y co-ordinates (20,10) are added to the current (30,30) cursor co-ordinates to give a point at (50,40).

Should the cursor have already been at the first point before the program loop, then the initial POINT statement would not have been required; the program becomes even simpler. Since no numeric expression has to be computed the execution time around the loop will be faster, giving a more rapid display.

LINE_R

This example neatly allows regular polygons to be drawn:

```
100 REMark * regular polygons *
110 MODE 4 : WINDOW 465,200,15,15
120 PAPER 7 : INK 2 : CLS
130 INPUT "number of sides?"! sides
140 INPUT "length of side (scale units)?"! length
150 INPUT "starting angle (degrees)?"! ang
160 LET angle = RAD(ang) : LINE 75,20
170 FOR number = 1 TO sides
180   LINE_R TO length*COS(angle),length*SIN(angle)
190   LET angle = angle+2*PI/sides
200 END FOR number
```

Line 160 defines the start of the polygon, all subsequent lines being drawn using relative co-ordinate expressions in line 180.

ARC_R

This time a star has been produced by linking four arcs together and plotting them at random.

```
100 REMark * arc stars *
110 MODE 8 : WINDOW 400,200,40,30
120 PAPER 1 : INK 7 : CLS
130 FOR stars = 1 TO 10
140   LET x = RND(30 TO 120)
150   LET y = RND(5 TO 50)
160   LINE x,y
170   ARC_R TO -30,30,PI/2 TO 30,30,PI/2
180   ARC_R TO 30,-30,PI/2 TO -30,-30,PI/2
190 END FOR stars
```

CIRCLE_R

The only parameter that can be a relative co-ordinate is, of course, the centre point for the circle. Again, incrementing this point can be simpler using the relative form of the keyword. The following example generates lines of interlocked circles.

```
100 REMark * circle lines *
110 MODE 8 : WINDOW 465,200,16,16
120 PAPER 0 : CLS
130 FOR y = 20 TO 80 STEP 20
140   LINE 8,y
150   FOR number = 1 TO 7
160     INK RND(1 TO 7)
170     CIRCLE_R 20,0,20
180   END FOR number
190 END FOR y
```

ELLIPSE_R

Like CIRCLE, it is the centre co-ordinate of the ellipse that can be expressed in the relative form. Here is a simple example showing ellipses being drawn in a diagonal line.

```
100 REMark * ellipse line *
110 MODE 8 : WINDOW 400,200,16,16
120 PAPER 5 : INK 2 : CLS
130 SCALE 200,-30,-20
140 LINE 0,0
150 FOR number = 1 TO 5
160   ELLIPSE_R 40,30,15,2,0
170 END FOR number
```

Straightforward enough, but notice that SCALE has been used to change the graphics origin. LINE 0,0 effectively moves the cursor to (30,20), which will become the centre of the first ellipse.

FILL

Standard use of the graphics keywords that we have looked at in this chapter generally results in a line drawing of single pixel thickness on the background colour. For many applications this is sufficient but often it is required to colour within the outline produced. This can be done by careful repetitive programming of the same figure on a reducing or increasing scale. The earlier example 'Olympic' demonstrated this effect. Fortunately QL users are supplied with a FILL keyword which allows much easier colouring of shapes.

The keyword turns the fill operation on with:

FILL 1

It turns it off with:

FILL 0

So to fill a circle, for example, we write:

```
100 FILL 1
110 CIRCLE 45,50,30
120 FILL 0
```

The FILL colour will always be the current INK colour.

There is one point you must remember about this keyword. When you have used it to fill up an area, *always* turn it off. Like the OVER keyword (Chapter 2), the effect will remain turned on until cancelled, even if you deleted the program.

FILL AREA SELECTION

Filling up closed areas such as circles and ellipses is straightforward, but if parts of unclosed areas or areas containing several lines are to be filled then a little more care is needed. FILL works horizontally. In other words, only when there are two points with the same Y-axis co-ordinate will a fill operation occur between them. The following example demonstrates this effect:

```
100 CLS : FILL 1
110 ARC 50,20 TO 100,20,-1.5
120 FILL 0
```

A filled-in dome is produced, but change line 110 to: ARC 50, 20 TO 50,80, −1.5 and not only is there no filled-in area, there is no arc! The phenomenon can best be explained by a further example:

```
100 REMark * shrinking arc *
110 CLS : ARC 50,50 TO 100,80,-3
120 FILL 1
130 ARC 50,10 TO 100,40,-3
140 FILL 0
```

You will find yourself faced with one normal arc towards the top of your screen, and a smaller filled-in arc at the bottom. But the two arcs should have been the same size (draw them on graph paper to check)! The reason is as follows.

The action of filling an area can be regarded as the drawing of lines in the current ink colour between two horizontal points, progressively moving up or down the screen. Where a figure cannot provide two horizontal points, no filling occurs. Any 'single-point' parts of that figure whose statement is contained within the FILL statements (e.g. line 130 above) will not be displayed. So the lower left-hand end of the filled arc has been omitted in our second example above. This also explains why no arc was visible in the earlier example too. All the points of the arc were 'single-points'.

Depending upon the figure's shape, the fill action can remove the need to program horizontal lines. A triangle can be programmed by:

```
100 CLS : INK 4
110 FILL 1
120 LINE 45,30 TO 75,80 TO 105,30
130 FILL 0
```

But rotating the triangle will require all sides to be defined, otherwise, like the arc, we will lose part of the triangle. Change line 120 to:

```
120 LINE 15,30 TO 75,80 TO 80,10
```

Specifying all the sides gives the correct result. Change line 120 to:

```
120 LINE 15,30 TO 75,80 TO 80,10 TO 15,30
```

Multi-statement FILL sequence

If several graphics statements are included within a common FILL sequence, then many interesting effects can be obtained — some being unexpected! The following program provides a simple illustration. Like other programs in this section it has been provided with PAUSE statements which allow you to control the running of the programs by pressing any key to continue on to the next stage.

```
100 REMark * fill in *
110 CLS : FILL 1
120 INK 7 : LINE 20,70 TO 20,10
130 PAUSE
140 INK 6 : LINE 60,50 TO 80,10
150 PAUSE
```

```
160 INK 5 : LINE 80,50 TO 60,10
170 PAUSE
180 INK 4 : LINE 120,70 TO 120,10
190 FILL 0
```

If the figures were drawn without FILL they would appear like this:

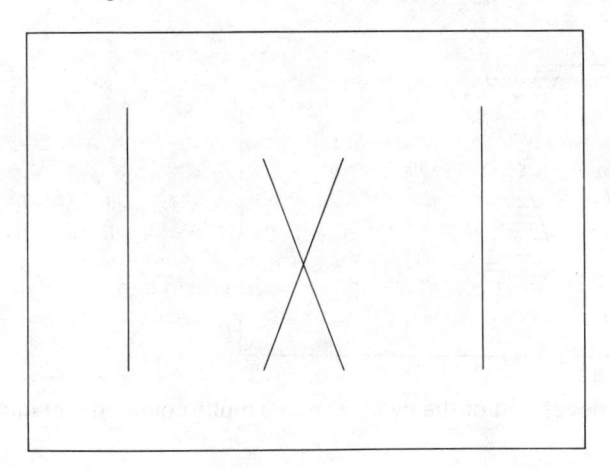

Although INK 7 was specified in line 120, no white colouring appears. In fact, nothing appears until the first PAUSE is passed when line 140 is executed. The reason is that whilst line 120 and its LINE points are read by the QL, the previous FILL 1 statement causes the points to be stored while the QL looks for matching horizontal points. Before line 140 none exist, therefore no filled area (and hence no line) is seen. The second line statement does provide corresponding points and the following figure results:

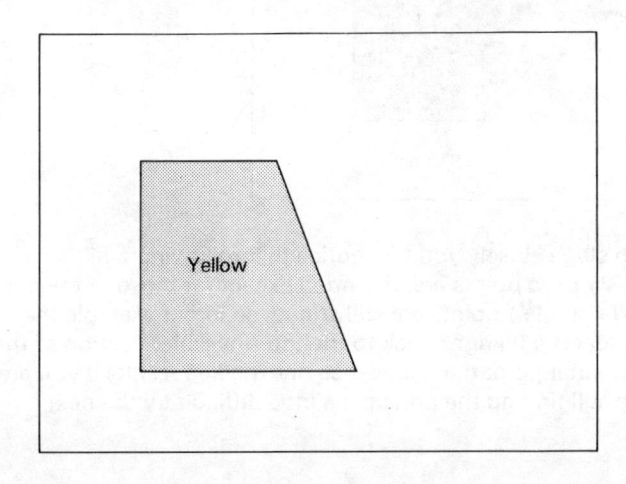

At the next stage of the program (line 160) the 'X' is filled in with cyan colour:

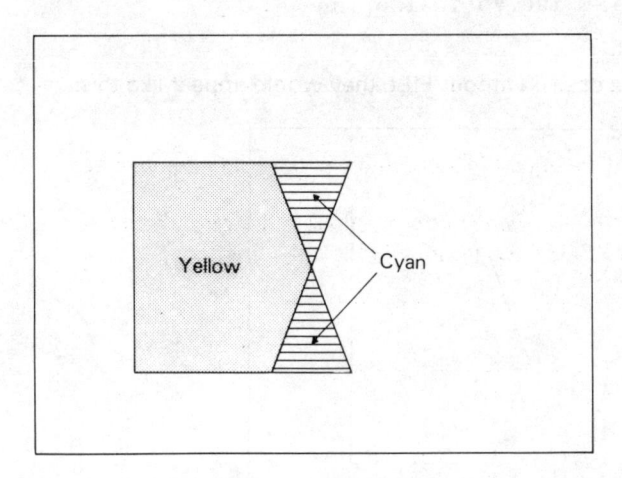

[Figure: rectangle containing a yellow triangle on the left and a cyan hourglass shape on the right, with labels "Yellow" and "Cyan"]

The final stage removes part of the cyan 'X' and a multi-coloured rectangle is produced:

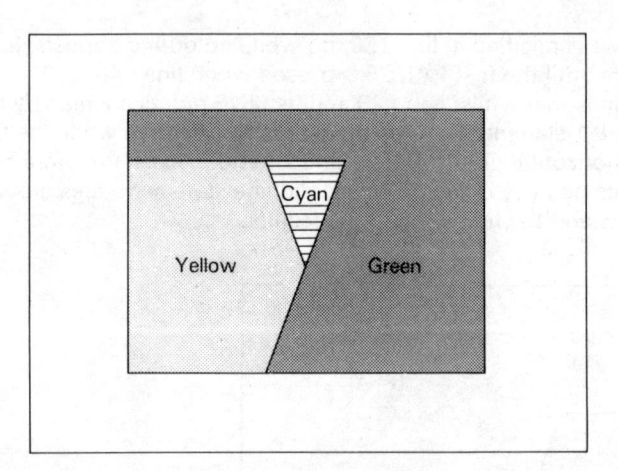

[Figure: rectangle with yellow region on the left, cyan triangle in the middle, and green region on the right, with labels "Yellow", "Cyan" and "Green"]

If you look at each stage closely you will notice that following a fill operation, all previously *used* points are discarded except for those of the most recent figure. Unused ('single') points are still stored, so in our example the last LINE statement creates a fill right back to the top (invisible) section of the very first line. It is this latter point that can cause unexpected results if you are not careful. If you are still finding the principle a little difficult try the next example:

```
100 REMark * fill test *
110 MODE 8 : PAPER 2 : CLS : FILL 1
120 LINE 20,50 TO 20,10 : REMark * line A *
130 INK 6 : LINE 60,50 TO 60,10 : REMark *line B *
140 PAUSE
150 INK 5 : LINE 100,50 TO 100,10 : REMark * line C *
160 FILL 0
```

Three vertical, parallel lines within a common FILL sequence have been programmed.

The first stage of the program shows a yellow rectangle towards the right of the screen. After the PAUSE the figure will look like this:

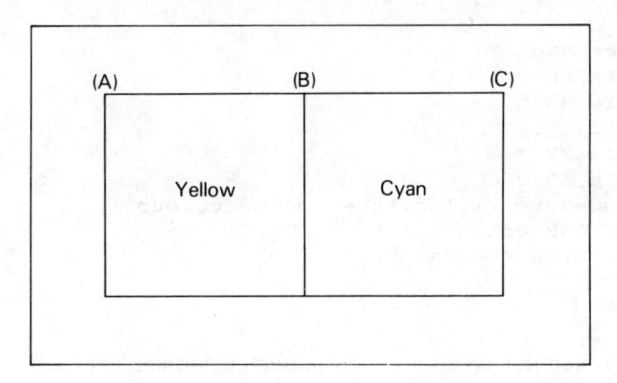

```
       (A)           (B)           (C)
        ┌─────────────┬─────────────┐
        │             │             │
        │   Yellow    │    Cyan     │
        │             │             │
        └─────────────┴─────────────┘
```

Now we will reverse the programming order for lines A and B. Change lines 120 and 130 as follows:

```
100 LINE 60,50 TO 60,10 : REMark * line B *
110 INK 6 : LINE 20,50 TO 20,10 : REMark * line A *
```

Run the program again. The first stage will be as before but the second stage will now reveal a completely cyan-coloured rectangle.

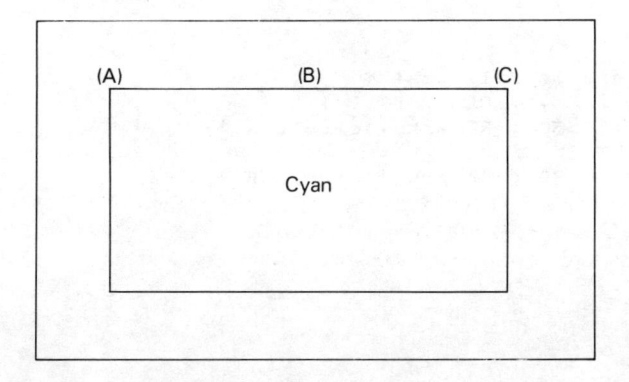

```
       (A)           (B)           (C)
        ┌───────────────────────────┐
        │                           │
        │           Cyan            │
        │                           │
        └───────────────────────────┘
```

Having selected matching horizontal points between lines A and B, the QL discards line B points (the first line programmed) and creates the second fill between line A and line C points. The yellow area is overprinted.

So it is important to remember that the order in which you write down your graphics statements within a FILL sequence will determine the final result.

FILLING CIRCLES AND ELLIPSES

Working with these shapes is quite interesting. Containing them individually within separate FILL sequences allows normal overlapping of colours. For instance:

```
100 REMark * roundel *
110 MODE 8 : PAPER 0 : CLS
120 fill_circle 38,6
130 fill_circle 35,1
140 fill_circle 22,7
150 fill_circle 10,2
160 DEFine PROCedure fill_circle(radius,colour)
170   FILL 1 : INK colour
180   CIRCLE 75,50,radius
190   FILL 0
200 END DEFine
```

Note the order in which the circles were programmed; largest first then progressing to the smallest.

Containing more than one circle (or ellipse) within a single FILL sequence creates a variety of effects depending upon the relative positions of the circles. We can understand the FILL action better if we imagine each circle split vertically into semicircular arcs, left and right. The points of the right-hand arc are stored first, the left-hand arc points stored second. The fill will occur, as with our earlier vertical lines, between horizontal points of the current figure and the left-hand arc. The points for the right-hand arc have been discarded. The next sequence of programs, all in MODE 8, should help to explain the action.

```
100 REMark * circle fill test *
110 PAPER 2 : INK 4 : CLS : FILL 1
120 CIRCLE 45,50,30 : REMark * circle A *
130 PAUSE : INK 3
140 CIRCLE 90,50,30 : REMark * circle B *
150 FILL 0
```

Stage 1	[box containing circle labeled "Green"]
Stage 2	[box containing rounded rectangle labeled "Magenta"]

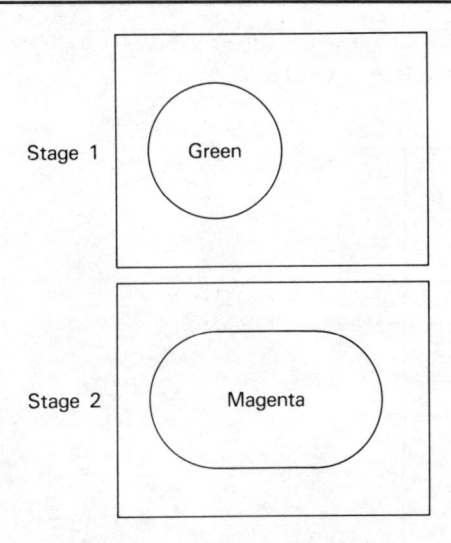

Now edit the program to swap over the two circles so that A is at line 140 and B is at line 120 and run the program again. The following effect is produced:

Stage 1	[box containing circle labeled "G"]
Stage 2	[box containing overlapping shapes labeled "M" and "G"]

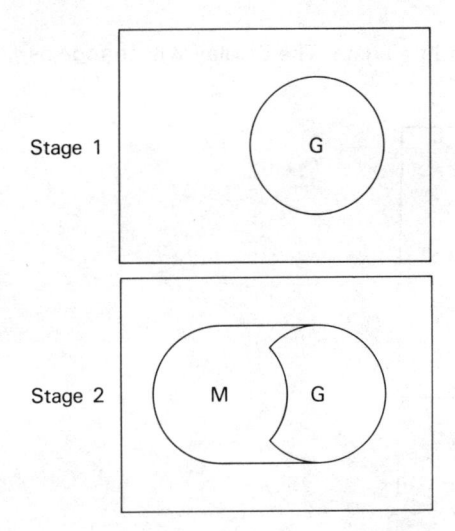

Finally we will offset the two circles:

```
100 REMark * circle fill test 2 *
110 PAPER 2 : INK 4 : CLS : FILL 1
120 CIRCLE 90,65,30 : REMark * circle A *
```

```
130 PAUSE : INK 5
140 CIRCLE 45,35,30 : REMark * circle B *
150   FILL 0
```

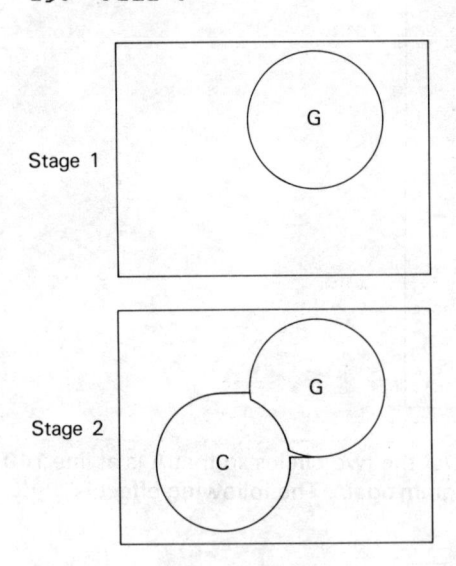

Stage 1

Stage 2

Now swap lines 120 and 140 and try again. The display will change as follows:

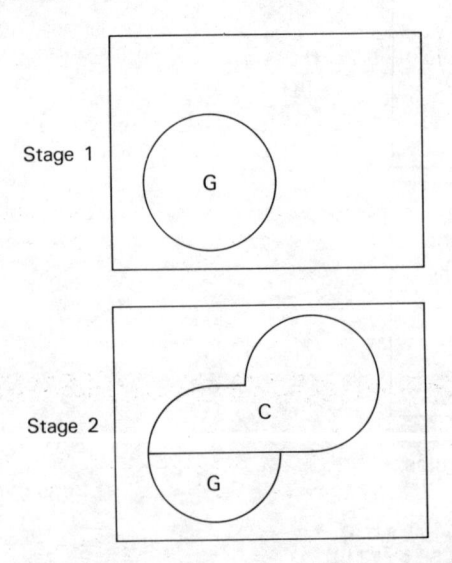

Stage 1

Stage 2

Ellipses, arcs and circles in combination can give such a wide variety of effects with the FILL keyword that they are best explored further by experiment.

Here are two more programs to whet your appetite!

```
100 REMark * fill blocks *
110 MODE 8 : PAPER 7 : CLS : FILL 1
120 OVER -1
130 REPeat loop
140     LET x1 = RND(50)*10
150     LET y1 = RND(20)*10
160     LET x2 = RND(50)*10
170     LET y2 = RND(20)*10
180     INK RND(7)
190     LINE x1,y1 TO x1,y2
200     LINE x2,y1 TO x2,y2
210     IF INKEY$<>"" THEN EXIT loop
220 END REPeat loop
230 FILL 0:OVER 0
```

The OVER −1 statement has been included to enhance the effect, but if you wish to see the FILL operation alone, just edit out the OVER −1 in line 110. The blocks of colour are simply produced by filling in between two vertical randomly positioned lines of random length.

```
100 REMark * turn ellipse *
110 MODE 4 : PAPER 4 : CLS
120 LET angle = 0
130 REPeat loop
140     FILL 1 : INK 0 : CLS
150     ELLIPSE 110,50,15,2,angle
160     INK 2
170     ELLIPSE 40,50,15,2,angle
180     FILL 0 : PAUSE 25
190     LET angle = angle+.2
200 END REPeat loop
```

Containing two ellipses within the FILL statements creates an interesting effect, especially as the ellipses rotate. Look carefully and you will be able to see the order in which the filling actually occurs.

PROBLEMS

1. With a scale factor of 180 and graphics origin (0,0), write a program to draw a square of 120-units-long sides with its centre at (80,100). Redraw the square with a scale factor of 300, then move it so that its centre is back at its original position.
Note: The use of graph paper, marked with scaled axes, will be found invaluable for working out this and other graphics exercise. Indeed, it is most useful for arranging the layout and co-ordinates of any graphic display.

2. Using WINDOW 350, 220, 20, 20 write a program to draw a large capital 'H' on a blue background. The vertical lines must be white and the horizontal line, of length 30 pixels, must be alternate red and white groups of twenty-five pixels. (Use the POINT keyword for the horizontal line.)

3 Write a program to draw a cosine curve in the range $-\pi$ to $+\pi$ with the graphics origin at the centre of a 490 by 220 window. Use high-resolution mode. (The basic formula is $y = COS(x)$)

4. Write a program to draw two diagonal lines between opposite corners of a square window with a scale factor of 200. On each half-diagonal produce two arcs on opposite sides to give a petal effect. Use a subtended angle of 30 degrees. Work in MODE 256.

5. Draw an ellipse of eccentricity 1.5 and height 20 units that touches two circles. One within the ellipse, of diameter equal to the minor axis, and the other outside the ellipse of diameter equal to the major axis.

6. Design a program that places a red, 30-unit radius disc central on a black background. A 10-unit radius white-coloured disc appears then disappears at random positions around the disc, always touching the circumference. A yellow line joins the centres of the two discs each time the white disc appears.

CHAPTER 5
CHARACTER STUDIES
CSIZE, CURSOR, AT, PRINT TO, UNDER

INTRODUCTION

We have now covered all the pixel graphics keywords and the scale graphics keywords, but there is one visual aspect common to both that has yet to be investigated. That is text or characters. Most programs require some form of text or character annotation, but it is no good paying great attention to the detail of the graphics if text is not accorded the same concern. A 'scruffy' display would result. A number of keywords are available to help us in text presentation.

The manipulation of printed information has been deliberately left until both groups of keywords had been explained. Occasionally you would have noticed a CSIZE or a CURSOR statement in some of the examples. As stated at the time, they were included to help you understand the graphics keyword being explained and were not individually mentioned.

We are able to control two main aspects of text. Its size and its position. Let us look at size first.

CHARACTER SIZE

The keyword CSIZE is used to define the size of all characters that follow it. When text is displayed on the screen, you can think of every character as being contained within a rectangle whose shape is the same irrespective of the character it contains. There is no proportional spacing here! Character size is expressed in terms of the width and height, in units of pixels, of this rectangle. CSIZE requires a maximum of three parameters:

CSIZE [# n,] width, height

Channel number is optional as always.

Width can have values from 0 to 3, height can have values 0 or 1. For instance:

CSIZE 2, 1
CSIZE # 6, 3, 0

Either parameter can exist in the statement as a numeric expression.
The related pixel values are as follows:

Width	Pixels	Height	Pixels
0	6	0	10
1	8	1	20
2	12		
3	16		

All possible combinations of the two parameters are permitted in MODE 4. MODE 8 allows widths of only 12 or 16 pixels.

You will already be aware of the different-sized cursors displayed in the two resolution modes. These represent the default CSIZE parameters which are:

MODE 8 : 2, 0   (12 pixels by 10 pixels)
MODE 4 : 0, 0   (6 pixels by 10 pixels)

Here is the full range of sizes available. View them first in MODE 4 then run the program in MODE 8.

```
100 REMark * character sizes *
110 FOR height = 0 TO 1
120   FOR w = 0 TO 3
130     CSIZE w,height
140     PRINT "SIZE"! w!","! height
150   END FOR w
160 END FOR height
```

Having set a CSIZE value in a program, that character size will remain effective until it is changed by a further CSIZE statement. For example:

```
100 REMark * size change *
120 MODE 8 : PAPER 7 : CLS
125 INK 2 : CSIZE 2,0
130 PRINT"CSIZE is effective until";
140 CSIZE 3,1
150 STRIP 6
160 PRINT !"altered"
```

The initial character size was the default value for MODE 8. STRIP was 'thrown in' for good measure just to confirm that the strip height is related to the character height.

We have tended to ignore the use of the channel selection parameter in previous keywords but it is worth mentioning that, used with CSIZE, it allows

you to create text of varying size in different windows. This can be an effective
means of achieving emphasis for a particular window's information.

```
100 REMark * emphasis *
110 MODE 8 : WINDOW 512,256,0,0
120 PAPER 7 : INK 2 : CLS
130 PRINT : PRINT"        NEXT RANDOM NUMBER IS:"
140 WINDOW 260,40,126,40
150 PAPER 5 : CLS
160 GO TO 180
170 PRINT "NEXT RANDOM NUMBER IS"
180 OPEN#5,scr_56x24a223x80
190 PAPER#5,6 :CLS#5 : INK#5,1 :BORDER#5,2,0
200 CSIZE#5,3,1
210 REPeat loop
220   LET number = RND(200)
230   PRINT#5,number
240   CLS 3 : PRINT "NOW";
250   PAUSE 50 :CLS#5
260   IF KEYROW(1) = 64 THEN EXIT loop
270 END REPeat loop
280 CLOSE#5
```

Lines 110 to 150 have cleared the screen, established a small default window and printed some text using the default character size for MODE 8. Lines 160 to 180 have set up a window on channel 5 and selected a character size of 16 by 20 pixels. The loop generates, and prints, random numbers within this window.

CHARACTER POSITIONING

When we send text to the screen using PRINT, the QL outputs the characters at a spacing of 40 per line (MODE 8) or 80 per line (MODE 4) to a maximum of 25 lines. In other words, there is a predefined format for the placing of characters on the screen. Successive PRINT statements will cause the QL to automatically increment the cursor down the screen to the left-hand starting position of each lines. An automatic 'carriage return and line feed' operation!

However, we do not always want to display text or characters at the beginning of a line. Also, particularly with graphics, we may wish to position text at a specific pixel point on the screen. This problem we can solve with our next keyword.

CURSOR

The CURSOR keyword allows the pixel graphics cursor to be placed anywhere on the screen. This frees us from the standard row/column restriction. It has the following general format:

CURSOR[#n,][scale graphics position,] pixel graphics position

The 'position' refers to the scale or pixel co-ordinates which can be numeric expressions if required.
Note that the scale graphics parameter is optional. For the moment we shall see what happens when we use just the pixel parameter. For example:

CURSOR 100, 50

This will place the pixel graphics cursor at the position 100 pixels across and 50 pixels down relative to the top left-hand corner of the current window. This was the type we used occasionally in our earlier chapters.

CURSOR#5, 100, 50

This will do the same for channel 5, and will therefore not affect the current cursor position of the default window, as our next example shows:

```
100 REMark * dual cursor *
110 MODE 8 : WINDOW 400,200,30,30
120 PAPER 5 : INK 2 : CLS
130 OPEN#5,scr_150x100a60x100
140 PAPER#5,4: INK #5,0 : CLS#5
150 CURSOR 200,30
160 CURSOR#5,3,45
170 PRINT "DEFAULT WINDOW"
180 PRINT#5,"CHANNEL FIVE"
190 CLOSE#5
```

Lines 150 and 160 set up the cursor positions for the two windows. The following PRINT statements are each controlled by their own window's cursor value. Do note, however, that if a second PRINT statement is used it is not controlled by any previous CURSOR statement. It will have its text positioned according to the normal rules since CURSOR defines only the cursor position for the *start* of any following text. For example:

```
100 CLS : CURSOR 50,20
110 PRINT "HELLO"
120 PRINT "EVERYONE"
```

'HELLO' appears to the right of the cursor position, but 'EVERYONE' appears at the beginning of the next line.

Cursor/character relationship

To be able to accurately place characters we must also know which part of the character rectangle is actually at the pixel graphics cursor position. This is always the top left-hand corner.

```
         Top left-hand
         corner of cursor
```

```
                    Character
                    rectangle
```

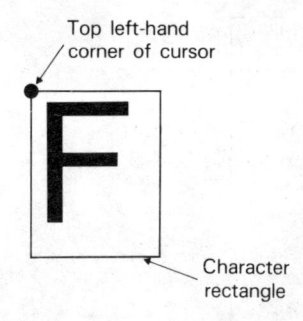

The characters themselves are not placed exactly in the middle of their
character rectangles but displaced slightly to the left. Lower-case (small)
characters are central in the vertical axis but upper-case (capital) characters are
naturally offset towards the top. The next example shows a 'staircase' of letters
to demonstrate the displacement:

```
100 REMark * character offset *
110 MODE 8 : CLS : STRIP 0
120 CSIZE 3,1
130 CURSOR 150,70 : PRINT"A"
140 CURSOR 166,90 : PRINT"I"
150 CURSOR 182,110 : PRINT"M"
160 CURSOR 198,130 : PRINT"a"
```

If you wanted to be particularly accurate about positioning characters then
the displacement should be taken into account, but it is only a matter of a few
pixels which are best adjusted after having seen the screen display.

Scale/pixel relationship

When planning the layout of a screen containing mixed graphics and text, it is
often necessary to place text in association with a specific graphics figure. This
entails finding out the relationship between scale co-ordinates and pixel co-
ordinates. Fortunately we do not need to delve into mathematics. The long
form of the CURSOR keyword provides us with the solution. If we write
CURSOR 100, 50, 16, 5 then the pixel cursor will be placed 16 pixels across
and 5 pixels down from the scale graphics co-ordinates (100,50). Try this
example:

```
100 REMark * scale/pixel match *
110 MODE 8 : WINDOW 400,200,10,10
120 PAPER 6 : INK 2 : CLS
130 CSIZE 3,0
140 CURSOR 90,50,16,-5
150 ELLIPSE 50,50,20,2,0
160 PRINT"ELLIPSE"
```

Your screen should look like this (without the annotation):

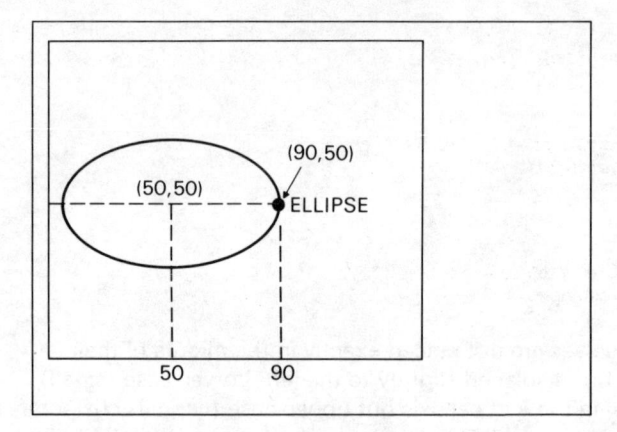

With the ellipse centred at (50,50) and the eccentricity at 2, the right-hand end of the major (horizontal) axis has co-ordinates (90,50). This position is the scale position in the CURSOR statement. The resulting pixel cursor is displaced from this co-ordinate by 16 pixels across (to the right) and 5 pixels up. This has enabled the text's character rectangles (height 10 pixels) to be placed centrally in line with the ellipse's major axis and to the right of it by one character space (16 pixels).

Remember, the pixel graphics cursor defines the location of the top left-hand corner of a character rectangle. To place a character centrally about this point we must offset the actual cursor position. The following program should help to clarify the technique required.

```
100 REMark * offset *
110 MODE 8 : WINDOW 400,200,20,20
120 PAPER 1 : INK 7 : CLS
130 CSIZE 3,1 : OVER 1
140 LINE 30,90 TO 60,90
150 CURSOR 60,90,0,0
160 PRINT "X"
170 LINE 30,60 TO 60,60
180 CURSOR 60,60,-8,0
190 PRINT "X"
200 LINE 30,30 TO 60,30
210 CURSOR 60,30,-8,-10
220 PRINT"X" : OVER 0
```

Loops have deliberately not been used so that you can easily see the parameters implemented at each stage. Line 150 places the character below and to the right of the end of the line, line 180 places it below and centrally about the X-axis, while line 210 places it fully central on the end of the line. If you are puzzled about the negative sign for the y pixel value in line 210, which moves the cursor upwards, do not forget that in the pixel co-ordinate system the origin is at the top left-hand corner of the window. So y pixel positive movement is downwards, and conversely for the negative values.

Use of this form of the CURSOR keyword makes character positioning a much simpler operation than perhaps originally envisaged, as the next example will show.

```
100 REMark * ellipse line *
110 MODE 8 : WINDOW 465,200,15,15
120 SCALE 200,0,0 : PAPER 6 : CLS
130 CSIZE 3,1
140 LET x_position = 45
150 LET word$ = "ELLIPSE"
160 FOR y_position = 180 TO 60 STEP -20
170   INK 1
180   ELLIPSE x_position,y_position,15,2,0
190   INK 0
200   CURSOR x_position,y_position,-8,-10
210   PRINT word$(10-y_position/20)
220   LET x_position = x_position+40
230 END FOR y_position
```

The CURSOR statement this time takes its scale graphics parameters as the centre of each ellipse. Since the character size is set to 16 pixels wide by 20 pixels high, offsetting the pixel graphics cursor position by (−8, −10) places each character centrally in the ellipse.

Many board games played on a computer require some form of grid with identifying numbers for reference. CURSOR can help to simply achieve it.

```
100 REMark * game board *
110 MODE 8 : PAPER 0 : INK 6 : CLS
120 FOR increment = 0 TO 90 STEP 30
130   LINE increment,0 TO increment,90
140   LINE 0,increment TO 90,increment
150 END FOR increment
160 LET number = 1
170 FOR y = 90,60,30
180   FOR x = 0,30,60
190     CURSOR x,y,2,0
200     PRINT number
210     LET number = number +1
220   END FOR x
230 END FOR y
```

Lines 120 to 150 draw the board. Line 190 uses CURSOR to place the pixel graphics cursor 2 pixels right of the scale graphics co-ordinates at the top left-hand corner of each of the nine squares.

The next example, though a little more involved, shows how CURSOR can be used to annotate the axes of a graph.

```
100 REMark * axis notation *
110 MODE 4 : WINDOW 365,220,40,20
'120 PAPER 0 : INK 7 : CLS
130 SCALE 150,-30,-30
```

```
140 LET d$ = "MONTUEWEDTHUFRISATSUN"
150 LET y_lab$ = "ENTRIES"
160 REMark * draw axes *
170 LINE 0,0 TO 140,0
180 LINE 0,0 TO 0,100
190 REMark * x-axis scale *
200 FOR x = 20 TO 140 STEP 20
210    LINE x,0 TO x,-5
220    CURSOR x,-5,-9,0
230    LET position = 1+3*(x/20-1)
240    PRINT d$(position TO position+2)
250 END FOR x
260 REMark * y_axis scale *
270 LET x = -6
280 FOR y = 10 TO 100 STEP 10
290    IF y = 100 THEN x = -12
300    LINE 0,y TO -5,y
310    CURSOR -5,y,x,-5
320    PRINT y/10
330 END FOR y
340 REMark * x-axis label *
350 INK 2 : CSIZE 3,0
360 CURSOR 80,-15,-24,0
370 PRINT "DAY"
380 REMark * y-axis label *
390 LET y = 80
400 FOR letter = 1 TO 7
410    CURSOR -5,y,-36,0
420    PRINT y_lab$(letter)
430    LET y = y-10
440 END FOR letter
```

The program has been split into identifiable sections to allow easier analysis. The following points may also help. Lines 210 and 300 generate the X- and Y-axis scale division marks and the ends of these short lines are used as scale graphics references in the CURSOR statements. The days are placed centrally below each X-axis mark, whilst the numbers are placed to the left of each Y-axis mark. No character size has been specified for these characters so the default size (6 × 10) will be automatically used. Changing the character size for the axis labels requires larger pixel co-ordinate offsets in lines 360 and 410 when positioning the labels. Finally, lines 230, 240, 420 involve SuperBASIC character string handling, line 230 being a convenient way of relating the string position to the loop variable *x*.

Now let us move on to look at other ways of positioning characters.

AT

Characters, of course, are not always positioned in relation to graphics figures. For instance, some programs may require separate windows containing text alone. The AT keyword enables characters to be positioned in terms of row and column within the current window. The format is:

AT[#n,] row, column

Numeric expressions are allowed as usual. Some of our earlier keyword examples used: FOR lines = 1 TO 6 : PRINT as a means of moving the cursor six rows down from the top of the window. With AT we simply write: AT 6, 0 which places the pixel cursor at the first character position on row seven.

A little confused? It is easier if you think of the first row and first column as:

row 0, column 0

So the fourth row down (0,1,2,3) is row 3, and similarly for columns. Specifying the sixth row and the eighth column would be written as:

AT 5, 7

For a given window size the number of characters per row and the maximum number of rows will depend solely upon one thing: character size. The AT statement is always relative to the current character size. No spaces are left between adjacent character rectangles in either rows or columns – it is simply the smaller-sized character within its rectangle that gives the appearance of spacing. You can see this with the following program, run in MODE 8 (with the overlapping channel 1 and 2 windows):

```
100 REMark * spacing *
110 CLS#2 : PAPER 2 : INK 0
120 CSIZE 3,1
130 FOR character = 1 TO 4
135   AT character,character
140   PRINT "HEHE"
150 END FOR character
```

The blue background of channel 2 is overprinted with the characters on their red rectangles.

So the maximum number of rows and columns for a particular window size and character size can be found by simple division. The AT parameters in the next program should not cause any problems:

```
100 REMark * mad at *
110 MODE 8 : WINDOW 400,100,75,75
120 PAPER 7 : INK 2 : CLS
130 PRINT "TEXT"
140 AT 3,5 : PRINT "CAN BE"
150 AT 6,16 : PRINT "PLACED"
160 AT 9,10 : PRINT "ANYWHERE"
170 PAUSE 100 : CLS : INK 4
180 CSIZE 3,0
190 AT 3,10 : PRINT"OR..."
200 PAUSE 100 : CLS : INK 1
210 FOR row = 1 TO 7
220   AT row,9
230   PRINT "CENTRAL"
240 END FOR row
```

We cheated, of course! A character width of 16 pixels gives 25 columns on a 400-pixel-wide window, enabling the 'T' of 'CENTRED' to be positioned exactly in the middle at column 13.

PRINT TO

The last character-positioning keyword included has the format:

PRINT[#n,] TO column

It is the word 'TO' that really performs the action of moving the pixel graphics cursor to a specified column – rather like tabulation on a typewriter.

It is always used with the preceding 'PRINT' and enables text positioning and printing to be achieved in one line. For example, to print 'hello' at column 28 we can write:

PRINT TO 28, "HELLO"

If required, you can use the statement on its own without following text:

```
100 PRINT TO 15
110 PRINT "HELLO"
```

You may wish to do this if you have a particularly long PRINT statement to follow, or intend using other printing control keywords before the text statement.

Here is a simple example of its use:

```
100 REMark * print to *
110 MODE 8 : WINDOW 512,256,0,0
120 PAPER 7 : INK 2 : CLS
130 AT 10,4 : PRINT "SPACED";
140 PRINT TO 19, "OUT"; TO 31, "TEXT"
```

UNDER

The final keyword in this chapter allows you to switch underlining of text either on or off.

UNDER #n, 1 switches it on
UNDER #n, 0 switches it off

You are left to work out an example!

CHARACTER MOVEMENT

Being able to position characters at a specific pixel point also means that we can move characters in pixel increments. For example:

```
100 REMark * moving text *
110 MODE 8 : PAPER 7 : INK 2 : CLS
120 FOR text_lines = 1 TO 50
130   CURSOR 40+text_lines,80+text_lines
140   PRINT "MOVING TEXT"
150 END FOR text_lines
```

Each time the cursor point moves, the next PRINT statement causes the previous text to be deleted. Relating the effect to our character rectangles, any rectangle that overlaps any part of another will delete it.

If necessary we can prevent the deletion by using OVER 1. This allows us to create overprinting.

```
100 REMark * overprinting *
110 MODE 8 : WINDOW 140,100,180,50
120 PAPER 0 : INK 2 : CLS
130 OVER 1
140 CSIZE 3,1 : CURSOR 38,40
150 PRINT "OVER"
160 CSIZE 2,0 : INK 6
170 CURSOR 22,45
180 PRINT "PRINTING"
190 OVER 0
```

We can, of course, extend this idea by using OVER 1 in conjunction with our moving-text principle to create shadows similar to the effect shown earlier in Chapter 3 for the BLOCK keyword.

```
100 REMark * shadows *
110 MODE 8 : PAPER 7 : INK 0 : CLS
120 CSIZE 3,1 : OVER 1
130 FOR layer = 1 TO 20
140   CURSOR 160+layer,80+layer
150   IF layer = 20 THEN INK 2
160   PRINT "SHADOWS"
170 END FOR layer
180 OVER 0
```

The action of OVER 1 was originally described when used with STRIP (Chapter 2) but here you are seeing its full use with text. The shadow is produced by successive 'layers' of text overlapping in a diagonal direction down the screen. The effect can be made more interesting by varying the direction in which the cursor moves.

```
100 REMark * coshadow *
110 MODE 4 : WINDOW 400,200,20,20
120 PAPER 4 : INK 0 : CLS
130 OVER 1 : CSIZE 2,1
140 SCALE 272,-10,-100
150 FOR x = 0 TO 300
160   CURSOR 0,70,x,-INT(COS(x*PI/200)*70+.5)
170   IF x = 300 THEN INK 2
180   PRINT "WHOOPEE!"
190 END FOR x
200 OVER 0
```

By using a cosine expression for the y co-ordinate in the CURSOR statement the shadow has traced out part of a cosine curve, albeit at a rather slow rate.

CHARACTER GENERATION

As with most high technology electronic products new computers tend to undergo development changes as time progresses. Old problems are solved and new facilities often added. The QL will probably not escape some modification in the future.

One absence that will be a cause of disappointment to some users is in the area of character generation. At present, no user-definable or special 'games' graphics characters are offered. To produce a complete program that enables you to generate, store and retrieve special characters, and incorporate them in other programs, is outside the scope of this book. However, a few ideas are included that could be used as a basis for designing your own characters using the graphics facilities that are available.

BLOCKS AND PIXELS

There are, in essence, two main styles of special characters – block and pixel. Block graphics characters are built up from similar-sized blocks of colour which may individually be composed of several pixels. They are frequently used in low-resolution modes and especially in programs for young children where 'chunky', colourful figures are excellent for gaining attention.

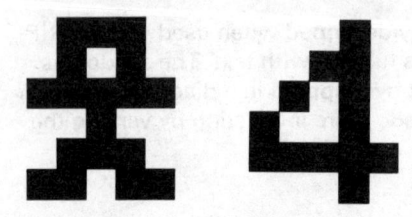

Block graphics

Pixel-based graphics are more apparent in high-resolution games displays and for the generation of special symbols not available in the computer's standard character set. As the name implies they are composed of individual pixels, and are therefore generally of small size.

Single pixel

Pixel graphics

We have already seen how pixel points and blocks of colour can be created on the QL. These facilities can be extended for the production of special characters, particularly with respect to block graphics.

Block graphics

The first thing to be decided is the nature of the figure, in particular size, shape and colour. Here graph paper is essential to allow the correct planning of these aspects and it is suggested that nothing smaller than 5 mm squares should be used. The screen size of the figure depends upon your own requirements. You will have to consider such things as its size in relation to other figures or standard characters being used or the number that may be required across or down a particular window size. This may be difficult to establish at the start, so it is best to make the size of each block that will make up the figure a variable that can be altered later to suit.

Design grid

Before creating your figure a standard square or rectangular grid should be designed containing sufficient squares to allow the figure's shape to be adequately defined.

It is best not to use too large a matrix otherwise the figure may take too long to be drawn on the screen. Again, it is a matter for you to decide just how fast or slow a speed is required for your desired effect. Indeed, the slow building-up of a figure block by block according to points scored may be the focal point of your program. The method about to be outlined does not display figures at a particularly high speed and could not be considered for fast animation effects. However, there are many applications where specially produced block graphics characters can be used outside the 'fast games' area. For instance, each element of a sales bar chart could be composed of proportional numbers of block graphics characters depicting each product. Large letters and numbers can be created for extra emphasis in educational programs for younger children.

Design method

We shall look at the following aspects:

1. Grid referencing.
2. Translation of grid references to programmable data.
3. Creation of a SuperBASIC Procedure to read the data and draw the figure at the defined screen location and of the required size.

Grid referencing

Having decided your grid size, fill in the squares that make up your figure using different hatching lines for different colours. Remember that if you are using a colour monitor, stipple colours can be used to good effect. Vertical bars of alternate colour make good teeth!

The illustration shows a six by eight grid containing a simple shape.

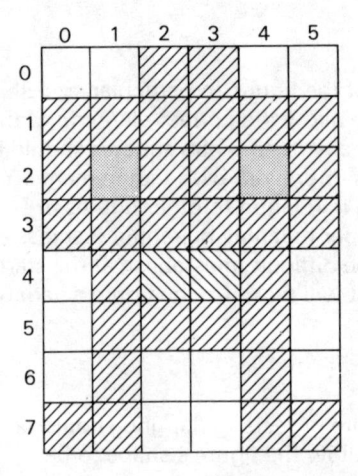

You will see that a numeric reference has been placed on two sides of the grid. Note that the numbers start from zero. Thus each square can be uniquely identified by a two-number reference. For example, the 'eyes' of our figure are represented by:

1,2 and 4,2

The references are always expressed with the horizontal value first.

The method is quite straightforward. Each square will be displayed using the BLOCK keyword. Here is a reminder of its format:

BLOCK[#n,] width, height, x origin, y origin, colour

The width and height is, of course, defining the size of the individual squares within the grid in pixels. It only remains to express the x and y origin co-ordinates of each square, relative to the top left-hand corner of the whole grid. This will be our screen reference point from which the figure will be drawn.

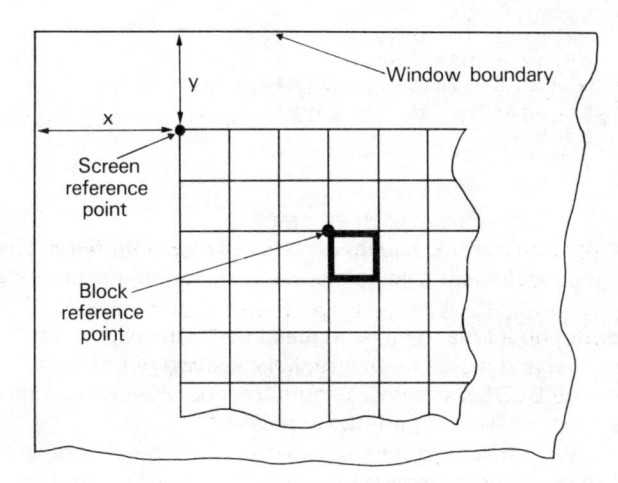

The two-number referencing system for the grid will allow us to define this relationship.

Reference data storage

Each square's reference can be stored using DATA statements. For example, the top two lines of our figure would be stored as:

DATA 2,0,3,0,0,1,1,1,2,1,3,1,4,1,5,1

By 'READing' values in pairs the position of each square in the grid can be made available to the program.

SuperBASIC procedure

Before listing a suitable procedure, we must define a few parameters:

    across = grid reference of square (X-axis)
    down = grid reference of square (Y-axis)
    x_origin = screen x co-ordinate of figure start position
    y_origin = screen y co-ordinate of figure start position
    width = width of individual square
    height = height of individual square
    number = number of squares filled-in on grid for each colour
    colour = colour of squares

The values in the above list from x_origin to colour will be passed to the procedure by the program using it. The procedure can be defined as follows:

```
1000 DEFine PROCedure figure(x_origin,y_origin,width,
        height,number,colour)
1010   FOR squares = 1 TO number
1020     READ across : READ down
         BLOCK width,height,x_origin+across*width,
         y_origin+down*height,colour
1040   END FOR squares
1050 END DEFine
```

(Line numbers from 1000 have been used arbitrarily.)

The BLOCK statement displays one square each time around the loop. The numeric expressions in the statement calculate the actual starting co-ordinates of the square.

To speed the procedure up a little there is no reason why the expressions could not be evaluated first and stored in an array, in a section of program outside the procedure. The BLOCK statement could then be reduced by simply accessing the array rather than working out the expressions.

The procedure will have to be called for each colour. It will be preferable to arrange your program to draw the squares with the predominant colour first. For instance with our figure we shall draw the body first, then add the eyes, then finally the mouth.

Here is a simple application of this method:

```
100  REMark * simple figures *
110  MODE 8:WINDOW 512,256,0,0
120  PAPER 3: CLS
130  FOR men = 25 TO 175 STEP 50
140    figure 30,men,8,5,30,1
150    figure 30,men,8,5,2,2
160    figure 30,men,8,5,2,6
170    RESTORE
180  END FOR men
190  figure 125,25,20,24,30,4
200  figure 125,25,20,24,2,1
210  figure 125,25,20,24,2,2
220  RESTORE
230  LET colour = 0
240  FOR men = 25 TO 175 STEP 50
250    figure 300,men,18,5,30,colour
260    LET colour = colour + 1
270    figure 300,men,18,5,2,colour
280    figure 300,men,18,5,2,0
290    RESTORE
300    LET colour = colour + 1
310  END FOR men
320  figure 440,115,4,4,30,0
330  INK 0
340  CURSOR 35,230: PRINT"8*5"
```

```
350 CURSOR 155,230: PRINT"20*24"
360 CURSOR 330,230: PRINT"18*5"
370 CURSOR 435,155: PRINT"4*4"
380 CLEAR
390 DEFine PROCedure figure (x,y,w,h,n,c)
400   FOR squares = 1 TO n
410     READ across : READ down
420     BLOCK w,h,x+across*w,y+down*h,c
430   END FOR squares
440 END DEFine
450 DATA 2,0,3,0,0,1,1,1,2,1,3,1,4,1
460 DATA 5,1,0,2,2,2,3,2,5,2,0,3,1,3
470 DATA 2,3,3,3,4,3,5,3,1,4,4,4,1,5
480 DATA 2,5,3,5,4,5,1,6,4,6,0,7,1,7
490 DATA 4,7,5,7,1,2,4,2,2,4,3,4
```

Do note that when all the co-ordinates stored as DATA statements have been read (i.e. a complete figure has been drawn) we must RESTORE the pointer back to the start of the first DATA statement. A CLEAR keyword is also required at the end of the main program (line 380) to enable the READ/DATA statements to be correctly executed when running the program again.

Lines 330 to 370 were included to display the pixel size of each grid square used.

Should you be using a colour monitor then line 210, for example, could have the colour code 2 replaced by 144 to give black and red vertical striped 'teeth'.

Hopefully, this example will help to trigger off some of your own ideas. Now we can move on to look at pixel graphics.

Pixel graphics

Within the character set provided in the QL there are a number of characters such as accented letters for use with foreign languages, Greek letters and arrow heads. Some may be used to represent characters, other than for their intended use, in games or other applications. They can be made to move around the screen at very high speed.

The characters are not represented by individual keys and so their character codes must be used in any PRINT statements. The following characters with their corresponding codes may be useful:

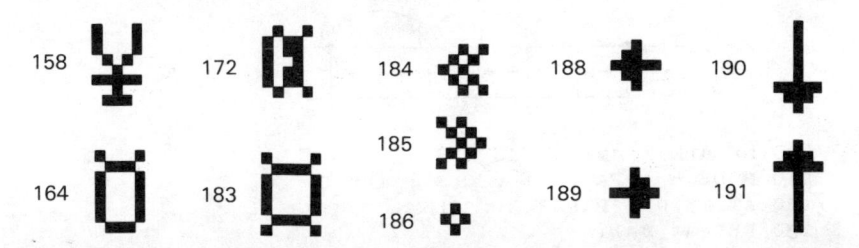

158 ⅄   172 ⌸   184 ❖   188 ✚   190 ⊥
                 185 ❥
164 ⊓   183 ⊔   186 ✦   189 ✚   191 †

If you wish to investigate the full range of this group of characters, the following program will display them together with their codes at the largest character size. Select MODE 8 default screen first.

```
100 REMark * special characters *
110 CLS : CSIZE 3,0
120 FOR codes = 129 TO 191
130    PRINT ! codes ! CHR$(codes);
140 END FOR codes
```

Below are three programs that demonstrate simple applications. The first simulates pipe flow diagrammatically.

```
100 REMark * pipe flow *
110 MODE 8 : PAPER 6 : INK 0
120 CLS : LET a=12
130 BLOCK 429,10,10,85,0
140 BLOCK 429,10,10,115,0
150 REPeat flow
160    FOR x = a TO 408 STEP 24
170       CURSOR x,100
180       PRINT CHR$(189); CHR$(32)
190    END FOR x
200    IF a=12 THEN
210       LET a=24
220    ELSE
230       LET a=12
240    END IF
250    IF INKEY$<>"" THEN EXIT flow
260 END REPeat flow
```

The variable *a* is used to alternate the CURSOR *x* parameter between 12 and 24. This causes the two printed characters (arrow and space) to alternately overprint each other giving the illustration of movement.

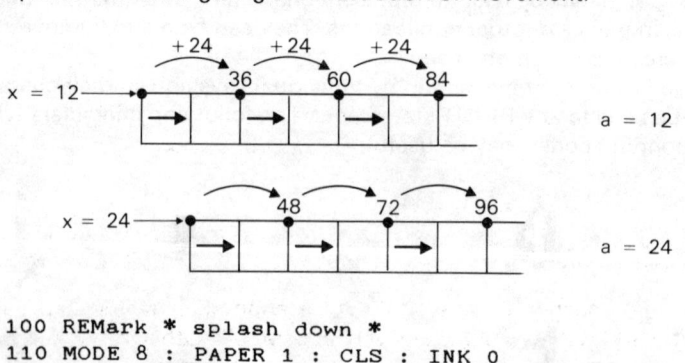

```
100 REMark * splash down *
110 MODE 8 : PAPER 1 : CLS : INK 0
120 AT 15,0 : PAPER 3 : CLS 1
130 REPeat fall
140    LET x = RND(10 TO 40)*10
```

```
150     FOR y = 0 TO 140 STEP 10
160        CURSOR x,y
170        PRINT CHR$(183): PAUSE 5
180        CURSOR x,y : PRINT CHR$(164)
190        PAUSE 10 : INK 3
200        CURSOR x,y
210        PRINT CHR$(32) : INK 0
220     END FOR y : INK 1
230     CURSOR x-10,y : PRINT CHR$(186)
240     CURSOR x+10,y : PRINT CHR$(186)
250     PAUSE 15 : INK 3
260     CURSOR x-10,y : PRINT CHR$(32)
270     CURSOR x+10,y : PRINT CHR$(32)
280     INK 0
290 END REPeat fall
```

This time the effect of movement has been achieved by printing the two characters in the same place with a suitable pause in between (lines 170, 180). Since printing a 'space' character would produce a blue square, the INK colours had to be reversed (lines 190, 210). The same principle was used to display the 'splashes'.

The final example shows a simple way to highlight titles.

```
100 REMark * highlight *
110 CLS : AT 4,9
120 PRINT"THIS IS THE TITLE"
130 LET NUMBER = 17
140 highlight 4,9
150 DEFine PROCedure highlight(x,y)
160    AT x-1,y : place 185
180    AT x+1,y : place 184
200 END DEFine
210 DEFine PROCedure place (char)
220    FOR position = 1 TO NUMBER
230       PRINT CHR$(char);
240    END FOR position
250 END DEFine
```

As long as the AT parameters are passed to the procedure 'highlight', and the number of character positions in the title are defined, the display can be used at any screen position. Different characters may also be selected by altering lines 160 and 170.

Special pixel characters

As we have already seen in Chapter 4, the generation of character shapes from pixels using the POINT keyword is not very acceptable. Other, more involved, methods must be used. Since these do not use SuperBASIC graphics keywords they are beyond the scope of this book.

PROBLEMS

We have looked at a number of methods and keywords available for the manipulation and positioning of text and graphics characters around the screen. Here are two problems on which you may like to practice.

1. Write a program to display your name at the top centre of the screen in red, then change it to green and make it move downwards until it comes to rest at the centre of a 200-pixel-high window with a circle of radius 30 units around it. (Twelve letters maximum.)
2. Generate a horizontal ladder on the screen with the numbers 1 to 6 centrally placed between the rungs. Use CSIZE 3, 1.

CHAPTER 6
TURN TURTLE
PENUP, PENDOWN, MOVE, TURN, TURNTO

INTRODUCTION

To many readers the words 'turtle graphics' are synonymous with Seymour Papert who, during the 1960s in America, utilised a programming language called LOGO for introducing children to the art of logical reasoning and self-discovery. His application centred around a small mobile robot connected by cable to a computer. This 'turtle' incorporated a pen at its centre that could be raised or lowered by program. Its movements in the X- and Y-axes were also controllable.

A simple set of program instructions allowed the children to control the turtle's direction, its distance travelled, and pen up/pen down operations. Moving the turtle over paper enabled shapes and patterns of a wide variety and complexity to be drawn.

QL turtle graphics can be regarded as a small sub-set of these instructions. It enables a single pixel point on the screen to be manoeuvred in 'turtle-like' fashion, permitting control of direction, distance and screen writing. Five simple commands are available and these can be used in direct command mode. That is, type in the command without preceding it with a line number, then press the ENTER key to see it immediately executed. As you will see though, many more interesting effects can be created when the commands are used within a SuperBASIC program. The command formats are:

PENUP[#n]

PENDOWN[#n]

MOVE[#n,] distance

TURN[#n,] degrees (relative)

TURNTO[#n,] degrees (absolute)

Channel numbers can be selected so that more than one window of turtle graphics can exist at the same time. First of all the action of each command will be described then we can look at their application.

PEN CONTROL

We can cover both pen commands together. No parameters are used apart from the optional channel number. The point on the screen can be imagined as being the tip of a pen, so a PENDOWN command followed by moving the point in a specific direction will draw a line. To raise the 'pen' so that drawing can start at another part of the screen, PENUP is used. Movement is then programmed in the required direction followed by a PENDOWN to prepare for drawing the next line. You see, we can still think of the point's position as being identified by the current scale graphics cursor position. A move following a PENUP command is really a re-location of the cursor with no visible display, like LINE x,y. The default condition of the 'pen' following a reset or power-on of the QL is up.

DIRECTION CONTROL

It will be easier to explain the two commands that control direction if we think of the point as being an arrowhead. TURN and TURNTO both affect the direction in which the arrowhead is pointing. Note that they do *not* cause any movement from the current position. Their parameters are in degrees not radians, and before any direction commands have been used, the arrowhead will be pointing to the right with a *heading* of 0 degrees, as shown below:

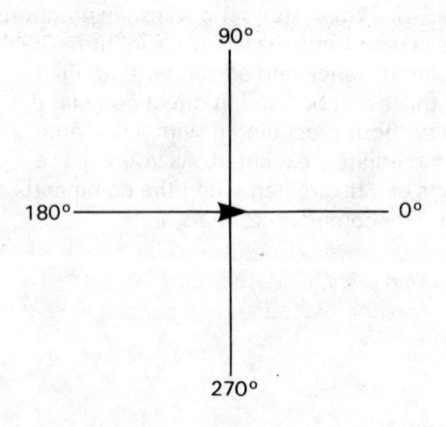

```
            90°
             |
             |
    180°─────▶─────0°
             |
             |
            270°
```

Default position

TURN

This command will cause the arrowhead to rotate by the specified number of degrees in an anticlockwise direction. If the arrowhead was already pointing vertically (heading 90 degrees) then: TURN 45 would cause it to point to a heading of 135 degrees (north-west), as shown below:

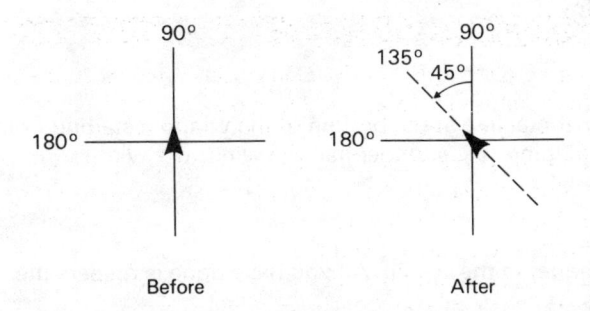

Before   After

So the angle parameter value is always added to the current heading in an anticlockwise direction. It is therefore a relative command.

TURNTO

With TURNTO, however, the arrowhead is rotated to point at a specified heading, its previous heading not being considered. TURNTO 180 will always cause the arrowhead to point to the left. This is an absolute command, always being referenced to zero degrees. It is the better turn command to use at the start of a program when often the current turtle cursor direction is unknown.

MOVEMENT

The final turtle command is MOVE, which simply causes the current cursor position to be altered by a specified number of units. Whether you see a resultant line or not depends upon any previous PENUP/PENDOWN command. The move is always made in the direction defined by the last-used TURN or TURNTO command. If a negative number of units is specified then the move will be backwards.

Do note that the units used are scale graphics units, not pixels. So if you should be programming moves that need a scale greater than the default setting (100) the MOVE commands must be preceded by an appropriate SCALE statement.

DIRECT COMMAND APPLICATION

Now that each command has been explained their uses can be shown, first of all in direct command mode. Remember to press the ENTER key at the end of each line.

To start with, press the RESET button on the QL and select low-resolution mode by pressing F2. Now type:

PENDOWN
MOVE 80

You will see a white horizontal line at the bottom of the window starting from the left-hand corner, extending to just under half the window's width. Continue with:

TURN 90

You will not see any change on the screen. All you have done is prepare the cursor to move upwards. Type:

MOVE 50

The line will extend vertically for 50 units.

PENUP
MOVE 10
PENDOWN
MOVE 30

This will display a gap of 10 units followed by the line continuing vertically for a further 30 units. We must always use PENDOWN before a move command that is to draw a visible line. Now follow on with:

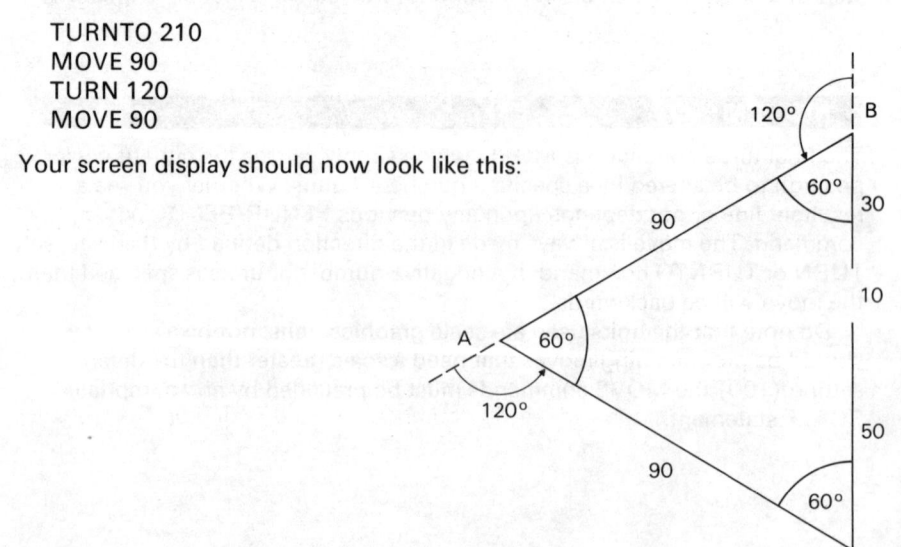

TURNTO 210
MOVE 90
TURN 120
MOVE 90

Your screen display should now look like this:

The dotted lines have been added to identify the angles through which the cursor has turned. At point B we made it turn to a bearing of 210 degrees, which is the same as using the relative command: TURN 120. The latter method was used for the second angle. Note that the angles are external, not internal, since the rotation is always anticlockwise, as the arrowheads show in the figure. Apart from the gap, an equilateral triangle has been drawn with internal angles of 60 degrees.

The following sequence will draw a square:

CLS
LINE 75, 50
TURNTO 90
PENDOWN
MOVE 40
TURN 90
MOVE 40
TURN 90
MOVE 40
TURN 90
MOVE 40
PENUP

The sequence was started with clear screen and line statements, both in direct command mode. The LINE statement has been used to set the turtle cursor at the scale graphics centre of the current window. We could have used two other methods: POINT 75, 50 if the first MOVE command were going to produce a visible line, or: SCALE 100, −75, −50 which could be used whether a line were to be visible or not.

It is becoming apparent that while many more complicated figures can be drawn with these direct commands, it will rapidly become laborious. It is, though, an excellent way of allowing young children to experiment with a very simple set of instructions to find out about lengths and angles.

EXPANDING TURTLE GRAPHICS

The absence of a *repeat* turtle command hinders sensible use of direct commands which are a basic feature of LOGO-derived turtle graphics. This is essentially because most regular figures are made up of repeated elements, often a MOVE/TURN pair. By combining turtle graphics commands with SuperBASIC keywords this problem can be overcome. We must, of course, revert to program mode and use line numbers, but this is of little consequence considering the great scope for inventiveness now available to the user.

The FOR/END FOR keywords provide us with the repeat facility and can be easily accepted by younger children. This extends their turtle vocabulary and enables them to produce very satisfying creations. The square drawn earlier can now be programmed in a more compact manner:

```
100 REMark * turtle square *
110 CLS : POINT 110,30
120 PENDOWN
130 TURNTO 0
140 FOR sides = 1 TO 4
150    TURN 90
160    MOVE 50
170 END FOR sides
180 PENUP
```

A triangle now becomes:

```
100 REMark * turtle triangle *
110 CLS : POINT 110,50
120 PENDOWN : TURNTO 120
130 FOR sides = 1 TO 3
140    MOVE 40
150    TURN 120
160 END FOR sides
170 PENUP
```

Although this particular example does not save many lines when compared with its direct command mode equivalent it does provide the structure on which any other regular polygon may be drawn. Replace lines 130 and 150 of the triangle program with the next two lines and run the program again.

```
130 FOR sides = 1 TO 6
150    TURN 60
```

A hexagon is displayed. But how did we arrive at the value for the angle? There are 360 degrees in a full circle, so for a polygon of n sides the external angle can be shown to be: $360/n$ degrees.

Diagonal lines are still 'ragged' and if too many sides are selected the outlines will tend to lose their polygon shape and approximate to a circle. Mode 4 can be used to improve the resolution, and attention can be paid to achieving maximum resolution in the X-axis by suitably choosing SCALE and WINDOW parameters. The next example will allow you to determine the polygon 'limits' of your system.

```
100 REMark * polygon resolution *
110 REPeat loop
120    CLS : PENDOWN
130    POINT 130,40
140    TURNTO 90
150    INPUT "HOW MANY SIDES?"; number
160    FOR sides = 1 TO number
170       MOVE 10
```

```
180        TURN 360/number
190        END FOR sides
200     PAUSE
210 END REPeat loop
220 PENUP
```

The following program 'nests' the polygon loop with a further loop that changes the number of sides. The INK colour is also varied.

```
100 REMark * turtle polygons *
110 PAPER 0: CLS: POINT 130,40
120 LET colour = 1
130 PENDOWN
140 TURNTO 90
150 FOR number = 3 TO 15
160    INK colour
170    FOR sides = 1 TO number
180       MOVE 20
190       TURN 360/number
200    END FOR sides
210    LET colour = colour+1
220    IF colour = 8 THEN colour = 1
230 END FOR number
240 PENUP
```

A square spiral design, impracticable in direct command mode, now becomes easy to achieve:

```
100 REMark * turtle squiral *
110 PAPER 1 : INK 6 : CLS
120 POINT 85,50
130 LET side = 2
140 TURNTO 270
150 PENDOWN
160 REPeat turns
170    MOVE side
180    TURN 90
190    MOVE side
200    TURN 90
210    LET side = side+2
220    IF side = 100 THEN EXIT turns
230 END REPeat turns
240 PENUP
```

Lines 170 and 180 are repeated to achieve the required offset as shown below:

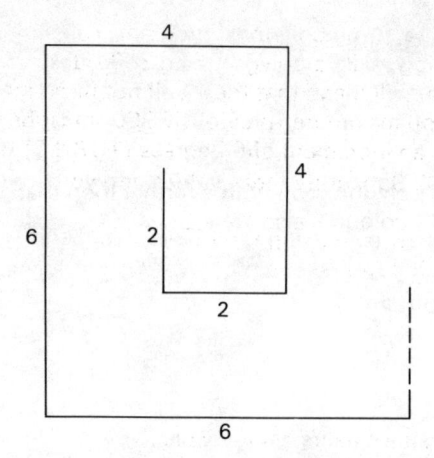

TURTLE CIRCLES AND ARCS

Drawing curves without the aid of SuperBASIC would be very time-consuming. To produce a circle a repeated sequence is again required, incrementing the angle at each step.

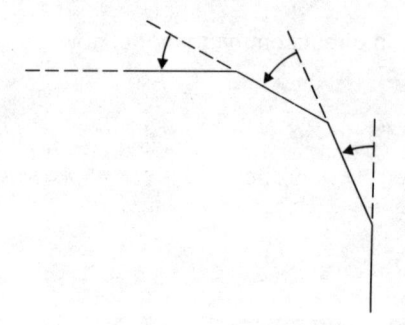

We can draw a circle like this:

```
100 REMark * turtle circle *
110 CLS: POINT 130,40
120 PENDOWN: TURNTO 90
130 FOR angle = 1 TO 360
140     MOVE 1
150     TURN 1
160 END FOR angle
170 PENUP
```

The circle is rather large! To create smaller, perhaps more useful circles, the TURN angle increment must be increased. In case you are not quite sure how the previous program did draw the circle, compare lines 130 and 150 of the program with lines 170 and 190 of the 'turtle polygons' program. You should be able to recognise our circle as being really a polygon with 360 sides! Increasing the angle parameter, then, will mean that there will not be so many 'sides' to the circle. Therefore the loop maximum (previously 360) must be appropriately reduced. For example, an increment of 5 degrees (TURN 5) will need a loop maximum of: 360/5 = 72. Substitute these values into your program and try it.

The circle can be reduced still further by making the MOVE parameter smaller. Change lines 130 to 150 as follows:

```
130    FOR angle = 1 TO 72
140      MOVE .5
150      TURN 5
```

Run the program and you will see that a smaller circle results.

To draw arcs it is only necessary to reduce the number of steps in the loop still further but keep the angle parameter the same. Try the program again, this time with line 130 containing:

```
130    FOR angle = 1 to 25
```

and you will produce an arc one-third the circumference of the original circle. Remember that MODE 4 will always give you better resolution.

TURTLE ROUTINES

LOGO-based turtle graphics allows the storage of command sequences as named routines, such as 'square', 'house', 'circle', 'petal'. We can emulate this using SuperBASIC procedures. For example, we can define *square*:

```
100 DEFine PROCedure square (wide)
110   PENDOWN
120   TURNTO 0
130   FOR sides = 1 TO 4
140     MOVE wide
150     TURN 90
160   END FOR sides
170   PENUP
180 END DEFine
```

We can define *triangle*:

```
200 DEFine PROCedure triangle (wide)
210   PENDOWN
220   TURNTO 0
230   FOR sides = 1 TO 3
240     MOVE wide
250     TURN 120
260   END FOR sides
```

```
270    PENUP
280    END DEFine
```

We could now draw a house:

```
300  PAPER 6 : INK 4 : CLS
310  POINT 75,30
320  square 20
330  TURNTO 90
340  MOVE 20
350  triangle 20
360  TURNTO 270
370  MOVE 20
```

We could also draw other figures as combinations of the two basic shapes. Note that lines 330 and 340 move the turtle (cursor) to the top left-hand corner of the square so that the triangle starts from the correct place. Lines 360 and 370 move the turtle back to the starting point (75, 30).

Edit lines 300 to 370 to program the following procedure:

```
300  DEFine PROCedure house (wide)
310     square wide
320     TURNTO 90
330     MOVE wide
340     triangle wide
350     MOVE wide
360  END DEFine
```

We can now draw the traditional turtle graphics 'street':

```
400  PAPER 7 : CLS : PENDOWN
410  DATA 20,20,40,10,15,25
420  FOR x_start = 10,35,60,105,120,140
430     READ size
440     INK RND(6)
450     POINT x_start,20
460     house size
470  END FOR x_start
480  PENUP : CLEAR
```

ROTATING FIGURES

Any figure built up from combinations of MOVE and TURN can be efficiently created using procedures, and it only needs the addition of an incrementing TURN command to rotate the figure and make some very effective patterns. Using the *square* procedure once more we can easily produce a rotating square. Either re-type the procedure again or delete line 120 and lines 200 to 490 of the previous routines.

```
500 REMark * square turns *
510 MODE 4 : PAPER 0 : CLS
520 REPeat outer_loop
530   FOR colour = 2,4,7
540     POINT 75,5
550     INK colour
560     LET angle = 0
570     REPeat inner_loop
580       TURNTO angle
590       square 20
600       LET angle = angle+30
610       IF angle = 360 THEN EXIT inner_loop
620     END REPeat inner_loop
630   END FOR colour
640 END REPeat outer_loop
650 DEFine PROCedure square (wide)
660   PENDOWN
670   FOR sides = 0 TO 4
680     MOVE wide : TURN 90
690   END FOR sides : PENUP
700 END DEFine
```

You will have to stop the program by pressing the CTRL key and the SPACE bar together. Try altering the angle increment at line 600. It is surprising just how many varied patterns can be generated from the rotating square.

QL TURTLE-TALK

There is one facility of the QL that allows us to simulate many of the LOGO turtle commands. SuperBASIC procedure definitions, after having been run in program mode, can be called up in direct command mode. Thus we can define the commands FORWARD, BACKWARD, RIGHT etc. in terms of the QL turtle graphics keywords and simulate true 'turtle-talk'. Press RESET, type in these next procedures then run them:

```
100 DEFine PROCedure forward (distance)
110   MOVE distance
120 END DEFine
130 DEFine PROCedure left (angle)
140   TURN angle
150 END DEFine
```

The screen will clear and nothing else is displayed. Continue by typing the following direct commands:

PENDOWN
FORWARD 20
LEFT 90
FORWARD 40

The new commands are obeyed in exactly the same way as MOVE and TURN. We can add two more procedures.

```
160 DEFine PROCedure backward (distance)
170    MOVE -distance
180 END DEFine
190 DEFine PROCedure right (angle)
200    TURN -angle
210 END DEFine
```

If you run the procedures again and type in some more direct commands you will see that the line continues from where the last FORWARD 40 left it. On RESET, of course, the turtle cursor starts from the bottom left-hand corner of the current window. What we need is the ability to specify a suitable starting point. In LOGO turtle this is normally at the centre of the screen with the turtle pointing upwards. Another procedure, *home*, provides the solution:

```
220 DEFine PROCedure home
230    POINT 75,50
240    TURNTO 90
250 END DEFine
```

Add and run the procedure, then try this:

PENDOWN
HOME
FORWARD 30
HOME
RIGHT 90
FORWARD 30
HOME
LEFT 90
FORWARD 30

You should have produced an inverted capital 'T'. Our procedure *home* always gives a visible point at the screen centre and should this be undesirable, the POINT keyword can be replaced by LINE.

We could cheat a little and generate a procedure for the LOGO turtle command MOVE X, Y which, since it defines a position on the screen in x and y co-ordinates, can use the QL keyword LINE. We must, however, give the command another name since MOVE is one of our keywords.

```
260 DEFine PROCedure position (x,y)
270    PENUP
280    LINE x,y
290 END DEFine
```

So a range of 'turtle-talk' commands can be created. By making up a program consisting of a number of these procedures, it can be loaded and run, then the QL can be 'handed over' to younger enthusiasts for LOGO-like creativity. Further additions to the program could usefully be the setting up of a suitable screen window, initial PAPER/INK colours and perhaps a 'prompt' list of commands available.

PATTERN GENERATION

As previous examples have demonstrated, turtle graphics can also be used to form patterns. These can, in themselves, be the basis of designs for fabrics, wallpapers and other materials, apart from being an art-form in their own right. The essence of pattern design is the creativity of the designer; rules are out! To this end are included a few programs, simple in construction yet visually effective, that hopefully some readers will like to use as the basis for further experiment.

```
100 REMark * turn turtle *
110 PAPER 0 : CLS
120 LET colour = 1
130 PENDOWN
140 FOR start_angle = 0 TO 350 STEP 10
150    POINT 85,50 : INK colour
160    TURNTO start_angle
170    FOR side = 2 TO 100 STEP 20
180       MOVE side : TURN 90
190       MOVE side : TURN 90
200    END FOR side
210    LET colour = colour + 1
220    IF colour = 8 THEN colour = 1
230 END FOR start_angle
240 PENUP
```

Try varying the STEP interval at lines 140 and 170.

```
100 REMark * turtle scrolls *
110 MODE 8 : PAPER 7 : CLS : PENDOWN
120 FOR scrolls = 1 TO 24
130    POINT 75,50
140    LET angle = 90
150    FOR steps = 1 TO 60
160       INK RND(6)
170       MOVE 4
180       TURN angle
190       LET angle = angle-3.5
200    END FOR steps
210 END FOR scrolls
```

What starts off as a spiral ends up as a scroll shape because the angle value changes its sign from positive (left-hand spiral) to negative (right-hand spiral) as 3.5 is successively subtracted from it. By varying the *angle* increment at line 190, and increasing the number of *steps* at line 150, a wide variety of linked scrolls can be obtained.

```
100 REMark * line spin *
110 MODE 8 : PAPER 0 : CLS
120 LET angle = 90 : PENDOWN
130 FOR start = 10 TO 154 STEP 2
140   INK RND(1 TO 7)
150   TURNTO angle
160   POINT start,50
170   MOVE 50 : MOVE -100
180   LET angle = angle + 2.5
190 END FOR start
```

Experiment with different values for the angle increment at line 180 and the maximum value for *start* at line 130.

```
100 REMark * flower *
110 MODE 8 : WINDOW 512,256,0,0
120 PAPER 0 : CLS : PENDOWN
130 POINT 75,50
140 LET colour = 1
150 LET offset = 0
160 REPeat flower
170   INK colour
180   DATA 0,180,90,270,180,0,270,90
190   FOR petals = 1 TO 4
200     READ outwards,inwards
210     petal outwards
220     petal inwards
230   END FOR petals
240   LET colour = colour + 1
250   IF colour = 7 THEN colour = 1
260   LET offset = offset + 20
270   IF offset = 80 THEN EXIT flower
280   RESTORE
290 END REPeat flower
300 PENUP : CLEAR
310 DEFine PROCedure petal(direction )
320   TURNTO direction + offset
330   FOR angle = 1 TO 30
340     MOVE 1.5
350     TURN 3
360   END FOR angle
370 END DEFine
```

Each petal is produced from two arcs starting at the centre of the screen, moving outwards then, on completion of the first arc, incrementing the heading by 180 degrees ready for the second arc.

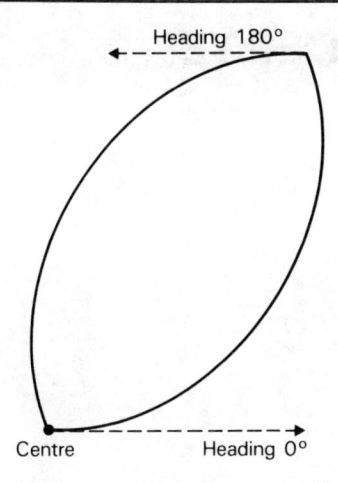

The *offset* parameter enables the gradual rotation of the petals in 20-degree steps.

Note that line 250 is redundant with the program in its present form; it is relevant only if the loop variable *petals* is increased beyond seven.

Try altering the DATA statement to give more petals, or vary the offset. If you modify lines 200 and 220 to the following, the petals can be coloured:

```
200 READ outwards,inwards : FILL 1
220 petal inwards : FILL 0
```

PROBLEMS

We have shown how the QL turtle graphics keywords may be used on their own in direct command mode, within programs and modified with the aid of procedures. Try your hand at the following problems, working in low resolution with a 512 by 256 window area.

1. Using the turtle keywords in direct command mode draw a large 'X' central on the screen, starting at the centre.

2. Create a procedure that draws a rectangle of size 25 units wide by 15 units high.

3. Using the above procedure write a program that displays a triangle of rectangles starting with a horizontal base of five rectangles. Fill in each rectangle with a random colour.

CHAPTER 7
EASEL: BASIC CONCEPTS

INTRODUCTION

The theme is now going to change from talking about writing programs that produce graphics, to using a program that produces graphics, or to be more precise, produces graphs. We are going to take a look at EASEL, described as a business graphics package, that is supplied on a single microdrive cartridge with the QL. It is essentially a large sophisticated program that can rapidly translate numeric information, entered by its user, into a visible graph. Several types and style of graph are available and most of the graphic elements that make up the graph may be altered if required. More than one graph may be displayed at the same time so that, for example, separate profit and sales graphs may be viewed as one.

With a description including the word 'business' you may be forgiven for thinking 'EASEL's not for me!' But if we stop and consider some of the possible applications where graphical results could be used, we should all realise EASEL's potential to be used in areas other than just for business. In schools and colleges graphs are used in scientific, statistical, chemical and mechanical analysis. Mathematical functions, a sine wave for example, can be much better understood graphically. Almost every subject can utilise, at some stage, a graph output for emphasis and clarity. From social studies on population and industrial statistics to harmonic analysis and the laws of physics, the scope is endless. Indeed, the transformation of numbers into visible quantities is an excellent way to teach young children about the relationships that exist between numbers. This could be an EASEL application area of interest to those involved in child education.

Certainly the small business user can benefit from the conversion of his figures into graph form, especially if figure-work is not his strong point! Although it will be explained in more detail further on, different formulae may be applied to a given set of figures and their effect visibly demonstrated with far greater impact than just by comparing sets of numbers. Graphs are particularly useful for displaying summaries and, in conjunction with a suitable printer, permanent copies may be obtained for distribution. Graphs may be created then stored on a microdrive cartridge for recall at some later date. They can then be modified, updated and re-stored as necessary. You can experiment with different graph formats without corrupting any existing graph but still using the same set of figures.

PRESENTATION

Although the theme may be changing the objectives are not. In these chapters devoted to EASEL the information will be presented in the same style as before, so that you will be able to understand all you need to know about EASEL, in order to use it as the very versatile tool it is.

| ENTER |

In this chapter and the next you will find the ENTER key symbol being used. Many EASEL operations do *not* require the ENTER key to be pressed so the symbol is used deliberately to emphasize the times when the key *must* be pressed.

EASEL OUTLINE

Before we start examining EASEL in detail let us take a quick look at the basic features available.

EASEL is 'user-friendly'. This essentially means that the program allows the user to understand and operate it with an easily acquired ability. EASEL achieves this by being interactive. For example, displayed information on the screen (**prompts**) assists the user in making his or her selections. Simple use of the cursor keys allows the user to indicate rapidly to EASEL where a particular number or text should be placed. At any stage, a **help** facility can be selected to provide successively more detailed levels of information relevant to the current action in progress. All typed inputs to the program can be edited before being incorporated on the final graph. Control of the various operating sequences is achieved with only a small number of keys.

GRAPH TYPES

Three basic types of graph can be displayed, **bar**, **line** or **pie**. The latter is often referred to as a '**pie chart**'. Each can exist in a number of different styles, sizes and colours. Backgrounds can be chosen in complementary colours or EASEL can be left to do it for you. The figure below shows outline graphs of the three types. Bar and line graphs may be horizontal or vertical. Line graphs can be filled in between the lines and the zero level.

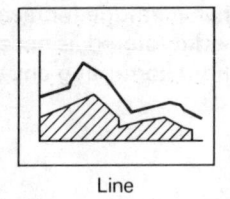

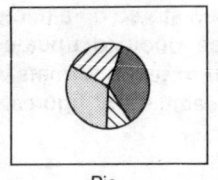

Bar   Line   Pie

As you will see in Chapter 8, the ability of EASEL to create different graph types and styles can be used as little or as much as you like. For instance, you can switch on the QL, load the EASEL program and immediately type in numbers that will be displayed as a bar graph. Alternatively, you can define the type of graph, colours to be used, size, axes increments and so on. Any requirement in between can be accommodated.

RESOLUTION

EASEL normally operates in MODE 4, but this is also a parameter that may be altered if required. Naturally, if you are using a colour or black and white monitor you would expect to stay with that mode. Should you be using the system with a conventional television then high-resolution mode will certainly given reduced clarity. EASEL fortunately allows you to select either 40, 64 (or 80) columns per line so that you may make the best use of your television resolution capabilities. A good quality television should be able to give reasonable definition of 64 columns per line. You will see how to set up this parameter early on in this chapter so that you can immediately use the best display for your screen.

COLOUR

When using EASEL in 64- or 80-column mode it is equivalent to setting high resolution, so only four colours (white, black, red and green) are available. However, 40-column mode allows the use of all eight standard colours in most of the selections you may make. It is best though, to limit the number of colours used for any one display, as too many can detract from the required impact.

EASEL CONTROL

Using EASEL at its highest level, numbers are typed and then automatically converted into a graph. If you wish to exercise any control over the operation then you will have to select an appropriate EASEL **command**. The commands enable control over a number of diverse operations from changing graph layouts to transferring graph files to the other software packages (ABACUS and ARCHIVE).

Should you want to manipulate the figures by applying formulae conversions then you can use EASEL Functions which modify existing values. If you have already studied SuperBASIC then you will have met all of them before (e.g. SIN, INT, SQR).

Function keys

Not to be confused with EASEL Functions, the five function keys F1 to F5 at the left-hand side of the QL keyboard are used to call up various facilities. These greatly reduce the amount of typing that would otherwise be necessary.

INPUT/OUTPUT

EASEL also provides for the storage, retrieval and movement of graph data, in the form of files, to and from the microdrives and to and from other software packages.

EASEL BACK-UP

At this point it is strongly recommended that you make a back-up copy of your EASEL program, just in case of any unfortunate accident that might occur to the cartridge. If you have not used the cartridges before you should read the section on microdrives (p. 2) concerning the precautions you must observe.

Before copying or storing any program onto a blank cartridge it must be **formatted**. Formatting is a process performed by the QL which prepares the tape for the storage of information. Once a tape has been formatted and programs stored on it, it would not normally be formatted again since the process effectively *wipes* the tape 'clean'.

The QL will accept an unformatted tape for the copying operation since it will perform the formatting first. However, it is advisable to format a new cartridge several times before use, since it helps to reduce possible data errors. The following program may be used to achieve this:

```
100 CLS:INK 0
110 FOR try = 1 TO 10
120 PRINT "Try =";try
130 FORMAT mdv1_
140 END FOR try
150 BEEP 20000,11,16,2,1
```

If required, you can add a reference to the end of line 120 (e.g. mdv1_ecopy). Type in the program, and with the blank cartridge safely installed in microdrive 1 (the left-hand unit) type RUN and press the ENTER key. The process does take a few minutes but BEEP tells you when it is finished and it really is worth doing.

To make a copy of EASEL, leave the formatted cartridge in microdrive 1 and load the EASEL master copy in microdrive 2. Now type:

LRUN mdv2_clone [ENTER]

The screen will clear and be replaced by a request to press the SPACE bar in order to format the cartridge in microdrive 1. You must do this for the program to continue. Over the next few minutes your screen should progressively display:

215/220 Sectors
Saving . . .
Copying BOOT . . .
Copying EASEL . . .
Copying GRAF_HOB . . .
Copying GPRINT_PRT . . .
Copying INTGX132_PRT . . .
Copying JX80_PRT . . .

The EASEL cartridge contains a suite of programs and a list (**directory**) of the programs now stored on the cartridge in microdrive 1 follows the above display. This allows you to check that all the programs have been safely copied.

The **sector** numbers deserve a short explanation. They refer to the cartridge's storage capacity (1 sector = 512 bytes). This can vary from cartridge to cartridge. The first number shows how many sectors are available for use. The second number shows the total number of sectors on the tape. The numbers shown above are therefore examples only.

Having copied your master cartridge, store it safely away and label the back-up copy.

LOADING EASEL

Throughout the chapter we shall be inviting you to try out the various EASEL facilities, so the next thing to do is load EASEL into the QL.

With the QL switched on and your television or monitor connected, press the RESET button then place the back-up EASEL copy into microdrive 1. Press either the F1 or F2 key, and it will load automatically. If you have already been using the QL, you can type:

LRUN mdv1_BOOT

The program is loaded in stages. After about 5 seconds from the start the PSION copyright display is shown, together with the EASEL version number:

```
LOADING QL EASEL

version 2.00

Copyright © 1984 PSION SYSTEMS

business graphics
```

Note that this is the version number of the EASEL package we have used as our source of information.

After about 10 seconds you will be presented with what is called the Main Display . . . a blank graph. EASEL is now in what we shall call **data entry mode**, since you will always have to return to this display format to enter graph data.

SCREEN RESOLUTION

Before its contents are explained, however, you may wish to change the resolution to match your own screen as explained previously. Decide on the number of columns per line you wish to try (40, 64 or 80) then perform the following operations:

1. Press F3

2. Type D

3. Type 4 or 6 or 8

The screen will now redisplay the Main Display at the selected size. Should you find the resolution still not acceptable then repeat the above sequence and make another selection.

MAIN DISPLAY

The illustration below shows what to expect from the Main Display in 80- or 64-column mode.

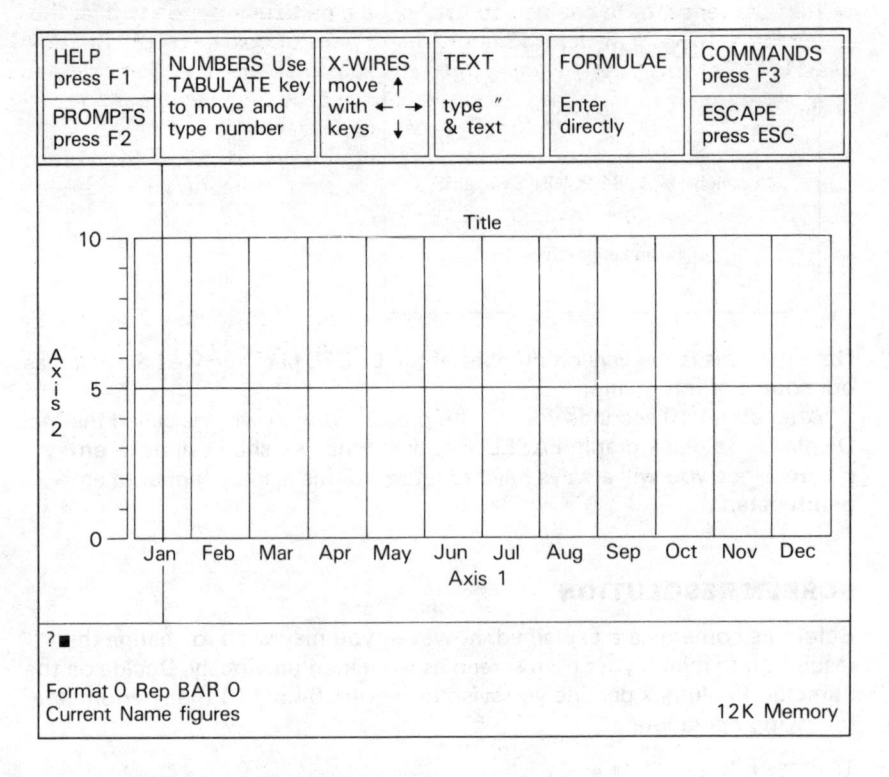

HELP press F1	NUMBERS Use TABULATE key to move and type number	X-WIRES move ↑ with ← → keys ↓	TEXT type " & text	FORMULAE Enter directly	COMMANDS press F3
PROMPTS press F2					ESCAPE press ESC

```
                               Title
      10 ┬───┬───┬───┬───┬───┬───┬───┬───┬───┬───┬───┐
         │   │   │   │   │   │   │   │   │   │   │   │
         │   │   │   │   │   │   │   │   │   │   │   │
  A      │   │   │   │   │   │   │   │   │   │   │   │
  x      │   │   │   │   │   │   │   │   │   │   │   │
  i  5 ─┤   │   │   │   │   │   │   │   │   │   │   │
  s      │   │   │   │   │   │   │   │   │   │   │   │
  2      │   │   │   │   │   │   │   │   │   │   │   │
         │   │   │   │   │   │   │   │   │   │   │   │
       0 └───┴───┴───┴───┴───┴───┴───┴───┴───┴───┴───┘
          Jan Feb Mar Apr May Jun Jul Aug Sep Oct Nov Dec
                              Axis 1
```

?■

Format 0 Rep BAR 0
Current Name figures   12K Memory

The screen is divided into four areas:

1. The Control Area: where your options are displayed.
2. The Display Area: where your graph will be assembled.
3. The Input Line: where anything you type will appear.
4. The Status Area: where the current state of the display is listed, together with any errors that may occur.

   We will look at each of these areas separately.

FORTY COLUMN MODE

A slightly different Main Display is created in which the Control Area layout has altered to accommodate the larger characters. The information content is the same. Additional colour has also crept in!

CONTROL AREA

The top section of our screen is reserved for the 'prompts'. Here, in various boxes, text is displayed to help you make the correct responses for the current or next sequence, or to enable you to choose a particular option to alter the sequence. Generally the left- and right-hand pairs of boxes (HELP, PROMPTS, COMMANDS and ESCAPE) remain on the screen all the time. The centre four boxes may change depending upon the current sequence being performed. Any operation involving the Control Area will cause the appropriate box to be highlighted to confirm your selection by changing the ink colour from green to white. The centre four boxes we will investigate in a moment. Let us take a closer look at the outer boxes.

HELP

This is one facility that is always available for use. At any time during the display, creation or editing of a graph, it is possible to call for HELP. Function key F1 will initiate it. It allows you to inspect successive levels of information concerning the options available to you at the time of pressing the F1 key. More detail is provided at each level accessed. The illustration shows the display created on pressing F1. Try it for yourself.

```
EASEL MAIN COMMAND LEVEL

ARROW KEYS      - move x-wires
F1              - help
F2              - prompts on and off
F3              - commands
F4              - delete an object
F5              - insert a gap
SHIFT F2        - status window off
ESC KEY         - cancel last entry
double or single quotes  - text
NUMBER          - value input
LETTER          - formula input
TABULATE        - cursor to next cell
SHIFT TABULATE  - cursor to previous cell

Additional information:

arrow_keys          commands          escape_key          formulae

function_keys       numeric_value     text_input


? ■◂──cursor
```

The Main Display disappears, the microdrive runs for about 15 seconds and brief details are given of the current options. Remember that we are in the default Main Display sequence and so at other times, for instance if creating a new colour sequence for your graph, pressing F1 for HELP will produce a different initial display.

At the bottom of the display is a list of topics, any of which may be investigated by typing in its name and pressing the ENTER key. There is one point here that applies to all the EASEL operations. When typing in a name that is displayed on the screen as part of an option list, only sufficient letters need be typed to distinguish it from the others in the list. This often means the first letter only. A useful timesaver! Press the A key followed by ENTER and see what appears.

```
ARROW KEYS
 - The arrow keys move the cross-wires at the top input level.
They are sometimes used to point at screen objects during
commands.
No additional information.
? ■
```

You should see the above message in the top left-hand corner of the screen.

There is one disadvantage with the HELP displays if working in 40-column mode. The text is always in high-resolution (80-column) mode, so readability can be impaired if not using a monitor.

HELP exit

Having entered the HELP mode, how do you return? One very sensible aspect of HELP is that you return to the same point in the sequence that you were performing before you pressed the F1 key. There are two methods of return. To exit directly from HELP back to your starting point press the escape key (ESC) to the right of the F1 key. Alternatively, if you want to 'back-track' through previous HELP display information press the ENTER key. Each time you do so you will return by one level until, eventually, you return to your starting point. Try this now. Return to the Main Display by pressing the ESC key then select HELP again, follow the 'commands' route: c,v,f,d each followed by pressing ENTER, then return in stages using the ENTER key. Do not worry about the content of the information – we will explain it all later. Altogether there are fifty pages of HELP information.

PROMPTS

Press function key F2 and its effect will be immediately obvious. The Control Area will disappear to be replaced by a larger Display Area. Press the F2 key again and the Control Area will return. There may be times when you need to produce a slightly taller graph in which case you can use F2 to enlarge the area. No other aspects of EASEL are affected, the 'invisible' Control Area parameters are still available to you.

COMMANDS

The F3 function key allows you access to use any of the command facilities, some more advanced than others, offered by EASEL. Press the F3 key and you will find the central four Control Area boxes replaced by a list, or **menu**, of commands available. We shall call this the **command area**.

COMMANDS	Files	Newdata	Rename
Change	Highlight	Olddata	Save
Defaults	Kill	Print	View
Edit	Load	Quit	Zap

To select any command it is only necessary to type in its first letter. It is not necessary to press ENTER. A number of options will be presented in the command area, some preceded by the microdrive running for a few seconds. If at any time you want to check the scope of a command just use HELP by pressing the F1 key. Remember, the ESC key allows you to return directly to your starting point, ENTER enables you to back-track. To give you an introduction to the command sequences, try the following:

Type C (for CHANGE). This command allows you to modify any feature of the graph. You should now be looking at a list of options in the command area.

Type B (for BAR) and press ENTER.
The display will present you with a picture of all the available bar styles.

Instructions for selecting a bar are contained within the command area. You had best not go on any further so return to the Main Display by pressing the ESC key. You will still be in command mode so press the ESC key again. All the commands will be explained in full as we progress through the EASEL chapters. The above is something to whet your appetite!

ESCAPE

We have already been using this key so let us summarise its actions. Pressing the ESC key allows you to:

1. Exit from a particular sequence of operations, e.g. HELP and COMMANDS.

2. Cancel any information you have typed into the Input Line before pressing the ENTER key.

INPUT LINE

Below the large Display Area you will find the Input Line which, in 40-column mode, will be two lines deep. In Main Display the line starts with a question mark followed by a square or rectangular cursor. Any typing you do will be copied into the Input Line and will normally be passed to the program by pressing the ENTER key. For some sequences EASEL prints a suggested input on this line which you can either accept by pressing ENTER or ignore by typing your own input. You may have noticed that when you pressed the F3 key for the command menu the Input Line also changed to display 'Command>'.

STATUS AREA

At the bottom of the screen is the Status Area where five parameters are normally displayed:

    FORMAT
    REP(resent)
    CURRENT NAME
    MEMORY

Format

When we move on to show you how to create your own graph types and styles you will find there are eight standard graph layouts, or **formats**, already available. They are numbered zero to seven and FORMAT will always display that number for the current graph. For example, in the Main display when EASEL is first loaded, a standard bar-chart type of graph is available for immediate use. This is FORMAT type 0. Should you want a pie-chart display you could select type 7 and FORMAT would be followed by that value.

REPresent

Apart from being able to define the type of graph there are a large number of different styles available. You may recall that a quick look at the CHANGE command earlier resulted in the display of a range of bar styles. Each bar had a number attached to it. Having appropriately made your selection you will find that the number, together with the graph type (BAR, LINE, etc.), will be displayed in the Status Area following REP.

Current name

EASEL allows you to create more than one type of graph at the same time, allowing that there may be instances when you wish to use or display the graph relating to a particular set of figures. To identify different sets of figures each must have a name, selectable by you, before entering them initially. The name that appears alongside the CURRENT NAME label is for the set of figures that can be currently processed.

Memory

The final label is used to keep you informed of the amount of QL memory currently available. It reduces as you supply EASEL with data. The amount is expressed as so many 'K', where K equals 1024 bytes.

Error messages

Finally, the Status Area will display any error messages from EASEL. They will tell you what has gone wrong and, in some instances, will let you know how to correct the error.

DISPLAY AREA

This is where it all happens! All the graphs are displayed in this area and, with the exception of pie charts, a blank grid will be displayed before you enter a new set of figures. On loading EASEL the Main Display already gives us a grid together with some axis markings. We shall utilise it to demonstrate operation of those remaining Control Area options still to be discussed. With the addition of appropriate axis and graph titles, however, you immediately have an acceptable graph format.

All the features shown on the graph may be changed if desired. Each time you do so you will be returned to the Main Display to see the overall effect. For the moment, though, let us look at the four Control Area options not yet discussed and see how they affect the Display Area.

X-wires

We will look at the action of the crosswires first, since their operation must be understood before explaining NUMBERS and TEXT. In the Control Area the box containing X-WIRES indicates that movement can be achieved using the cursor keys up, down, left and right. They are represented by their key symbols, the arrows.

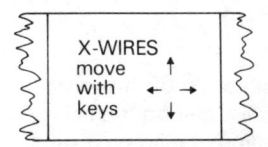

```
X-WIRES
move      ↑
with    ←   →
keys      ↓
```

First, a little explanation. Whenever you wish to place something at a particular position in the Display Area you will be identifying that position to EASEL by moving the crosswires to it. It makes the positioning of text, graphs keys and the graph data very easy. But where are the crosswires?

When viewing the Main Display that is created when first loading EASEL you will see a single narrow white vertical line, extending the full height of the Display Area from top to bottom and positioned central over the first section

(*Jan*) of the blank graph. In this mode EASEL is quite able to accept data and convert it into bar-graph form. Each time a number is entered the vertical crosswire will move to the next section (*Feb*), or **cell** as it is called. Successively entering numbers will cause the graph to be progressively created from left to right.

But you may not always wish to enter information at the extreme left, or alternatively you may be altering an existing value and wish to select a particular bar position on the graph, then re-enter a new value. To this end, crosswire control is achieved by a choice of two key selection methods:

1. TABULATE / SHIFT and TABULATE
2. CURSOR LEFT / CURSOR RIGHT

Try the operations as we discuss them. The TABULATE key, when pressed and released, will step the vertical crosswire one cell to the right. Pressing the SHIFT and TABULATE keys together will step the crosswire one cell to the left. Pressing and holding the key(s) down will move the crosswire rapidly in the appropriate direction. The cursor keys produce a slightly different effect. Press the cursor right key (→) and release it. The crosswire will move a short distance to the right. Press the key again and hold it down. The crosswire will now travel smoothly to the right for as long as you hold the key pressed. Movement in the opposite direction is produced in the same manner by using the cursor left key (←). So the TABULATE method produces a cell-stepping movement, the cursor keys produce a smooth movement.

Should you be in a display mode where the vertical crosswire is not visible, it can be activated by pressing either cursor left or cursor right. Note that the TABULATE method may be used only when entering data.

There is not just a vertical crosswire, however. Press either the cursor up (↑) or cursor down (↓) keys and a horizontal crosswire will appear. This can be moved by these cursor keys in exactly the same way as the vertical crosswire. By using both sets of cursor keys it is therefore possible to position the intersection of the two crosswires anywhere on the Display Area. It is rather like aiming a gun sight at a target.

Graph expansion

You may already have stumbled across a very useful action of the vertical crosswire. Move it using the TABULATE key to the last cell on the right (*Dec*). Then press it once more. The display will clear and be replaced by a similar grid but containing many more cells. The Axis 1 labels will have been compressed to the left. More cells of information can therefore be added.

An identical effect is achieved in the opposite direction by using the SHIFT and TABULATE keys.

The operation may be repeated several times until the limit of resolution is reached and individual cells cannot be identified. The facility can be usefully employed when creating trigonometrical graphs, as we shall see later.

To return to the standard twelve-cell display the F3, Z and ENTER keys are pressed in sequence. This is represented by:

[F3] [Z] [ENTER]

The actions involved will be explained later in this chapter.

Numbers

Let us look at the NUMBERS box in the Control Area, where the text should now make sense.

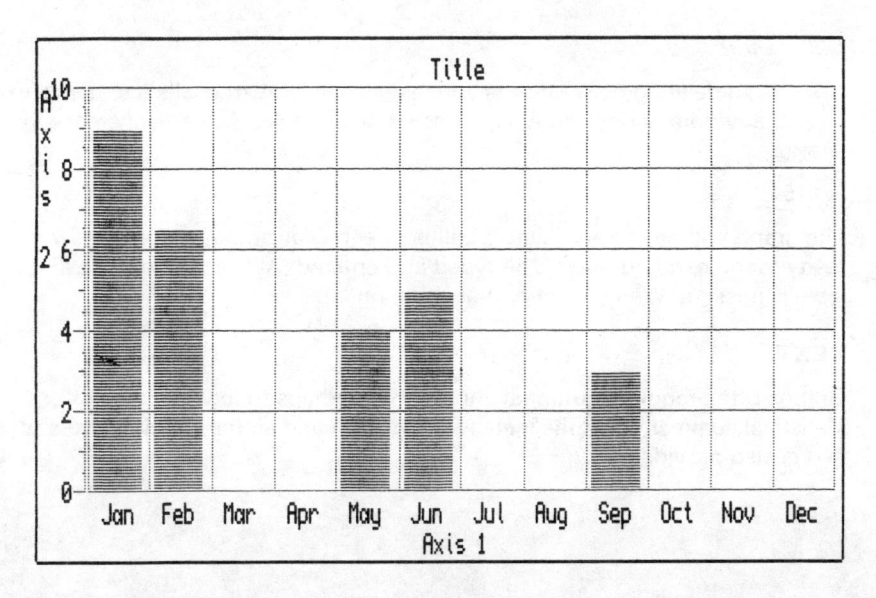

> NUMBERS Use
> TABULATE key
> to move and
> type number

If you have been experimenting with the cursor and TABULATE keys, the crosswires are probably off the initial left-hand cell. Using whichever method you wish move the vertical crosswire to the *Jun* cell. Type number 5. You will see the number appear in the Input Line. Now press the ENTER key. The *Jun* cell will rapidly fill up to the *5* mark on Axis 2 with a coloured bar, and the vertical crosswire will move to the next cell on the right. You have made your first graph entry! It really is as easy as that. Enter the following numbers and you should finish with a display that looks similar to that shown below.

Jan	9
Feb	6.5
May	4
June	5
Sept	3

Now type in for *Nov* the value 20. We have exceeded the Y-axis scale range but, on pressing the ENTER key, you will find the Display Area re-drawn with a new scale and all the previous inputs scaled down in proportion. Their numerical values will, however, still be the same. EASEL automatically adjusts the scale to the range of values you enter.

When you enter a value into the final cell (*Dec*), you will find that on pressing the ENTER key the graph is redrawn with eight more cells on the right. To return to the original twelve-cell graph perform the following sequence. Do not worry about the details – we shall explain them later in Chapter 8.

| F3 | V | ENTER | ENTER | ESC |

As with all EASEL operations always allow time for any screen changes to finish before making the next selection.

Number deletion

If a wrong number has been entered and displayed on the graph then it is a simple matter to delete it. Using the vertical crosswire, position it over the cell whose contents are to be deleted, then:

| F4 |

This is your delete key, and apart from numbers it can be used to delete text, axis labels and graph keys, as we shall see later. Having pressed the F4 key you will notice that the crosswire moves to the next cell on the right. Sequential bars can therefore be deleted quite conveniently by repeatedly pressing the F4 key. You can now type and enter the correct number, remembering to move the vertical crosswire to the correct cell first.

Cell insertion

Apart from deleting cell contents you can also insert extra cells and hence extra data at any point along the Axis 1. For instance, move the vertical crosswire to *May*.

| F5 |

The graph will be redrawn with a cell between *May* and *Jun*, the crosswire ready for an extra number to be typed and entered. At the moment the axis label is missing. We will rectify that situation later.

TEXT

Graphs often require additional annotation, perhaps to indicate a quick statistical summary ('profits increased to 29%') and so the capability to add text is also provided.

```
  ┌─────────────┐
  │    TEXT     │
  │   type "    │
  │   & text    │
  └─────────────┘
```

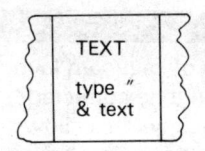

To enter this option you can type either a single (') or double (") quote mark. As soon as you have typed the quote mark, the Input Line will show:

TEXT:

On the Display Area the two crosswires will appear if they were previously absent. Type:

First for me

Watch it appear in the Input Line and also at the intersection of the two crosswires. Then press the ENTER key. Two things happen. First, the Control Area has its four centre sections replaced by text giving details of how to move the text. Second, the cursor keys can now be used to move the text to any part of the display. Note that the TABULATE key has no effect.

Using the cursor keys position the text in the top rectangle of the *Feb* cell. You will find that the text will disappear if you hold down any of the cursor keys to achieve a repeat action but will return on releasing the key. When satisfied, press the ENTER key. The crosswires will disappear, the Control Area returns to normal and the Input Line reverts to a simple question mark.

FORMULAE

The final option to look at in the Control Area is FORMULAE. It is a very powerful facility allowing you to apply a modifying formula to each value of an existing set of figures to create a new set. The formula is typed in as an equation, where the left-hand side must always be a name. It may be a new name or the current name as displayed in the Status Area. The right-hand side will generally include either the current name or other existing names. For example, if we wished to add VAT to a current set of figures named PRICE we simply type:

PRICE = PRICE + PRICE * 15/100
(or: PRICE = PRICE * 1.15)

If we wanted to produce a new set of figures rather than alter the current set, we could type:

VALUE = PRICE + PRICE * 15/100

On pressing the ENTER key the new graph would be displayed and the CURRENT NAME label in the Status Area will be followed by VALUE.

We shall return to the use of formulae in Chapter 8.

EDITING FACILITIES

It is possible that you may be unfamiliar with the QL style of keyboard layout and made a typing error when entering your text. How can it be corrected? Very conveniently EASEL incorporates a full-line editor facility. This allows any text entered in the Input Line to be corrected or modified as required before pressing the ENTER key. The facilities are, in fact, an extension of the normal QL SuperBASIC editing.

LINE EDITOR

Every time you type information into the Input Line the line editor is available. But the text to be changed must be editable. By that we mean it must have originally been typed by you and not displayed automatically by EASEL. You have already seen some operations where EASEL places informative text in the Input Line.

Editing within the Input Line is achieved by using an appropriate combination of cursor keys, SHIFT and CTRL keys. When typing out the text facility just now, you will have noticed the cursor on the Input Line. Each time you typed a character the cursor would move one place right and the new character would appear to its left. The editing facilities are linked to this cursor and are best described by a short table:

Action	Key
Move cursor one place left	←
Move cursor one place right	→
Move cursor one word left	SHIFT ←
Move cursor one word right	SHIFT →
Move cursor to start of editable text	↑
Move cursor to end of editable text	↓
Delete character to left of cursor	CTRL ←
Delete character under cursor	CTRL →
Delete all editable text to left of cursor	CTRL ↑
Delete all editable text from under cursor to right	CTRL ↓

Enter the text option again (single or double quotes) and try using all the line editor facilities on text of your own choice.

EDIT COMMAND

All the text editing we have discussed assumed that the text to be edited was in the Input Line. However, you may wish to alter or move text that is already in the main body of the graph, or perhaps on an earlier graph that you are in the process of modifying.

To alter this type of text we must use the EDIT command. First, create some text on the graph currently displayed. Then perform the following sequences. We shall explain each step as you progress.

[F3] [E]

The Input Line now contains:

Command > Edit

The command area displays a list of editing options:

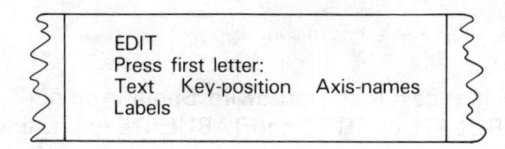

```
EDIT
Press first letter:
Text    Key-position    Axis-names
Labels
```

We will look at each option in turn.

Text editing

By 'text' we are including not only any text we have placed in the body of the graph but also the title and the two axis names.

[T]

The command area tells you what to do and both crosswires appear. Using the cursor keys move the crosswires so that their intersection is close to, or over, any of the text you wish to EDIT. The crosswires do not have to be exactly over the start of the text.
Then press ENTER.
Two things will happen. If the crosswires were not exactly at the start of the text they will move into that position. Also, the text will appear in the Input Line. If you wish to delete all of the text and not insert anything in its place then press the F4 key. This will automatically terminate the EDIT sequence. The graph will be redrawn without the text or crosswires but is still in command mode.
Alternatively, if you wish to alter the text in some way use the line editor that we have already described. When you are satisfied with the text press the ENTER key. Then reposition the text if required, using the cursor keys to move the crosswires. When satisfied, press the ENTER key once more. The graph is redrawn with the edited text in the correct position and the display in command mode.

Remember, pressing the ESC key will exit from command mode and allow further data or text insertion if required.

If you have not already tried to EDIT the Axis 2 name which is, of course, vertical, try changing it to:

£ * 1000

The method is exactly the same as for normal text. The only difference is that the final display will show the text positioned vertically as before with Axis 2.

Label editing

As far as the Axis 1 cell labels are concerned they can be changed or deleted but cannot be repositioned. To select the option from command mode:

[E] [L]

The vertical crosswire will appear to the left of one of the Axis 1 labels.
The Input Line will display:

Edit label:

followed by the label name which is next to the crosswire. Should you not wish to EDIT this label, use TABULATE or SHIFT and TABULATE to position the crosswire on the one you require to change. As the crosswire moves from cell to cell you will see the Input Line contents changing appropriately.

The selected label can either be deleted by pressing the F4 key or edited using the cursor keys. After the latter press the ENTER key, provided that no further labels are to be edited. Note that the labels are automatically centred within the cell.

Quite often you would wish to change all the labels – for example from months to days, or item references. The simplest method of achieving this is first of all to position the crosswire over the *Jan* label. Then press the F4 key twelve times (allowing the display to settle after each press). All the labels are now deleted. But we have also now been presented with an expanded Axis 1! To revert to the original twelve-cell display, press:

[ESC] [V] [ENTER] [ENTER]

To return to the label editing option, press:

[E] [L]

Note that this time the Input Line displays:

New label:

Position the crosswire at the first cell position (using SHIFT/TABULATE) and type in your new label name. It may contain as many as 10 characters, but it may be truncated to fit the cell width.

Having typed the name for the first cell press the TABULATE key to move the crosswire to the next cell. Now you can type in the second cell's name. Repeat the process until the final cell is completed. Then press the ENTER key to terminate the EDIT sequence. Provided that you did not press the TABULATE key after typing the last cell's label, you should still be looking at your edited twelve-cell graph in command mode. If you did, then correct the size, using:

|V| |ENTER| |ENTER|

Pressing the ESC key now returns you to data entry mode.

Cell quantity

It is quite possible that you may not want twelve cells on your graph, so we must be able to control the number of cells displayed. We can achieve this in one of two ways, both methods requiring all existing labels to be deleted first, as we have already shown by using the F4 key.

- Method 1: type in the required number of new labels then use the sequence:

  |ESC| |V| |ENTER| |ENTER| |ESC|

- Method 2: use the sequence:

  |ESC| |V| |ENTER| |ENTER| |ESC|

  This generates a single cell. Then press the F5 key to progressively insert the required number of cells.

The second method allows you to insert data without axis labels.

Cell deletion

Should you need to delete a cell entirely then you must delete not only the contents (the F4 key in data entry mode) but also the label. Then the following sequence will display the graph with the cell missing:

|V| |ENTER| |ENTER| |ESC|

Axes editing

There is a separate option for editing the axes names but we can achieve this by using the text option. What is different? Quite simply, it is a slightly quicker way of editing. Try it and see. Press:

|F3| |E| |A|

The command area changes to present a choice of V or H (or delete using the F4 key). Press the H key. Immediately the vertical crosswire moves to the left of 'Axis 1' and its name appears in the Input Line. Editing proceeds as normal. Replace it with:

Month

Reposition it between cells 6 and 7.

Key editing

The final option concerns the graph key. This is automatically created (and styled) by the QL when we display more than one set of figures on the same graph. We can only move the key (by using the cursor keys) or delete it (by using the F4 key). Multiple graphs will be explained in the next chapter.

GRAPH DATA DELETION

Sometimes it is necessary to delete one or more sets of figures and we can achieve this by using one of the following two commands, depending on the exact requirement.

KILL COMMAND

This command allows you to delete one or more sets of figures by identifying each by its name then pressing the ENTER key. We could delete our single set of figures by the sequence:

[F3] [K] [ENTER]

However, the KILL command does not delete any text that we may have placed on the graph. This is because text so placed is considered common to *all* sets of figures stored at the time. If we want to delete all the information we use the next command.

ZAP COMMAND

Using this command we clear out not only all text but every set of figures in the QL at the time. **Use it with caution!** In this instance if we want to clear our existing graph data and text before moving on to the next chapter, press:

[Z] [ENTER]

Note that on pressing the Z key you are given the choice in the command area of either deleting all or returning (with the data intact!) by pressing the ESC key.

EASEL EXIT

One further command we can explain before leaving this chapter is QUIT. This allows you to return from the EASEL program package to SuperBASIC, losing all stored data at the same time. It is really equivalent to removing the EASEL cartridge and pressing the RESET button. Like the ZAP command, you are able to confirm the selection by either pressing the ENTER or ESC keys.

PROBLEM

Before leaving this chapter, try the following problem using as many of the operational sequences explained in this chapter as are necessary.

Reset the QL and load in EASEL. Change the Axis 1 labels to the days of the week (seven cells only). Set up the following titles:

    Main title: INVOICES
    Axis 1:   DAY
    Axis 2:   QUANTITY

Enter the invoice quantities as follows (Sunday to Saturday):

    15, 230, 200, 126, 80, 75, 52

CHAPTER 8

EASEL: MORE ADVANCED FACILITIES

INTRODUCTION

In this chapter three main topics will be covered:

1. Multiple graphs.
2. Graph design.
3. Graph storage and transfer.

Understanding these topics will enable you to make full use of all the EASEL facilities currently available.

MULTIPLE GRAPHS

So far we have considered the display of only a single set of data on the graph. This, for many purposes, is sufficient but EASEL can store and display several sets if required. The exact number depends upon the number of cells in each set. For example, you can have about forty-four graphs of twelve cells each. Remember, you can always see how much storage space is left by observing the MEMORY display in the Status Area.

Should you attempt to insert data when there is no more memory left you will see appear in the Status Area:

ERROR – out of memory

It is worth remembering, though, that even when 'ØK Memory' is displayed for the first time there may still be about forty cells available. As much data as possible will be drawn on the graph but you can add more data only by deleting something; perhaps by removing an earlier set of figures no longer required. Alternatively, you can save the information on a cartridge, as will be explained later, then delete it.

There are many applications where the display of several sets of figures on a single graph is advantageous: comparing successive years of trading; plotting related electronic/mathematical waveforms; displaying statistics from different areas of the country; and many more.

To see how we can create and manipulate multiple graphs with EASEL we will start by considering the Formulae option in more detail.

FORMULA APPLICATION

We will assume that you are starting with EASEL loaded, no sets of figures entered and the display in data entry mode. Now type in the following set of figures, presented in cell one to cell twelve order:

   4, 9, 8, 6, 2, 3, 6, 7, 5, 1, 2, 3

The graph will appear as green vertical bars. Restore the display to twelve cells. The current name is 'figures' and applies to the set of numbers you have just typed. Type the following formula (it will appear in the Input Line as you type it):

   figures = figures * 2

Use the line editor if you make any mistakes. Press the ENTER key. By comparing with the list of numbers just entered, you will see that the new graph has each cell's value equal to twice its previous value (note the altered Axis 2 scale). In this way any set of figures may be altered. We have lost the original set of figures for *figures*, but could easily regenerate them by typing:

   figures = figures/2 |ENTER|

Try it. Should we wish to keep an existing set of figures but use them to create a new related set, we just use a new name. For example:

   product = figures * 4 |ENTER|

This will cause the display of a new graph, with white bars, whose current name in the Status Area is *product*. The cell values will be four times those of the previous graph.

We now have two sets of figures in the QL so it is appropriate to explain four further commands:

   VIEW, NEWDATA, OLDDATA, RENAME

VIEW command

We have used this a few times already. Basically the VIEW command enables you to select which sets of figures you wish to see displayed on the graph. For instance, you now have created two sets of figures called *figures* and *product* and wish to visually compare them on one graph. If you had input several more sets of figures then VIEW allows you to select just these two.

Having selected command mode and press the V key the command area prompts you to type in the required names, each separated by a comma. If you look at the Input Line you will notice that it displays:

command > View all Figures

The cursor will be positioned over the *a* in *all*. You could type in the name of a particular set of figures you want to view, but should you want to view all the sets of figures on one graph then the QL has already provided the Input Line text for you. Just press the ENTER key and the cursor moves to the end of *Figures*.

But now more information has appeared. The command area requests a format number while the Input Line suggests format 0. For the moment press the ENTER key. We shall be looking at graph formats in a later section of this chapter.

Having pressed the ENTER key the graph is redisplayed with two sets of figures and an appropriate Axis 2 scale. A key has also appeared displaying the bar colours chosen for each set of figures. Bar selection too will be dealt with in a later section.

If the key is obstructing any of the graph bars then use the EDIT command to move it.

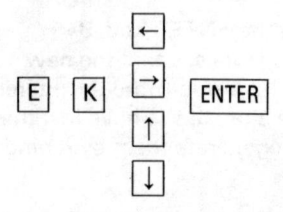

E   K   ←   ENTER
        →
        ↑
        ↓

Having moved the key or not, pressing the ESC key will exit from the command sequence back to data-entry mode.

If during Axis 1 label creation or cell editing there were any blank unlabelled cells, then using the VIEW command will display the graph without them. It is in this area that we have already used the command.

OLDDATA command

Using the VIEW command, alter the display to show the single graph *figures* and return to data-entry mode. Move the vertical crosswire to the *Jul* cell, type 4 into the Input Line and press the ENTER key. The display clears to be replaced by both graphs, but the *product* value for the *Jul* cell will be seen to change not the *figures* value. The reason is that the CURRENT NAME in the Status Area is showing *product* not *figures*, so we can alter values only in the set of numbers called *product*.

Whenever a new set name is created in EASEL it always becomes the CURRENT NAME.

To access previous sets of information we must use the command OLDDATA.

Now press the F3 and O keys to select the OLDDATA command. The command area asks you to type in the required set name which is to become the CURRENT NAME. The Input Line suggests *product* but we are interested for the moment in *figures*. Type it in and press the ENTER key.

The graph is redrawn showing the same values as before but this time the CURRENT NAME is *figures*. Press the ESC key, move the vertical crosswire to the *Jul* cell and change it to 4. This time it works! Only the *figures* graph is displayed.

NEWDATA command

So much for retrieving previous sets of figures – if we want to create new sets we can use two methods. The NEWDATA command is one. Suppose you want to call a new set *deliveries*. Select the NEWDATA command:

[F3] [N]

Type *deliveries* into the Input Line followed by pressing the ENTER key. A blank graph appears with your new name as the CURRENT NAME. Data can now be typed in as normal.

The second method is perhaps easier. First clear out *deliveries* by pressing the F3 and K keys. Starting from data entry mode type in:

deliveries = 0 [ENTER]

The same result is achieved. We have, of course, input a formula allocating values of zero to all the cells of the set.

RENAME command

With this command you can change the name of any of the stored sets of figures. But it will work only if the set to be renamed is the current set (in other words, named in the Status Area). It is particularly useful for the very first graph you create since EASEL, as you will have seen, assumes it is called *figures*.

To use the command make the selected set the current set (if not already so) by using the OLDDATA command. When RENAME is selected the command area asks you to type in the old name, followed by pressing the ENTER key. The Input Line copies your input and you then type the new name, again followed by pressing the ENTER key. The display is redrawn with the new name in the Status Area.

When selecting an appropriate name bear the following points in mind:

1. The name must be continuous with no spaces, e.g. 'sales' but not 'sales figures'. ('sales_figures' is permitted).

2. It must always start with a letter, but following numbers are allowed, e.g. sums123.

3. The name must contain less than fourteen characters. If you use more, EASEL will truncate it to thirteen.

Disobeying these limitations will bring up an error message in the Status Area (with the exception of point three). Simply edit the name to correct it and press the ENTER key.

Number source

Returning to the use of formulae to create graphs, there is one particular facility within EASEL that can be very useful for creating sets of figures. By using the word **cell** within a formula, EASEL will create a set of figures equal in number to the total number of cells currently displayed in data-entry mode. But in addition, EASEL provides a set of values that start at one for cell one and progress to twelve for cell twelve (or up to the maximum cell number displayed). These values can be used by the formula. For example, clear the display back to data-entry mode and enter this formula:

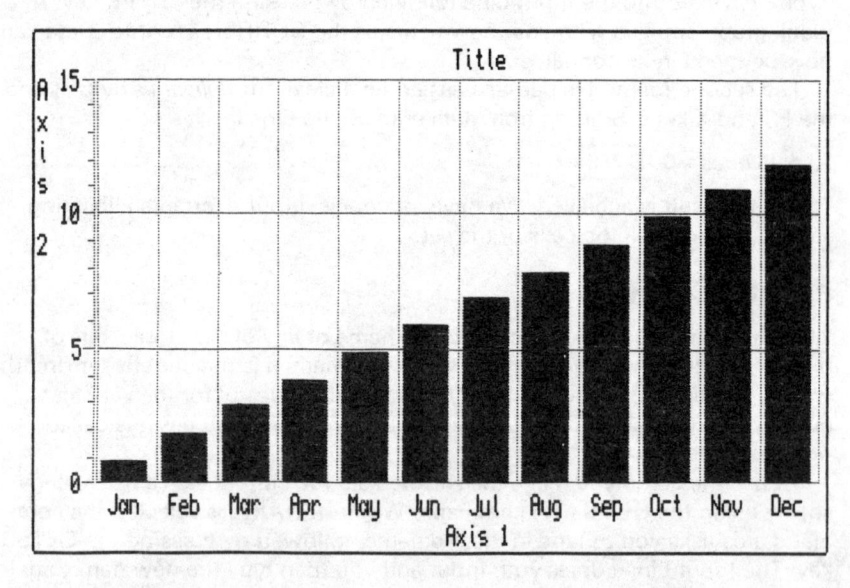

steps = cell ENTER

You will be presented with a display of what could be described as ascending steps from left to right. In other words, the cell values from one to twelve have been made equal to a new set of numbers with the name 'steps'. So there are values of one in the first cell, two in the second, all the way up to twelve in the last.

Now type in another formula:

graph = cell*5 ENTER

This time the graph will display ascending steps in increments of five, up to sixty. So by modifying the values of *cell*, new sets of figures may be created. If you would like something a little more interesting, try this one:

cosine = cos((cell − 1) /2) [ENTER]

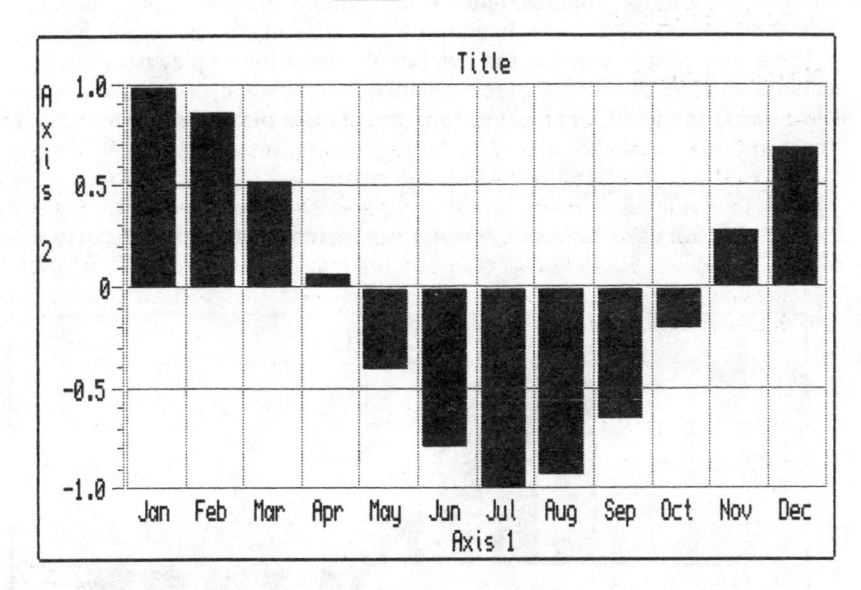

The graph displayed is showing a cosine wave represented in bar form. Note that Axis 2 is now showing positive and negative values. The 'minus 1' is included to allow cell one to have the value of one. Waveforms of this nature are generally not viewed in bar-chart form but as continuous lines. We shall see how to achieve the same effect with EASEL later.

The *cell* facility is most useful for applications where a regularly increasing scale of values is required. Let us go on a little further.

Clear EASEL's memory of the earlier names by using ZAP, then enter the next formulae in succession:

a = 1/cell [ENTER]

b = SQR(cell)/2 [ENTER]

c = a + b [ENTER]

Look at all three sets together on one graph using the VIEW command. The key identifies which is which. Note that *figures* is shown in the key but we have not allocated any values to it. Particularly remember waveform c.

Return to date entry mode and type in:

b = cell − cell + 0.5 [ENTER]

The graph for *b* will be drawn with all cells filled up to value 0.5. View all three sets on one graph again. You will see that waveform c is the same as before. This emphasises an important point. When a formula is used to create a set of figures, changing any of the variables in that formula at a later date will not affect the previously stored set of figures. So although we altered the set of figures for b, c's set of figures remains unchanged. There is no automatic updating of formula values. You need the ABACUS software package for that!

When drawing waveforms the number of cells in the display naturally affects the final result. For instance, to display a complete cycle of a sine wave (between 0 and 2∗PI) we must include the number of cells in our formula. Try this:

sinewave = sin (2∗PI()∗(cell − 1)/11) ENTER

Note that we use eleven not twelve to allow the last cell to have a true value of 2PI.

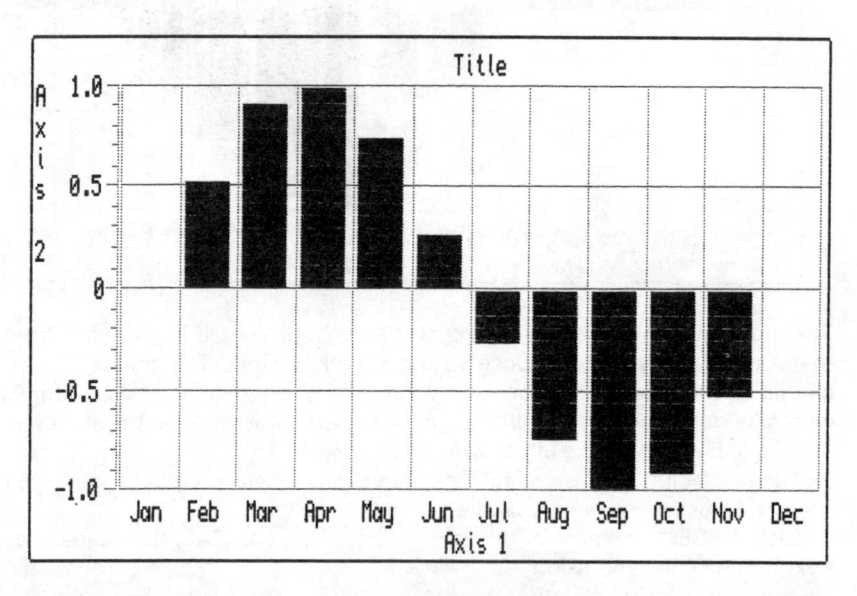

[Bar chart titled "Title" showing sine wave values across months Jan–Dec, y-axis labeled "Axis 2" ranging from -1.0 to 1.0, x-axis labeled "Axis 1"]

The resolution with only twelve cells is not too good, so we could expand the graph by using the TABULATE key to add extra cells as explained earlier. We would then have to count up the number of cells. This could become awkward if we created a large number of cells. Fortunately EASEL provides us with an easy way out. The word **cellmax** can be used in the formulae. It always has a value equal to the **maximum** number of cells currently displayed. To demonstrate this use the TABULATE key to create a larger number of cells (about 30).

Now type in:

sinewave = sin(2∗PI()∗(cell − 1)/(cellmax − 1)) ENTER

You will have to wait several seconds while EASEL calculates all the values before the display changes. When it does you will be presented with a complete sinewave cycle.

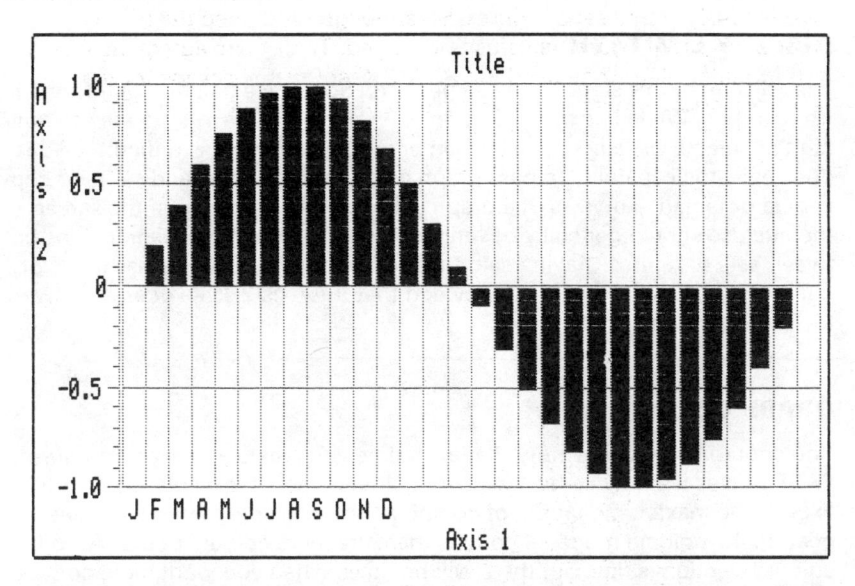

[Bar chart titled "Title" showing a sinewave cycle across months J F M A M J J A S O N D on Axis 1, with Axis 2 ranging from -1.0 to 1.0]

Try altering the number of cells again and re-type the formula just to confirm that it works for any number of cells.

The basic principle applied in the formula is to take the maximum desired Axis 1 scale length (2*PI in our example) and multiply it by a scaling factor of:

(cell − 1)/(cellmax − 1)

The technique can be applied to any formula where you need a particular range of progressively increasing values over the length of the Axis 1 line. If we wish the first cell to start at a particular value then we can use the general expression:

cell increment = cell 1 value + (maximum value − cell 1 value)*
(cell − 1)/(cellmax − 1)

If we were to start the sinewave at PI/2 instead of zero, our formula becomes:

sinewave = sin (PI()/2 + (2*PI() − PI()/2)*(cell − 1)/(cellmax − 1))

We can type this in as:

sinewave = sin(PI()/2 + 3*PI()/2*(cell − 1)/(cellmax − 1))

For those readers who do not have mathematical leanings we do hope that the examples above have helped you to understand some of the ways in which we can use the FORMULAE option to good advantage. Perhaps for some, sines and cosines may take on a new meaning!

DISPLAY LIMITATION

It is relevant at this stage to say something about the extraction of information from graphs. While it is true that graphs on paper can be interpolated to quite high accuracy, visually on a television or monitor screen it is difficult. EASEL does have the capability to pass graph data out to a printer and so 'hard copy' can be obtained. However, if a graph is to be produced only on the screen, then its use should generally be limited to display trends, or relationships between sets of figures. Having said that, reasonably accurate assessments of numerical values can be made provided that the Axis 2 scale does not cover too large a range.

GRAPH COLOUR

You should be aware by now that each time you create a new set of figures, EASEL gives it a new colour or mix of colours when it is displayed. If you exceed the maximum number of combinations available then the colours repeat. In 40-column mode, of course, there are more colours to use. Automatic colour selection is fine, but there will be times when you want more control over the final product. The next section on graph design will be covering this aspect in detail.

Before we leave the FORMULAE option there is one piece of advice we would offer. If you do experiment with different formulae in the process of creating a particular graph, do remember to write down the formulae as you develop them. Once a graph is displayed the formula is deleted from the Input Line and cannot be retrieved.

GRAPH DESIGN

So far all the examples we have used have resulted in the display of a bar graph in colours automatically selected by EASEL. In many instances the displays will be quite satisfactory but if you take a look at books, magazines and other documents where graphs are used, you are bound to see a number of different styles. Some have a particular style simply to attract; others use a style more suited to a specific application. Variety increases interest.

EASEL has the capability to give variety. In fact, almost every item on a graph may be changed, from the overall type of graph down to the colour of associated text. This section will reveal how you can rapidly master the design capability of EASEL and create a wide variety of graphic styles.

GRAPH FORMATS

We have already said that there are three types of basic graph format you can choose:

1. Bar graph.
2. Line graph.
3. Pie chart.

Eight styles exist for these and the easiest way to see them all is to use the Change command in the following sequence:

[F3] [C] [F] [ENTER]

Seven 'mini' graphs are displayed.
   The displays look rather cluttered if you are working in 40-column mode; you may find it better to change to 64-column mode, though it does give a hint of the colour combinations possible.
   All the graphs, with the exception of the pie chart, show typical layouts for two sets of figures. We will look at each style in turn but it must be appreciated that all the colours, text and graph paper designs, can be altered.

FORMATS 0 and 1

We can cover these two together. FORMAT 0 is the style you have been seeing up to now, a standard vertical bar graph where the bar for each set is separated from its neighbour within a cell. FORMAT 1 is the same except that the bars of each set overlap within the cells.

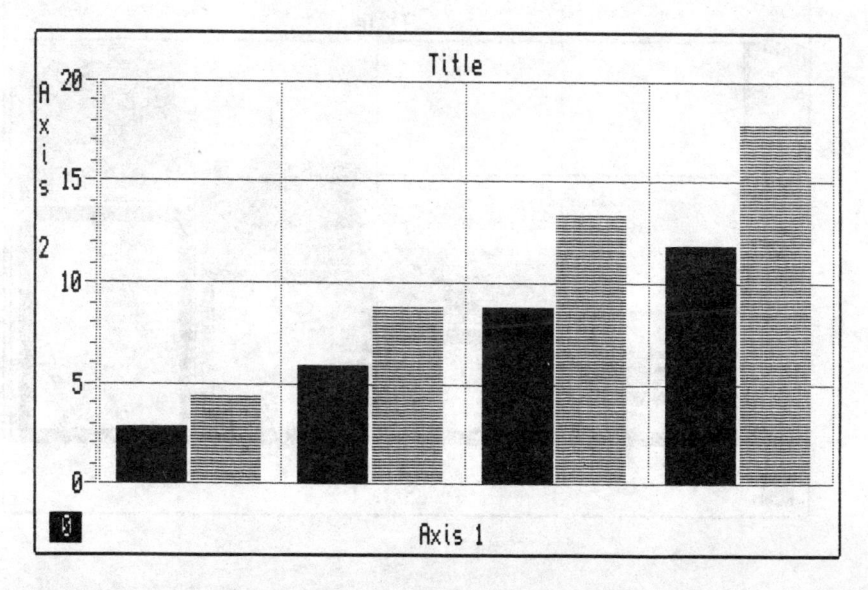

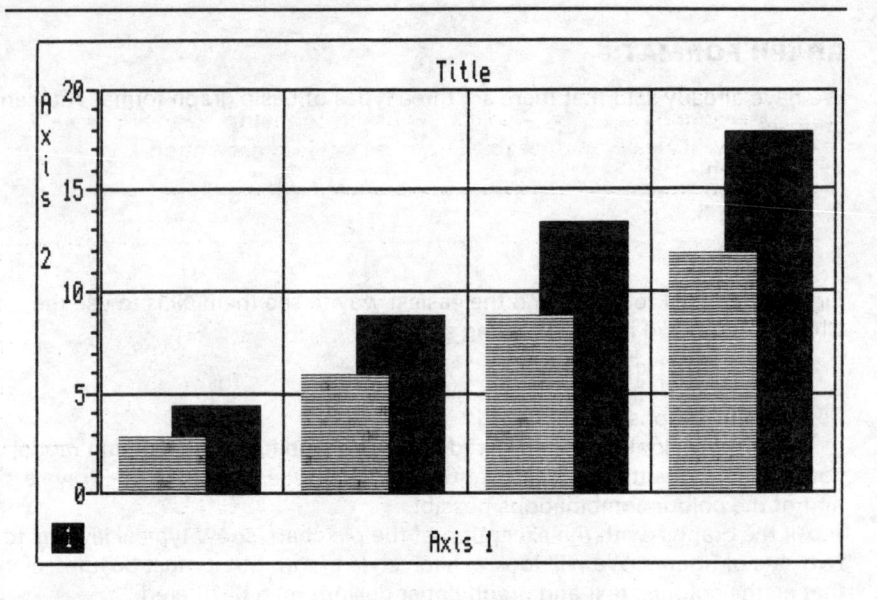

FORMAT 2

A very useful format where each cell's value is made up of the sum of each set's value. A typical application could be a car sales chart where each month's cell contains the quantities of different makes sold, the total quantity showing total sales for that month. The style allows very bold graphs to be created.

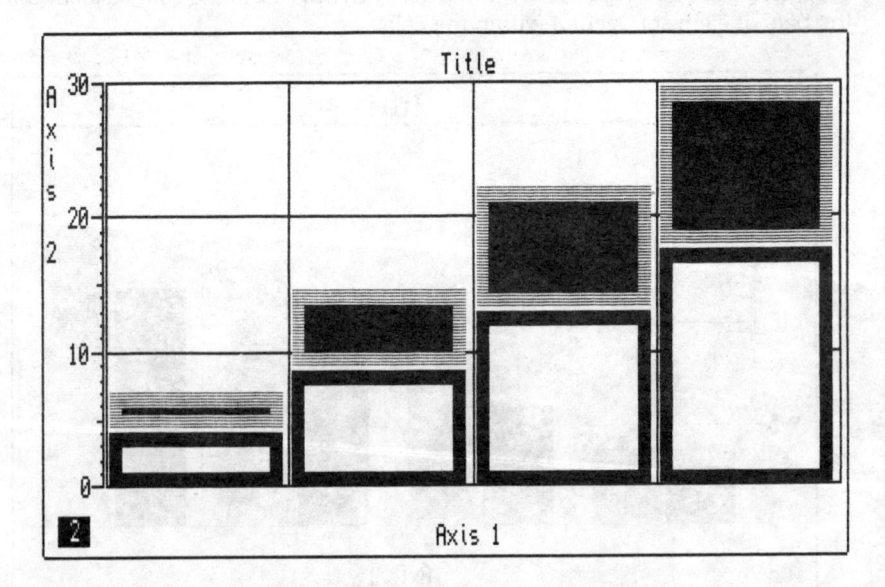

FORMAT 3

This is the style most suited to the display of waveforms where lines or 'filled to zero' lines can be selected. Application of this format to some of our earlier examples will create a noticeable improvement in presentation.

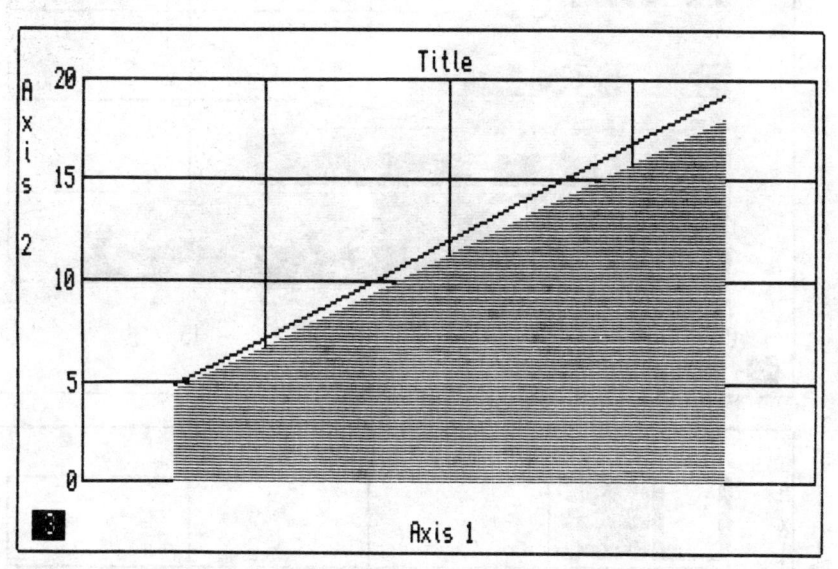

FORMATS 4, 5, 6

FORMATS 4 to 6 create identical structures to FORMATS 0 to 2 but in horizontal bar form. This gives plenty of scope for variety in your designs.

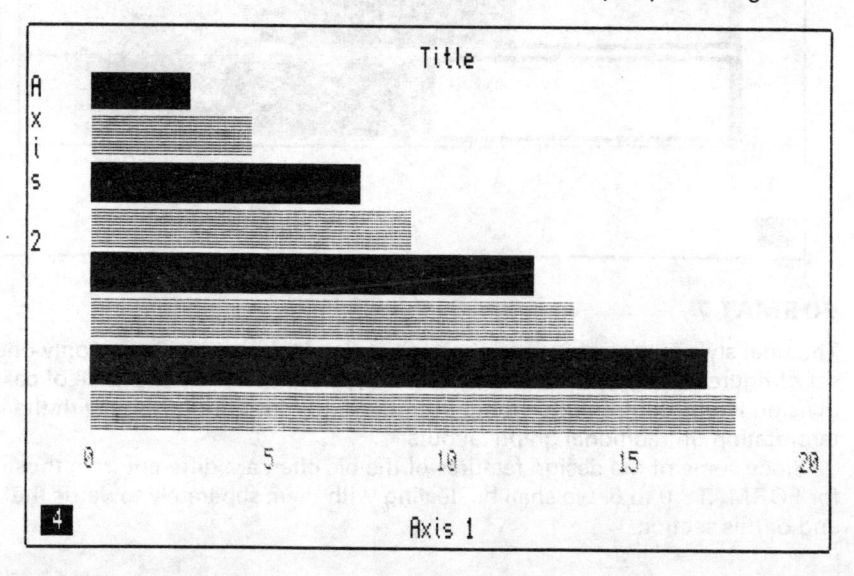

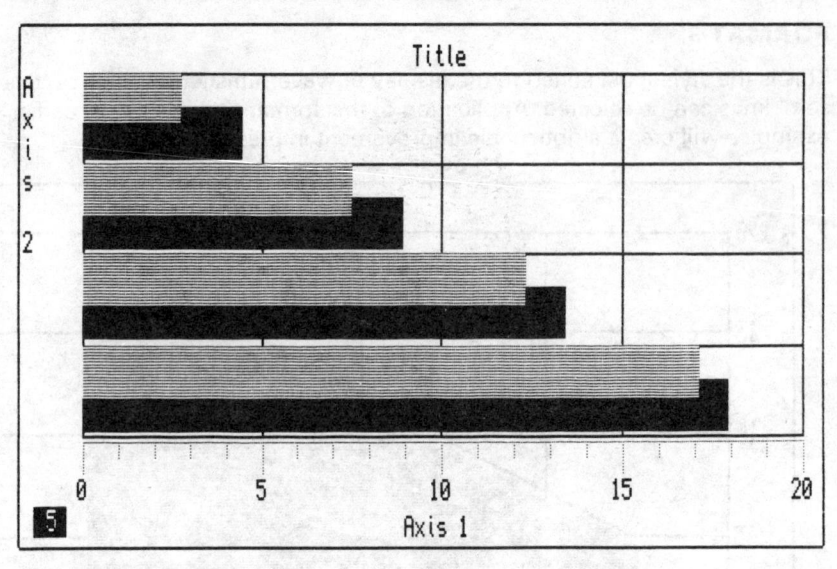

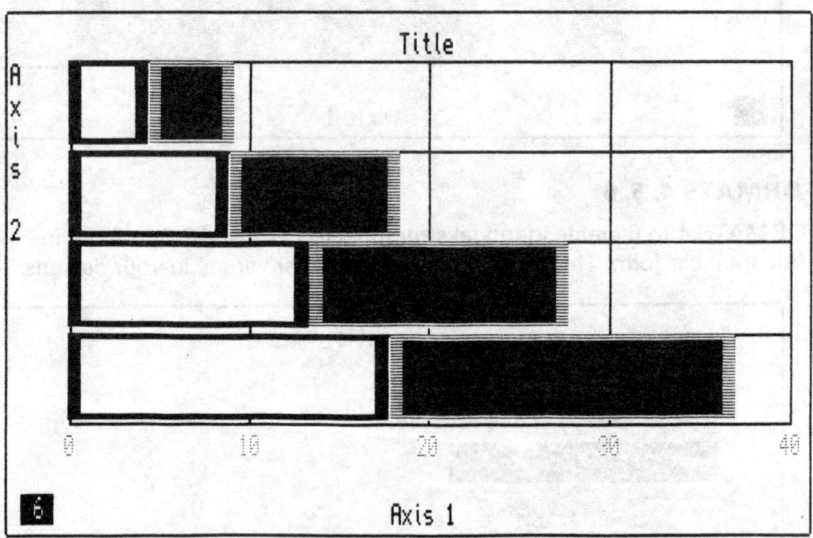

FORMAT 7

The final style is the unique pie chart which is capable of displaying only one set of figures at a time. It is a very popular type of style since the 'slice of cake' division it represents is often more acceptable to those not familiar with the interpretation of traditional graph layouts.

Since some of the design features of the pie chart are different from those for FORMATS 0 to 6, we shall be dealing with them separately towards the end of this section.

171

[Pie chart showing segments labeled 9, 4.5, 13.5, and 7]

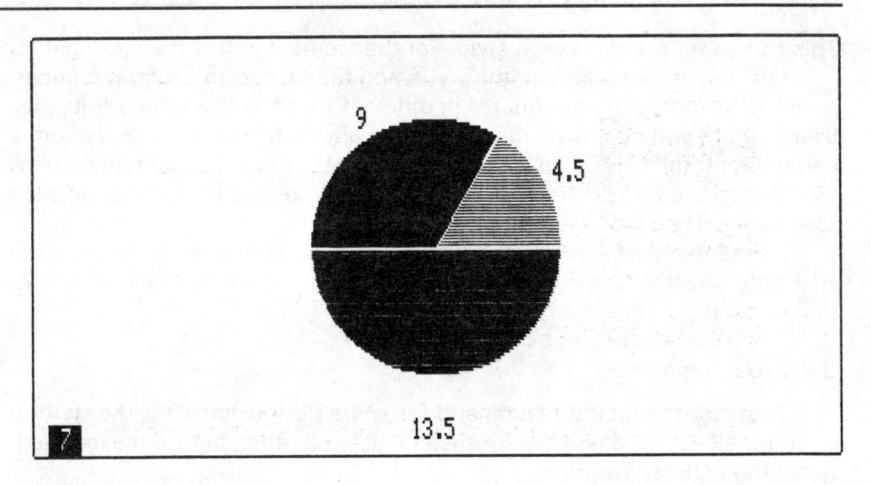

Format selection

Those are the formats available; how do we select them? There are two main methods involving two commands, both of which you have already met: VIEW and CHANGE. The former has been explained previously but at the time we did not discuss format selection. You have just used CHANGE to display all eight formats. Selection is achieved as follows:

VIEW command

Using ZAP clear the EASEL's memory. Enter in these two sets of figures using the FORMULAE option:

    figures = cell [ENTER]

    numbers = cell/2 [ENTER]

Then select the VIEW command with:

    [F3] [V] [ENTER]

This accepts the display of all figures. The Command Area now asks for a format number. Type in:

    1 [ENTER]

Your figures will quickly be displayed in FORMAT 1 style complete with a key (which may, if you wish, be moved using EDIT). If you had pressed the ENTER key without typing a format number then FORMAT 0 would have been automatically selected. This we had done earlier in the chapter. However, once a new format is selected it appears in the Status Area and will also become the recommended format number in the VIEW command's Input Line. Having displayed the figures in FORMAT 1, press the V key again, followed by the ENTER key and you will see what we mean.

To see how your figures look in all the other formats, use the sequence:

    [V] [ENTER] [format number] [ENTER]

This can be repeated for each style. For the moment ignore the pie-chart style.

Once you are familiar with the styles and their respective format numbers, it is very easy to try out your figures in different styles to find which suits the best. Should you be unsure of a style, then after selecting the VIEW command and pressing the ENTER key for the first time, type in a question mark followed by pressing the ENTER key and the display will present all eight formats as we saw earlier. Then make your choice.

Do note that pressing the ESC key to return to data-entry mode does not affect the selected format. Any further sets of figures entered will be in that same format.

CHANGE command

This is the most important command for graph design since it is the starting point for all design changes. We shall be using it often, but for the moment select the FORMAT option:

[F3] [C] [F]

This creates the same Command Area display as the latter part of the VIEW command. We can either type in the required format number or press the ENTER key (no question mark this time) for a display of all eight. Why two commands for the same thing? Essentially you would normally use the Format option when creating a new graph style *before* entering in any sets of figures. The choice is yours.

DESIGN IMPLEMENTATION

We will now turn our attention to how design selections are made and what features of the graph we can control The CHANGE command is the starting point, so select:

[F3] [C]

Your Command Area should look like this:

```
CHANGE              Axis
Bar                 Line        Graph_paper
Segment             Format      Text
press first letter
```

FORMAT we have just covered, so that leaves six possible options. We will look at them individually.

Bar

Select BAR by pressing the B key and the Command Area will display:

> CHANGE REPRESENTATION
> Enter new object number
> if known.
> ? for choice by example.

You will also see this display when selecting Axis, Line or Graph_paper. It invites you to either type in a design number relating to a particular representation or press the ENTER key to have all the choices displayed. It is very similar in operation to the FORMAT option.

Bar choice

At this stage we have not met all the possible representations available for bars, so press the ENTER key to continue. The Display Area will change to show all the variations possible. The command area gives further details of how to make the selection. It could not be easier. Using the cursor left/right keys, we move the white rectangle outline onto the desired design then press the ENTER key for EASEL to accept our selection and re-draw the current set of figures using it.

Note that each bar contains a number. This is the object number we could have used to select a known bar type. It is also the number you will see in the Status Area following *Rep*. At the moment it should be displaying:

Rep BAR 3

This is because the CURRENT NAME, *numbers* was drawn using white bars. Users of 80- or 64-column mode will see some duplication of bar types. This is to achieve compatibility with 40-column mode where more colour is available.

Bar design

We can go even further. Should you not like any of the choices presented, place the rectangle on the last bar containing a question mark then press the ENTER key. The Display Area changes once more and we can design our own bar. We are presented with a menu on the left and a large bar in the current representation on the right. The four cursor keys control the selection sequence. A colour palette at the top of the menu gives four choices in 80-/64-column mode and eight choices in 40-column mode. The options beneath are identical in any mode. They allow us to change any of three parameters:

   Fill colour
   Border colour
   Border thickness

Using either up or down cursor keys you can cyclically move the green highlight through the options. Stop at *Fill colour* then press the ENTER key. A white square outline will appear around the left-most palette colour and the bar will change to that colour. The selected text colour changes from green to white. Now we use the left/right cursor keys to select the desired colour. Each time you press the cursor keys the bar reflects the selected colour, giving an immediate check on the final appearance. Once satisfied, press the ENTER key. The white outline disappears and the next option is highlighted in green. Pressing the ENTER key allows the border colour to be changed in the same way. If it is not required to be changed, simply use the down cursor key to skip to the next option.

Border thickness is initially set to twenty, but as the Status Area shows, it can be anything from zero to one hundred. Just type in the desired thickness which is expressed as a percentage of half the bar's width.

The final option, *Satisfied*, should be selected – by pressing the ENTER key – only when your design is complete and you wish to see the current set of figures (*numbers* in our case) displayed with the new bar style.

Design storage

Once a new bar style has been created it is remembered by EASEL for the duration of the program residing in the QL, so that you do not have to re-create a particular style each time. EASEL also allocates a new object number to it. You can check this by calling up the bar design palette again:

[F3] [C] [B] [ENTER]

You will find your new design with a number of sixteen, the 'question mark' example having moved to the right.

When you switch off the QL all new design styles are, of course, lost. Fortunately we are able to save graphs on cartridge, as we shall be explaining later. Also stored at the same time are any new styles, so all is not really lost!

Multiple bar design

It is important to remember that any bar design change affects only the CURRENT NAME set of figures. When using multiple graph displays you must use the OLDDATA command each time before designing new styles for each of the sets of figures. We can do this now with our existing sets of *figures* and *numbers*. The latter we have just changed. First of all use VIEW to look at both sets together:

[F3] [V] [ENTER] [ENTER]

The *figures* set is still in BAR 0 style. Change it to BAR 8, or even better design your own style for it, then view them both together.

Line

We can now move on to see how line graphs may be designed. First select the LINE option with:

[F3] [C] [L]

You have already met the command area contents before. Press the ENTER key to view the choices possible.

Line choice

Apart from different colours, a number of other variations are available. Lines may be thick or thin, centre-cell values may be marked with a cross, or lines may be filled in down to the zero value on the Axis 2. Since the background colour is black, line styles three, seven, eleven and twelve are invisible. Style three is a black thin line, seven is thick, eleven is thin with point crosses added, while twelve is filled in black with point crosses added.

Using the left/right cursor keys we select any desired style then press the ENTER key to see it displayed, just as we did for bars.

Line design

The design procedure is also the same. Place the white rectangle outline on the line with the question mark and press the ENTER key. This time we have options for:

   Line colour
   Symbols on?
   Symbol colour
   Line filled?
   Line thickness

Selection is the same as for bars so we shall confine comments to a few observations.

The options *Symbols on?* and *Line filled?* are on/off selections; if you want that option press the ENTER key, if not move on to the next option. Should you select, for example, symbols, then decide you do not want them, position the green highlight on *Symbols on?* again and press the ENTER key. The option will then be deleted.

Line thickness is selected by typing in a number between zero and one hundred but numerically bears no relationship to the border thickness option for bars.

Having finished your design pressing the ENTER key with the *Satisfied* option selected returns you to command mode with the current set of figures displayed.

Line example

Earlier in this chapter we used several waveforms that we said could be better represented in LINE format. To demonstrate this, and provide a little revision at the same time, perform the following sequences:

1. Clear out any current sets of figures:

   |F3| |Z| |ENTER|

2. Use TABULATE eight times to create thirty cells, deleting the Axis 1 labels in the process:

   ×12   ×8
   |F3| |E| |L| |F4| -------- |TABULATE| -------- |ENTER|

3. Replace the name *figures* with *sine*:

   [R] [ENTER] sine [ENTER]

4. Return to data entry mode:

   [ESC]

5. Type in the formula:

   sine = sin(2*PI()*(cell − 1)/(cellmax − 1)) [ENTER]

6. Type in the formula:

   cosine = cos(2*PI()*(cell − 1)/(cellmax − 1)) [ENTER]

7. View both waveforms in FORMAT 0:

   [F3] [V] [ENTER] [ENTER]

8. View both waveforms in FORMAT 3:

   [V] [ENTER] 3 [ENTER]

9. Change *cosine* waveform to filled red line (LINE 14):

   [C] [L] 14 [ENTER]

10. Change current name to *sine*:

    [O] sine [ENTER]

11. Change sine waveform to filled white line (LINE 13):

    [C] [L] 13 [ENTER]

12. View both waveforms in FORMAT 3:

    [V] [ENTER] [ENTER]

13. Move the key towards the top of the graph:

    [E] [K] [←] [→] [↑] [↓] [ENTER]

14. View the waveforms in FORMAT 0 again:

    [V] [ENTER] 0 [ENTER]

Hopefully you have successfully performed the sequences and have observed the following points.

Having typed in the two formulae and viewed them in the default format (0), you will have seen two sets of bar graph information.

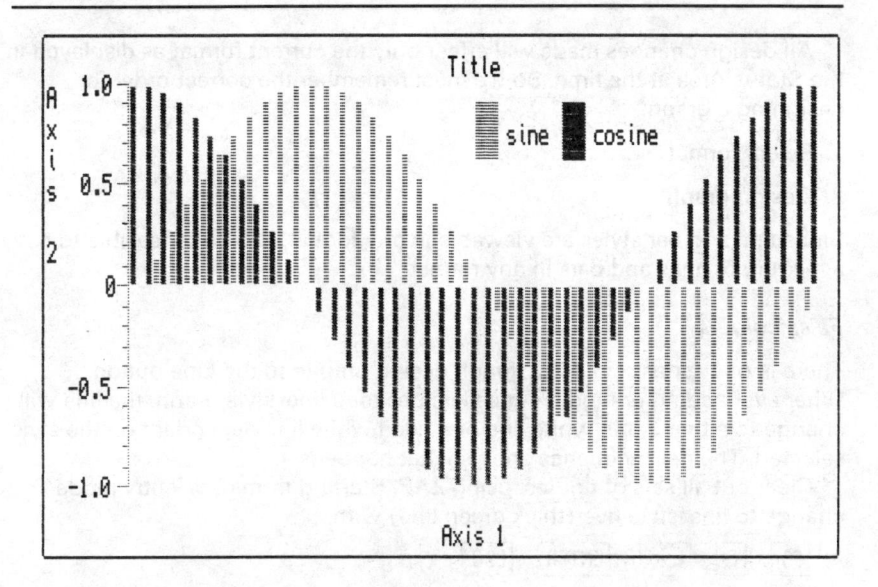

Viewing them in FORMAT 3 produced EASEL-controlled line styles of a single green line for 'cosine' and a single white line for 'sine'. The ensuing changes created two filled line waveforms which should have demonstrated the suitability of this format for these types of waveforms.

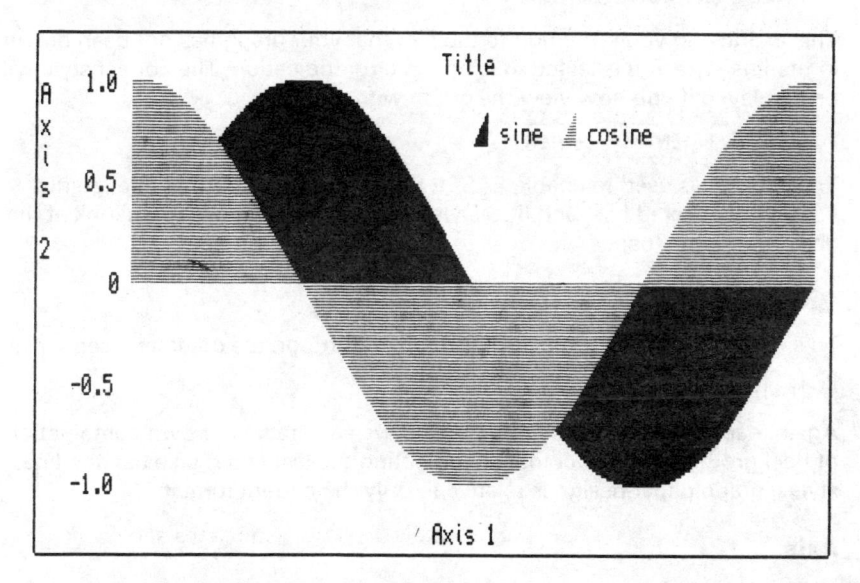

Sequence fourteen, however, showed that the bar graph styles originally viewed in sequence seven were still available. This emphasizes an important aspect of EASEL.

All design changes made will affect only the current format as displayed in the Status Area at the time. So we must remember the correct order for designing a graph:

1. Select format
2. Design graph

Since line and bar styles are viewable in any format, it is quite feasible to have a mixture of lines and bars in any format.

False colours

There is one aspect of EASEL graph design unique to the Line option. Whenever adding or modifying cell values for a line-style graph, the line will change to either a thin white line or a filled white line dependent on the style selected. The next sequence shows what happens.

Clear out all sets of figures, using ZAP. Starting from data-entry mode, change to line-style five (thick green line) with:

|F3| |C| |L| 5 |ENTER| |ESC|

Enter any data you wish into a few cells. As soon as you enter the first cell's data the graph will be drawn with a thin white line. In the Status Area on the right will be displayed:

FALSE LINE COLOURS

This is drawing your attention to the fact that your graph has not been drawn in the line style you selected. It is not an error indication. The correct style will be displayed if you now view the graph with:

|F3| |V| |ENTER| |ENTER|

This method is used to enable EASEL to change your display more rapidly.

Having covered bar- and line-style design we shall move on to look at the design of graph 'paper'.

Graph paper

To see the design variations for this item go through the command sequence:

|F3| |C| |G| |ENTER|

Again, each is selectable by number and we can create our own combination of background and grid colours by selecting the last entry. Like bar and line styles, graph paper design is relative to only the current format.

Axis

Axis design relates only to Axis 2, its method of selection being the same as for the previous items. We can change axis colour, label colour and whether or not we actually display an axis. In addition, the axis limits can be changed. There are three choices:

- EASEL automatically selects the upper and lower limits of the axis values to give maximum graph readability.
- EASEL automatically selects the upper limit; the lower limit always being zero. This is the normal, default, condition.
- You can set the upper and lower limits. However, EASEL will overide your choice if all of a graph cannot be displayed within your limits.

Note that FORMATS 2 and 6 will *always* include zero irrespective of your selection.

Confirm the selections available with:

F3 C A ENTER

Two styles do duplicate in 80-/64-column mode, again for compatibility with 40-column mode.

Text

The design of text encompasses the following options:

Text ink
Text paper
Transparent?
Direction?

When selecting the text option you press only:

F3 C T

The design menu is immediately displayed. There are no pre-defined text styles. Ink and paper should be self-explanatory. Selecting *transparent?* allows the text to be superimposed on the background graph colour. Each time you select this option (or the next) the opposite facility is created (as happened for *Symbols on?* in the Line option). You would not expect to set up a text paper colour *and* the transparent option since the latter cancels the effect of the former!

The final option, again an on/off selection, selects either horizontal or vertical text printing.

When a text design has been made it affects only text created afterwards. All existing text remains unchanged. This allows a wide variety of text styles to be simply created on one graph. Remember, text means not only additional information you may add to the graph but also axis names and the graph title. Note that the direction of the axis names and title cannot be changed.

Another point to remember: text design is the only CHANGE option that does affect all formats. Once it has been altered it remains in that style until changed again.

Segment

The final CHANGE option refers to changing segment colour of a pie chart. Since it is operable only when FORMAT 7 has been selected, we shall discuss it in the separate section on pie charts.

HIGHLIGHT command

There are times when it is necessary to draw attention to a particular cell value or perhaps to emphasise all the negative values on a graph. HIGHLIGHT allows us to do this by selecting a different bar style or designing our own. It is not possible to HIGHLIGHT line graphs, and only single segments can be highlighted in pie charts since negative values cannot be represented. The following sequence demonstrates the HIGHLIGHT action:

Using ZAP clear all existing sets of figures and RENAME *figures* as *a* with:

| F3 | | R | | ENTER | a | ENTER | | ESC |

Type in the formula:

$a = 2*(cell - 6)$ | ENTER |

Now select the HIGHLIGHT command:

| F3 | | H |

The command area changes to inform that:

V will highlight a single bar (or segment).
N will highlight all negative bar values.

Select the V key and the vertical crosswire will appear. Use the TABULATE key to place it on the *Mar* cell (a negative value). Then press the ENTER key. The familiar bar-style selection menu is displayed. You choose your highlight style in exactly the same way as you did for bar styles earlier. Select style ten, press the ENTER key and the graph is redrawn with the *Mar* cell highlighted.

Should you wish to delete a highlight and restore the cell to its original style simply press the F4 key after selecting the cell using TABULATE following the selection of the V key.

Continue by selecting HIGHLIGHT again, this time choosing the N key. We are presented with the same bar-style menu. Select style nine and press the ENTER key. The graph will shortly be drawn with all negative values in style nine *except* the *Mar* cell which is still in style ten. This can be changed by:

| H | | V | | TABULATE | ———to *Mar* cell——— | F4 |

All negative cells are now in style nine.

To delete negative cell highlighting it is necessary to go through the design process again to select the same bar style as the rest of the original graph.

Do note that, like most of the other design facilities we have covered, highlighting affects only the current format.

PIE CHARTS

The principle of data entry for pie charts is similar to that used for bar and line graphs, but since the pie display format is so different we are treating all of its features separately.

Pie creation

To start with there are two ways in which a pie chart can be created. We can select FORMAT 7 first then progressively enter data until the pie is complete, or we can enter data in one of the other formats (BAR 0 is the easiest), then view the figures in FORMAT 7.

The displayed pie is not very large so you must always try to keep the number of segments down to a viewable maximum. If labels are used they will overlap if the segments are too close together. This is especially relevant since the numerical value of the segment (equivalent to Axis 2 information) is also displayed with the label.

Method one

Start by clearing out any previous sets of figures. Change to FORMAT 7:

|F3| |C| |F| 7 |ENTER|

A 'blank' pie chart is drawn in red with *Jan* to its left.

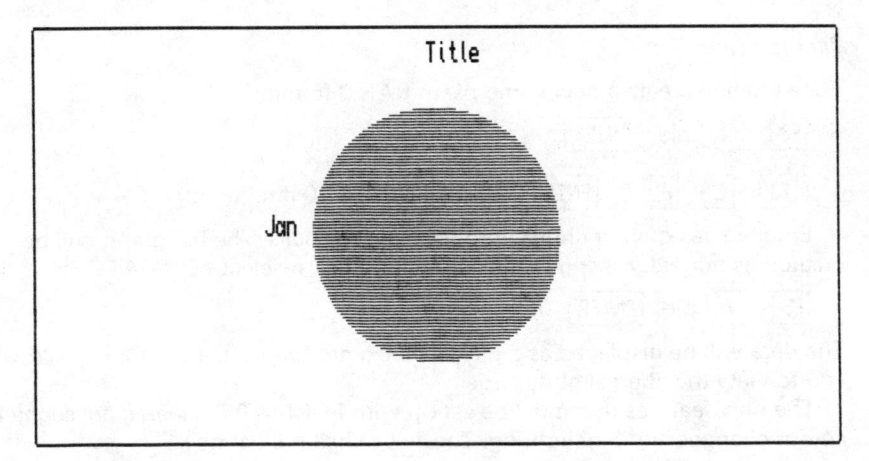

Press the ESC key, type in 30 and press the ENTER key. The chart is redrawn exactly as before but displayed with *30* underneath *Jan*. *Feb* has also appeared, highlighted in white, in the bottom left-hand corner.

Press the TABULATE key and *Feb* is replaced by *Mar*. In other words, highlighting, under the control of the TABULATE (and SHIFT/TABULATE) key, is used to identify the segment ready for data entry.

Return the highlight to *Feb* and enter the value 50. The chart is redrawn to look like this:

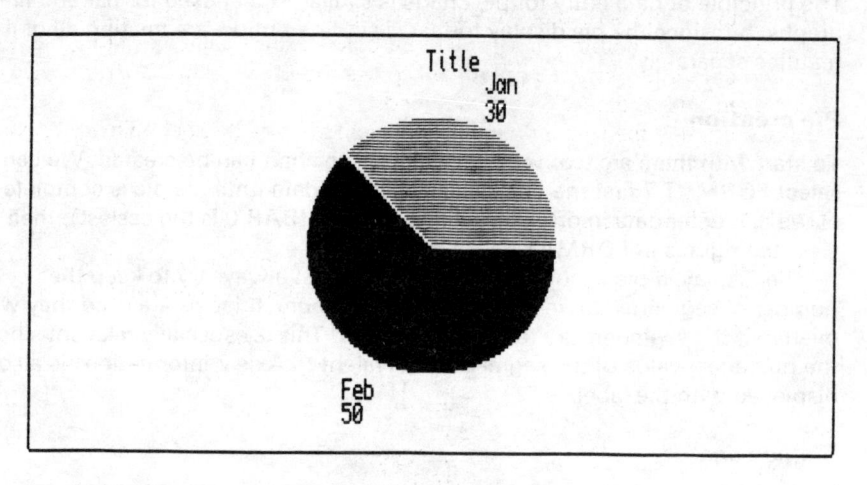

Note that *Mar* has now appeared in the corner. Enter a value of 20. Again the chart is redrawn. This time the *Mar* segment appears in green.

We will not proceed any further since the design sequence has been well demonstrated. Let us go on to the second method.

Method two

For a change create a new name *pie* in BAR 0 format:

[F3] [N] pie [ENTER]

([F3] [C] [F] 0 [ENTER] selects FORMAT 0 if required)

Enter values of your choice into the first four cells. The bar graph will be created as normal. Having completed your entry, reselect FORMAT 7:

[F3] [V] pie [ENTER] 7 [ENTER]

The data will be displayed as a pie chart. Do not forget that the F2 key allows you to view the chart slightly larger.

The only features that must be set up with FORMAT 7 selected are segment colour changes and highlighting. These we shall look at now.

Segment option

This option was mentioned earlier when discussing the CHANGE command. We can now try it out. It enables us to change the colour of one segment only per sequence. Select the option with:

[F3] [C] [S]

With the current pie chart displayed, use the TABULATE key to select any segment of your choice then press ENTER.

A colour palette is displayed at the top left-hand of the Display Area. If you are viewing in 40-column mode, all eight colours are available. Using the left/right cursor key select a colour and press the ENTER key. The chart will be redisplayed with the new colour included.

Unfortunately the selection sequence must be repeated each time you wish to change a segment's colour.

HIGHLIGHT command

The effect of this command on a pie chart is to detach the selected segment slightly from the rest of the chart. Only one segment per chart may be highlighted.

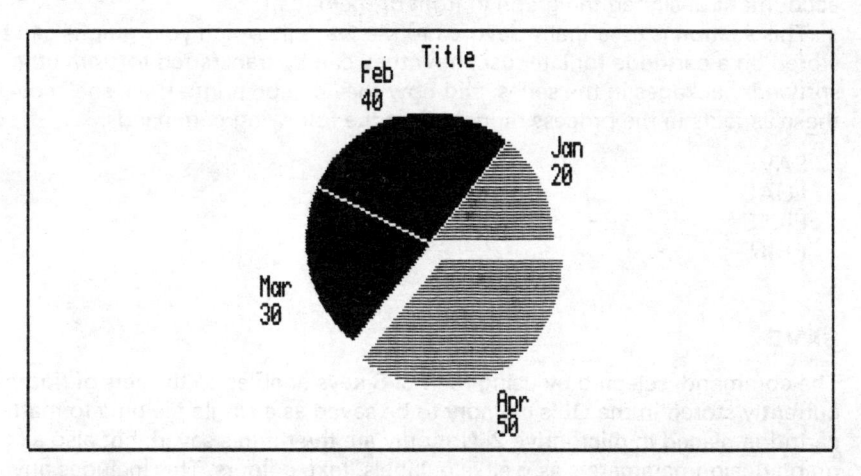

Highlighting affects only the current name's chart. We select it with this sequence:

|F3| |H| |TABULATE| -- to required segment -- |ENTER|

To remove highlighting, simply select the option then use the TABULATE and TABULATE/SHIFT keys to select a label in the bottom left-hand corner of the display Area.

Editing

As far as pie charts are concerned editing of labels is the only option which is slightly different from bar graph editing. Both additional text and the main title can be edited in the normal manner. There are no Axis 1 or Axis 2 labels used.

When you select label editing (F3, E and L keys) one of the labels will appear in the Input Line for editing. Depending upon the previous selection that had been made the label may or may not have been highlighted in white.

You can now use the SHIFT/TABULATE, F4 and cursor keys to move to, delete, or edit labels as required. Should you be presented with an 'unnamed' label you can edit it out by typing a space using the SPACE bar.

Remember that the editing facility cannot remove the segment value, only its label.

GRAPH STORAGE AND TRANSFER

For many applications the creation of a graph and its subsequent use would take place at different times. The advantage of a rapidly presented financial summary would be defeated if the boardroom members had to wait while the accountant designed the graph in front of them first!

This section is essentially devoted to the ways in which your graphs can be stored on a cartridge for later use, how they can be transferred to/from other software packages in the series, and how they can be printed. We shall cover these aspects in the process of looking at the following commands:

SAVE
LOAD
FILES
PRINT

SAVE

The command, selected by using the F3, S keys enables *all* the sets of figures currently stored in the QL's memory to be saved as a single file on a formatted cartridge placed in microdrive 2. Not only are the figures saved, but also all the graph design parameters as well, e.g. labels, text, colours. This includes any design styles you may have created so your own styles will be available as 'standard' designs when reloading the file at a later date and accessing the design menus. This is irrespective of whether they have been used in the stored graphs or not.

File name

So that EASEL can identify every file it stores each must have a file name. The name can be any alphanumeric combination up to a maximum of eight characters. The first character must be a letter and there must be no spaces included. When saving a file for you EASEL automatically attaches the following suffix to the name:

_grf

You do not need to type it. The reason for the suffix will be more obvious when we look at the way in which we transfer graph data to/from other

PSION software packages. Basically it enables the QL to differentiate between the same files (with the same names) stored for different purposes.

Default microdrive

While on the subject of file names it must be pointed out that EASEL will assume that any file to be accessed will be in microdrive 2. In the future we shall no doubt see external add-on microdrive units. To access other drives it is simply a matter of typing the microdrive number before the file name. For example:

   mdv3_graph1

We shall make use of this format when we look at the BACKUP command.

SAVE method

The best way to understand what happens is to try it. First of all, create a graph of your choice, perhaps consisting of two sets of figures. The next thing you require is a formatted cartridge. If you do not have one already formatted then perform the following sequence:

1. Place the unformatted cartridge in microdrive 2.
2. Type in:

   [F3] [F] [F]

The Command Area requests a name to be typed but this is not a file name. It is a name, optionally added, which identifies the whole formatted cartridge. You could, for example, type in:

   graph1 [ENTER]

The cartridge in microdrive 2 will run and be formatted in about 30 seconds. Your screen will then return to command mode. You may recall, though, that in Chapter 7 we advised formatting new cartridges several times before use. This routine formats only once, so it would be preferable to format the cartridges you intend to use with EASEL *before* you load EASEL.

With the cartridge now formatted, press the S key to select the SAVE option. At this point you have a choice: either to go ahead and save the stored sets of figures or just request a list of the files already stored on the cartridge in microdrive 2. Not having any files stored yet we will continue by typing in a suitable file name. We shall use 'figures'. Press the ENTER key, microdrive 2 will run and the file will be saved. The display will be returned to command mode.

To follow up the other selection we can now request a list of all the files on the cartridge. Press the S key and type in a question mark. The Input Line will have added to it:

   dir mdv2_

Simply press the ENTER key. Microdrive 2 will run and the directory will appear in the top left-hand corner of the cleared Display Area. Only *figures* will be listed if you have used a newly formatted cartridge. Note that the suffix _grf has been added and the heading includes our cartridge name *graph1*. The directory also tells us how many sectors are available for use (the left-hand number).

When you have finished with the directory option (which can be used to list any cartridge's files) press the ESC key to return to your original display in command mode.

Note that this option is also available with several of the other commands and selections we shall be discussing.

Having saved a file, let us see how we can load it back in again.

LOAD

Clear out the graph data you have just saved by using the ZAP command. The LOADing sequence is very similar to the SAVE sequence in that you either type in the name of the file you wish to LOAD, or can request a directory. Type this sequence:

[F3] [L] figures [ENTER]

Microdrive 2 will run for a few seconds then, after about a 6 second pause, the graph will be displayed, just as it was when you saved it.

If necessary you could EDIT or alter its design further. Do note that LOADing a file will delete any graph figures already held in the computer. This brings us to an important point.

Graph file protection

Once a file name has been allocated to a file and the file saved on a cartridge, any attempt to save another or the same, modified, file with the *same* name will be detected by EASEL. To show you this feature, having loaded the graph *figures*, alter it in some way – perhaps change the line or bar style – then go through the SAVE command routine. When you press the ENTER key having typed in the same file name, the Input Line changes. You are given the option of either allowing the file to be overwritten with the new graph by pressing the ENTER key or abandoning the attempt by pressing the ESC key.

Your stored files are therefore protected from accidental overwriting unless you deliberately allow it.

FILES

Moving on to the FILES command, select it with:

[F3] [F]

Five commands are available, one – FORMAT – we have already covered. The others are:

    DELETE
    BACKUP
    IMPORT
    EXPORT

DELETE

This command gives a similar command area display to SAVE and LOAD. To delete a file from the cartridge in microdrive 2 simply type in its name, then press the ENTER key. The process is irreversible, so make sure you really do want to delete the file. Also, when typing in the name you must include the suffix. We have met only _grf so far, but others exist and it is quite possible to have the same file name with different suffixes.

BACKUP

The command is designed to allow the copying of a stored file from one cartridge to another. The necessity for backing-up EASEL was discussed at the beginning of Chapter 7, and is equally important for any graph data you store.

After selecting the command you are asked to type in the name of the file to be backed-up. Let us assume it is called *figures_grf*. Type in its name and with its cartridge in microdrive 2, press the ENTER key. Easel checks that the file is present and if not it tells you in the Status Area: *file not found*.

The Input Line should now contain:

    command > Files : backup from figures_grf to

Your back-up cartridge must now replace the EASEL cartridge in microdrive 1. This is the only time when it is permitted to remove EASEL.

To continue you must type the backup file name which can either be a new name or the original. EASEL will automatically add _grf. In fact, it does not need to be typed when entering the file name to be copied. You must also type the microdrive used. So it we were retaining the old name the Input Line could look like:

    command > Files : backup from figures_grf to mdv1_figures

Finally press the ENTER key and the copying will start. It takes about 25 seconds for a two-sector file. If you do not specify the microdrive used then the file will be duplicated on the same cartridge.

IMPORT and EXPORT

The last two command options will be explained together.

Much of the information that is used by the three QL software packages EASEL, ABACUS and ARCHIVE is very similar in nature, being essentially tabular. EXPORT allows the creation of files, in a common format, by any package while IMPORT reads the files.

EASEL cannot exchange information with the word-processing package QUILL, since the latter uses a formatted text which is incompatible with the EXPORT structure.

To explain the procedures for these two commands we shall use an example of part of an ABACUS grid shown below. If you have not yet used ABACUS a quick scan through the *QL User Guide* should help you understand the format.

	A	B	C	D	E	F
1	Temp.	January	February	March	April	May
2	Bath	5	5	7	9	12
3	Dundee	3	4	5	7	9
4	Newquay	7	6	7	9	11

The EXPORT command, performed in this instance by ABACUS, will store the table of data on a cartridge file, its name automatically suffixed with _*exp*.

With EASEL loaded in the QL the IMPORT command is selected:

[F3] [F] [I]

You are asked for the file name of the ABACUS-exported file. Since there may also exist a similar named file with the _*grf* suffix, you must type in the full name, e.g. *temps_exp*, and press the ENTER key. The file will be loaded and then displayed in BAR format 0 as three sets of figures called:

Bath
Dundee
Newquay

The month names are used as Axis 1 cell names. If we had exported from ABACUS just the five 'cells' of numbers shown there would be only these five displayed. Note that the grid heading of *Temp* is not used by EASEL.

We could now amend the graph style if required, or simply arrange for it to be printed out as a hard copy for future reference.

The rules concerning the use of EXPORT with ABACUS and ARCHIVE are explained elsewhere. However, it should be pointed out that if EASEL imports a file that contains more than one set of textual information, it will use the first set as the cell labels and ignore the rest. It converts only true data into cell values. Conversely, if cell labels are numeric, they will be displayed as a set of graph figures and the Axis 1 labels will remain as *Jan* to *Dec*.

Exporting graph data

The procedure for exporting from EASEL is quite straightforward. Having created your set of figures, select the EXPORT command with:

[F3] [F] [E]

You will be asked to type the file name you wish to use. Again, you do not need to add the suffix _exp as EASEL does it for you. Press the ENTER key and all the sets of figures in the QL will be stored in export file format.

We mentioned that EASEL will discard the heading *Temp* from the ABACUS cell 1A when it imports a file. Conversely it adds a heading of *label* when creating the export file to maintain compatibility.

PRINTING

The final section concerns perhaps one of the most rewarding aspects of EASEL. It is all very well creating a graph and displaying it on a screen, but this is not always the most convenient method of presentation. The ability to provide an output of the graph data to give a permanent paper copy, via a printer connected to the QL, makes all the difference. Graphs can now be included in reports; they can be transported easily and duplicated further if necessary.

A printer capable of high-resolution graphics is essential, and the QL serial interfaces have been designed so that many makes of printer can be satisfactorily connected. For connection details you should read the 'Concepts' section of the *QL User Guide* entitled 'communications RS-232-C' in conjunction with the manual for the printer you are considering. Perhaps the best advice to offer is to take your QL along to the dealer selling the printer and try it first!

The PRINT command is selected by:

[F3] [P]

Three choices are presented in the Command Area:

- Print the graph
- Install a new graphics driver
- Save a screen dump on a microdrive

If your printer is a dot matrix type and is compatible with the Epson FX80, then your graph can be printed immediately by pressing the P key. You can create a larger picture by pressing F2 before pressing P, to remove the Command Area from the screen.

The display will clear, the Display Area only will be redrawn and the printer should then print the graph. Depending upon the speed of the printer, it may take a few minutes. Upon completion the Control and Status Areas will be added to the screen and EASEL will be back in command mode.

Printer driver

The printer is controlled by a separate program called a printer (or graphics) driver. The default printer driver is held in the file *GPRINT_PRT* on the EASEL cartridge. Pressing 'P' simply selects this default driver and initiates the printing operation.

EASEL printing requires the printer to operate in graphics mode, so it is not possible to create your own printer drivers using the ABACUS or QUILL file *INSTALL_BAS*. The latter assumes the printer will operate in character mode. However, additional printer drivers are provided on the EASEL cartridge to allow a range of colour printers to be used.

- *INTGX132_PRT* for Integrex 132, Okimate 80 and similar types.
- *JX80_PRT* for epson JX80 and similar types.

To use an alternative driver, you must *install* it by typing in its file name (preceded by *mdv1_*) following the selection of the I (install) option.

The installation is *not* permanent. Reloading EASEL at a later date will result in the original default printer driver (*GPRINT_PRT*) being used. To change the driver type permanently, you must rename the files on the EASEL cartridge. Remember that you can only alter your back-up copy of EASEL. The master copy cannot be overwritten.

For example, if the colour printer driver *JX80_PRT* was to be permanently installed, the following sequence could be used:

1. Load the back-up copy of EASEL.

2. Copy the default file to another file (so that it may be used later if required):

   a) Place the EASEL cartridge in microdrive 2 (this saves having to precede each file name with *mdv1_*)

   b) [F3] [F] [B] GPRINT_PRT [ENTER]

   c) DEFAULT_PRT [ENTER]

3. Delete original default file:

   [F] [D] GPRINT_PRT [ENTER]

4. Copy colour printer driver file to new default file:

   a) [F] [B] JX80_PRT [ENTER]

   b) GPRINT_PRT [ENTER]

5. Replace EASEL cartridge in microdrive 1.

One further point, the Integrex 132 printer operates at a different transmission rate (4800 BAUD) from that of the default setting (9600 BAUD) so this parameter must be changed before printing begins. There are two ways to do it, one temporary, one permanent.

To temporarily change the BAUD rate, type in (before loading EASEL):

BAUD 4800 [ENTER]

Then type:

LRUN mdv1_BOOT [ENTER]

A permanent change can be achieved by altering the *BOOT* program on the EASEL cartridge. Following RESET, and either F1 or F2, place the cartridge in microdrive 1 and type the following sequence:

LOAD mdv1_BOOT [ENTER]

RENUM 10, 10 [ENTER]

5 BAUD 4800 [ENTER]

DELETE mdv1_BOOT [ENTER]

SAVE mdv1_BOOT [ENTER]

Future printing operations using this cartridge will now always select 4800 BAUD.

Should you be using different types of printer, then it may be more convenient to produce several copies of EASEL each with a different default printer driver.

Screen dump

The second PRINT option (S) allows a screen dump of the total contents of the display to be made to a specified file. This includes the Control Area, which if not required, must be removed by using the F2 key before typing the file name. The Input and Status Areas are automatically removed before the file is written.
byte by byte, that you see on the screen. A screen dump is simply a copy of all these bytes. There are a very large number of them and the storage of the dump on a file can take several minutes. Generally no more than about three screen dumps can be kept on one cartridge.

The dump may be a more acceptable source of graph data for some printers not able to receive the information via the EASEL PRINT command, and it would normally be used in a SuperBASIC data transfer program.

Device selection

EASEL normally assumes that the EASEL program suite (including the printer drivers) will be in microdrive 1 and storage files will be in microdrive 2.

As additional external devices become available, e.g. disks or microdrives, you may require to alter these default devices. For instance, you may wish to save your graph files on an external disk drive.

You can achieve this change by loading the file *CONFIG_BAS* from the ABACUS cartridge. A simple menu selection routine then allows you to change the default devices as required.

CHAPTER 9

A SOUND AT THE END

BEEPING, BEEP

INTRODUCTION

It could be said that sound has no place in a book on graphics so why include it? It can be argued that sound may be applied in many forms of programs using graphics, and indeed it can enhance the interaction of the graphics with the user. Rather than stand over the QL waiting for a complex diagram to be drawn or for results to be analysed, an engineer, scientist or student can be called from other duties by an appropriate sound.

Different sounds can be used to identify various stages in an experiment, to indicate particular errors or request more information. Sound can be an effective way of showing that the QL has accepted data that has been input by an operator. And, of course, there are the games applications . . . how could you possibly shoot down an alien spacecraft without a 'zap'?

QL SOUND

The standard QL is not provided with particularly sophisticated sound capabilities, being intended for a much wider, more useful range of applications than simply games. Nevertheless it is still quite capable of meeting all the situations outlined in the previous paragraphs and, when appropriate external add-on hardware is available, will no doubt exceed them.

Two keywords are available, one generates the sound (BEEP), the other monitors it (BEEPING). The latter will be explained first.

BEEPING

This is really a SuperBASIC function which will return a value equal to 1 if a sound is still being generated by any earlier BEEP statement or 0 if the sound has ceased. Without going into technical details the QL sound is controlled by a separate microprocessor. Once a sound has been started the main microprocessor can continue with the next statement in your program, leaving the sound electronics to carry on for the required duration. Should it be necessary to wait for the sound to end before continuing the program the main microprocessor must be halted. BEEPING can be used to achieve this by allowing us to program a wait condition until the sound ends. For example, we could simply write:

    50 IF BEEPING THEN GOTO 50

The QL will cycle continuously at this line until the sound stops, when the next statement in sequence will be executed. A further use of BEEPING will be met when we discuss the BEEP keyword itself.

BEEP

The QL has a single sound channel which is activated by BEEP, the keyword being followed by up to eight parameters. Each parameter controls a particular aspect of the sound generated. The contents of this chapter will be confined to describing the action of each parameter, each time giving a variety of examples for you to try (experiment with) and so develop your own sound requirements. We shall not be covering every possible sound . . . there are over two and a half billion parameter combinations, excluding variations caused by altering the duration of the sound!

SOUND-SELECTION

Attempting to type in BEEP statements for different combinations of such a vast range would be extremely tedious without some form of programming aid. At the end of this chapter you will find a program (*sound selection*) which has been developed with the following requirements in mind:

1. Quick insertion/deletion of any of the parameters.
2. Ability to select a range of values for a specified parameter, then play them in sequence.
3. Provision of a quick reference menu including range limits for each parameter.

   The program is the longest in the book, but advantage has been taken to include a number of the QL graphics features discussed in earlier chapters.

Carefully type the program into the QL and save it. It can be used to try out some of the BEEP statements you will meet in the following pages. It should also be of use later on if you wish to develop your own sounds.

Should the program stop for any reason (for instance, pressing the ENTER key following a request for input, with no value typed) then typing CONTINUE should allow it to carry on from the next statement.

Note that if a range of values for a parameter has been played, and then cleared, the maximum range value selected will remain as that parameter's value (it can, of course, be changed).

BEEP FORMAT

The eight parameters follow BEEP in this order:

BEEP duration, pitch 1, pitch 2, grad_x, grad_y, wrap, fuzzy, random

Each parameter can be a number or a numeric expression. Fortunately, not all the parameters need to specified; it depends upon the complexity of the sound required. There are five permitted combinations. If we assign the letters A to H to the parameters in the order in which they appear in the full format, we can represent these combinations as follows:

A, B
A, B, C, D, E
A, B, C, D, E, F
A, B, C, D, E, F, G
A, B, C, D, E, F, G, H

If BEEP is used on its own without any parameters, then any sound currently being generated will cease. So to test for – then silence – any sound, we could use:

    50 IF BEEPING THEN BEEP

We shall start, then, by examining each parameter within its permitted combination.

DURATION

This parameter sets the duration of the sound. The range of values it can accept is:

    − 32768 TO 32767

A value of 13889 would create sound for 1 second. If 0 is used then the sound would continue indefinitely until BEEP, reset or a re-defined shorter duration BEEP occurred.

Positive values have a linear relationship with time, being in units of 72 microseconds. The following program accepts your input of a required duration, generates a sound for that time and prints out the equivalent parameter value.

```
100 REMark * BEEP timing *
110 CLS
120 REPeat times
130   PRINT "Maximum time : 2.36 seconds"
140   INPUT " duration in seconds?"!duration
150   LET parameter = INT(duration*13889+.5)
160   CLS: BEEP parameter,100
170   PRINT duration!"seconds ="!"parameter of"!parameter
180 END REPeat times
```

BEEP repetition

The maximum positive value (32767) gives a duration of about 2.4 seconds, so for longer periods the BEEP statement would have to be repeated. This can be achieved by including an appropriate PAUSE statement between the BEEP statements. Remember, once a BEEP has been started, the main microprocessor carries on with the program. If it meets another BEEP statement while the first is still sounding, the sound logic will be started again with the parameters of the second BEEP. The first would be cancelled and, if two BEEP statements were consecutive, the first would not even be heard. Try the following sequence:

BEEP 13889, 100
BEEP 13889, 50

This is just to hear two different pitches (we shall be discussing these shortly). Now type in:

```
100 BEEP 13889,100
110 BEEP 13889,50
```

RUN the program. Only the second sound will be heard.
Now add in:

```
105 PAUSE
```

RUN the program. This time the first sound is heard and pressing any key will cause the second sound to be heard too.

```
105 PAUSE 100
```

Using this will do the same, but automatically, with a gap between the two sounds. By reducing the PAUSE parameter, the second sound can be made to immediately follow the first with neither a gap nor loss of part of the first sound. The time duration used here requires a PAUSE of 45. If the BEEP duration is changed then an appropriate PAUSE time must be found. For example:

```
100 BEEP 26778,100
110 PAUSE 60
120 BEEP 26778,100
```

This generates a continuous four second note.

You must also be careful if a BEEPING statement immediately follows a BEEP statement. Try this:

```
100 BEEP 20000,100
110 IF BEEPING THEN PRINT "OK!"
```

On running the program the sound will be heard but 'OK' will not appear on the screen. The problem is that the main microprocessor has moved on to line 110 before the sound generation logic has started, so BEEPING effectively misses the sound. The solution is to insert a delay between the two statements, either using a PAUSE or another statement.

```
100 BEEP 20000,100
110 PRINT "sound on"
120 IF BEEPING THEN PRINT "OK!"
```

This now works, as it also would if line 110 became:

```
110 PAUSE 5
```

Negative values

So far we have avoided negative parameter values. Not a bad idea since they are far from linear in their relationship with time! However, since they can produce much longer durations (best found by experiment) they can be useful. A few examples should suffice (times shown are approximate):

Parameter	Time (seconds)
−30000	2.5
−10000	4
−52 TO −1500	4.5
−50	10
−40	27

PITCH

When a string is plucked on a musical instrument, the sound we hear is caused by the vibrations of that string being passed on through the air and vibrating our ear-drums. Rapid vibrations from short strings produce notes of high **pitch** whilst slower vibrations from longer strings produce notes of low pitch. The rate of vibration per second is called the **frequency**.

Sound on the QL is generated by electrical oscillations passed to a small loudspeaker mounted between the microdrives. The frequency of the sound is controlled by the PITCH parameter. An integer range of 0 TO 255 is allowed. The higher the number, the lower the pitch. You can hear the full range with this:

```
100 FOR pitch = 0 TO 255
110     BEEP 1000,pitch : PAUSE 4
120 END FOR pitch
```

Musical scale

Simple tunes can easily be programmed, though the QL is a rather expensive way of doing it. However, by selecting appropriate pitch values, a musical scale can be established – albeit not to the satisfaction of a trained musician! The scale is biased towards the lower pitches and unfortunately the relationship between parameter value and musical pitch is not linear. Values must be found by experiment. Here is a non-musical scale:

```
100 FOR pitch = 0 TO 100 STEP 4
110     BEEP 2000,pitch :PAUSE 8
120 END FOR pitch
```

Every musical note is represented by one of the first seven letters of the alphabet and has a defined pitch, the internationally agreed standard (Concert Pitch) being based on 440 vibrations per second for note 'A'. We can obtain this frequency (approximately) with a parameter of 15. The following table gives reasonably acceptable values for a range of notes.

Parameter	Note	Parameter	Note	Parameter	Note
2	A	20	F#	62	D#
3	G#	22	F	67	D
4	G	24	E	72	C#
5	F#	26	D#	77	C
6	F	28	D	81	B
7	E	30	C#	86	A#
8	D#	32	C	91	A
9	D	35	B	97	G#
10	C#	38	A#	104	G
11	C	41	A	110	F#
12	B	44	G#	119	F
14	A#	47	G	127	E
15	A	51	F#	134	D#
17	G#	54	F	143	D
18	G	58	E	153	C#
				165	C

For those of us not too familiar with music fundamentals the following information may prove useful.

Any group of eight consecutive letters, for example C(32) to C(11) in our table, has an equivalent set of consecutive white keys on a piano. The group is called an **octave**. The following program plays this octave:

```
100 FOR pitch = 32,28,24,22,18,15,12,11
110   BEEP 2000,pitch : PAUSE 8
120 END FOR pitch
```

With reference to the physically central key ('Middle C') on a piano, the notes would be found like this:

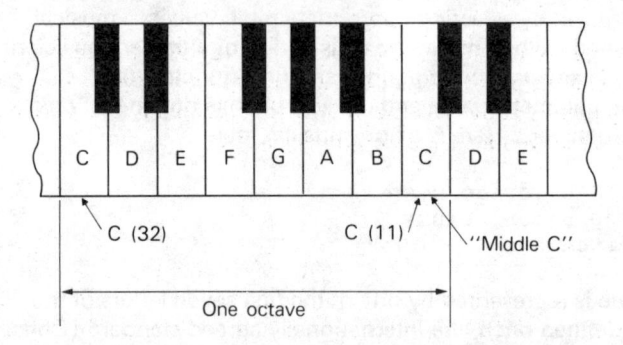

C	C#	D	D#	E	F	F#	G	G#	A	A#	B	C
	Db		Eb			Gb		Ab		Bb		

The pitch interval between two adjacent white notes is called a **tone**, except for B to C and E to F where the interval is a **semi-tone**. Each black key is spaced a semi-tone from its nearest white notes and can have two names. For instance, the note between G and A can be G# **(sharp)** or A♭ **(flat)**. Our table has used # throughout for convenience. When converting from sheet music to computer, the following may help.

Adding in the sharpened notes to the octave gives a twelve-note **chromatic** scale. Modify line 100 and you can hear the difference:

```
100 FOR pitch = 32 TO 18 STEP -2,17,15,14,12,11
```

In musical notation, pitch is conveyed by placing note symbols on horizontal lines called the **stave**. Sharps and flats are indicated by placing the appropriate symbol either in front of the note or at the beginning of the stave.

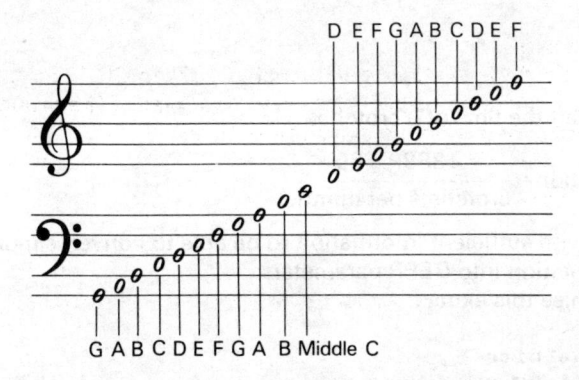

Since the pitch range of the QL does not cover all the notes of the top (treble) stave, it is best to transpose the pitch values up an octave so that 11 is now the C note one octave above Middle C. Any tune copied in this way will, of course, sound one octave lower than originally written.

Timing

To produce a tune, however, not only must the pitch of each note be correct but also its duration. Musical timing usually involves selecting a fundamental unit of time then successively dividing it by two to obtain the duration for each type of note. The principal note symbols and their time-relationship is shown below:

Note Symbol	Note Name	Fraction of unit time	BEEP parameter	Rest symbol	PAUSE value
o	Semi-breve	1	27778	■	100
d	Minim	1/2	13889	■	50
♩	Crotchet	1/4	6945	𝄽	25
♪	Quaver	1/8	3473	𝄾	13
♫	Semi-quaver	1/16	1736	𝄿	6

Note: BEEP and PAUSE values shown for tempo of 120 crotchets per minute

The symbols used for **rests** (periods of silence) are also shown with equivalent PAUSE values. So, for example, if we take a unit of time that gives us 120 crotchets per minute, then each crotchet of pitch p could be represented by:

BEEP 6945, p

A quaver would be:

BEEP 3473, p   i.e. half the time of a crotchet.

Hence: crotchet duration $= \dfrac{13889 \times 60}{\text{crotchets per minute}}$

You are now armed with sufficient information to be able to convert simple (single note) musical notation into BEEP parameters.

See it you can recognise this extract:

```
100 REMark * tune bits *
110 FOR notes = 1 TO 9
120    READ duration, pitch
130    BEEP duration , pitch
140    PAUSE 5
150    REPeat wait:IF BEEPING = 0 THEN EXIT wait
160 END FOR notes
170 DATA 6945,32,13889,22,6945,18
180 DATA 10418,15,3473,12,6945,15
190 DATA 13889,18,6945,24,10418,32
200 CLEAR
```

It is not really necessary to create a different complete set of duration values for tunes of different speed. Simply modify the 'duration' parameter in the BEEP statement. Our tune may be speeded up by changing line 130 to:

```
130 BEEP duration/3,pitch
```

If playing a tune slower, however, do be sure not to allow the duration to become greater than the maximum permitted (32767) otherwise an 'overflow' error message will result.

DURATION, PITCH_1, PITCH_2, GRAD_X, GRAD_Y

So far we have only looked at BEEP duration, pitch combinations. Let us now move on to consider the next permitted combination, which requires not only a second pitch value but also two further parameters. This immediately complicates the matter of sound selection by presenting us with a very large number of possible combinations. From now on you will find the program *sound selection* of great use! As you experiment you will find that many combinations produce the same sound, but conversely, some combinations will give quite different sounds with only a small change of one parameter. It is certainly best to change only one parameter's value at a time and to record the values used and (if you can describe it!) the type of sound.

Before having a closer look at this combination of parameters we will outline each parameter's action.

Pitch_1, pitch_2

These two parameters have the same range of values and produce the same frequencies as 'pitch' previously discussed. But now we are able to specify two pitch levels. You can use high- or low-pitch values for either; there is no precedence for which should come first.

Grad_x, grad_y

These parameters control the rate at which the sound will move between the two pitches. Grad_x controls the time intervals between increases (or decreases) in pitch controlled in turn by grad_y.

The range of permitted values suggested in the *Sinclair User Guide* is:

Grad_x: − 32768 TO 15
Grad_y: − 8 TO 7

While there is no advantage gained in extending the grad_y values more positively or negatively (sounds simply repeat), grad_x values are a different matter. Extending the range in the positive direction considerably increases the variety available. Conversely, *any* negative value for grad_x will give either a pitch_1 note or a pitch_2 note for the specified duration, dependent on the sign of grad_y:

Grad_y: − 8 TO − 1 gives pitch_2
0 TO 7 gives pitch_1

A better grad_x range would be:

− 1 TO 9000

Generally you will find that small values of grad_x and larger values of grad_y produce warbling or buzzing sounds. Large values of grad_x and small values of grad_y create ascending or descending pitches. Try these:

BEEP 30000, 255, 32, 30, − 7
BEEP 30000, 255, 32, 2300, 1

Speed is also a function of the pitch values selected.

BEEP − 40, 32, 160, 2300, − 1

This ably demonstrates the point, while the next is even more extreme!

BEEP − 40, 88, 160, 2300, 1

As grad_x increases, the warble rate reduces. Try the following parameters with a range of values for grad_x:

BEEP 10000, 100, 2, R, − 2

Suggested range:

1000 TO 7000 STEP 500

Making grad_x smaller provides us with some interesting warbles.

BEEP 10000, 100, 3, 900, −2
BEEP 10000, 100, 3, 300, −4

The latter a telephone sound perhaps?

Turning our attention to grad_y, negative values would appear to be more active in modifying the sounds. This may be so with the warbles just demonstrated since positive values have little controlling effect, but try this set of parameters for a range of −8 TO 7 STEP 1:

BEEP 10000, 255, 32, 3000, R

You will hear the ascending/descending pitch sequences for both positive and negative numbers. Duration changes reveal even more. Change the duration value to 32000 and listen to the result!

But pitch, too, controls the effect. Try the next parameters for the same range. This time the positive values of grad_y predominate in their controlling effect.

BEEP 32000, 0, 255, 3000, R

If you want a laser-type gun-fire, one statement can provide it:

BEEP −40, 255, 32, 30, 1

So everything effects everything else! Should you be 'sound-inclined' there is sufficient scope to keep you 'BEEPing' for hours . . . and there are three more parameters left!

Before moving on to the remaining parameters, a few more examples are provided.

A series of buzzer tones:

BEEP 10000, 11, R, 2, 1
Range: 13 TO 17 STEP 1

A whistle:

BEEP 10000, 255, 9, 300, −1

A warble:

BEEP 20000, 0, 255, 1000, 1

Another alien:

BEEP 20000, 11, 40, 2, 1

WRAP

The wrap parameter, when added to the previous combination of parameters, can modify most of the sounds further. It does not create very spectacular effects, often imparting a vibrato quality to the sound and causing the rate of change of pitch to alter. For example:

BEEP 32000, 255, 32, 30, 1, 5

This modifies the earlier laser-type gun-fire.
Our whistle takes on an almost echo-like quality:

BEEP 10000, 255, 9, 300, −1, 4

Changes are more noticeable with longer durations, though it has little effect on single tones (grad_x negative) or ascending/descending tones. Changes to gruff sounds, 'zaps' and 'growls' are more apparent.

The permitted range is:

0 TO 32767

Any values over 20 would seem to give repeats of sounds produced in the range 0 to 20.

Try hearing the changes created with a range of 0 to 20 for the telephone sound:

BEEP 10000, 100, 3, 300, −4, R

FUZZ

The next parameter that may be added is given a range of:

0 TO 15

It imparts a considerable change to most sounds! Fuzz is like distortion and is generally only effective for values in the range 8 to 15. Negative values simply repeat the sounds created by positive values.

Its effect is quite apparent, increasing in intensity as the parameter increases to 15.

Our laser 'disintegrates' into noise:

BEEP 32000, 255, 32, 30, 1, 0, 12

A previously pleasant sequence of descending tones now sounds like something about to crash!

BEEP 20000, 255, 32, 2300, 1, 0, 10

RANDOM

The final parameter, when added to the rest, produces random variations in pitch and hence varies the effect of grad_y. Being a random effect means, of course, that each time a particular combination is played, it will be different.

The range specified is:

0 TO 15

Again, like the fuzz parameter, it is values between 8 and 15 that are effective.

The randomness of pitch can be easily demonstrated by setting up a range of 7 to 15 for our earlier warble. Note that parameter value 7 will play the original sound.

BEEP 20000, 0, 255, 1000, 1, 0, 0, R

The variations can be quite amusing. The following could perhaps be an inter-computer chat!

BEEP −40, 1, 100, 560, −8, 0, 0, 14

Add a wrap parameter of 8 and the QL might be composing its own music, particularly if you start off with a scale of tones:

BEEP 32000, 2, 200, 2800, 1

Then add wrap and random parameter values:

BEEP −40, 2, 200, 2800, 1, 8, 0, 14

The duration has been increased to show one other effect of the random parameter. It modifies the duration since, as we have seen earlier, pitch values effect duration.

We can make it 'compose' for ever:

```
100 REMark * QL composer! *
110 REPeat phrase
120    BEEP 15000,2,200,2800,1,8,0,14
130    PAUSE RND(15 TO 30)
140 END REPeat phrase
```

Should you become tired (!) of the repeating pitch_1 note, for even more variety it can be replaced with a:

RND(11 TO 32)

MULTI-BEEP

We have been making sounds with only one BEEP statement, but by combining them or programming a range of values for various parameters, many more different effects are possible.

The following examples just scratch the surface:

```
100 REMark * siren *
110 LET grad_y = 1
120 REPeat siren
130    BEEP 10000,6,17,-1,grad_y
140    PAUSE 25
150    LET grad_y = grad_y *(-1)
160 END REPeat siren
```

```
100 REMark * battle fire *
110 FOR sound  = 1 TO 6
120    BEEP 10000,255,32,300,-1
130    PAUSE 15
140 END FOR sound
150 BEEP 20000,11,40,2,1


100 REMark * crash *
110 BEEP -50,88,160,2300,1
120 PAUSE 280
130 BEEP 20000,255,32,2300,1,0,11
```

SOUND SELECTION PROGRAM

A very small selection of the sounds available has been presented. It is hoped that enough material has been provided so that you can usefully experiment further without having to waste too much time with parameter values of little effect.

The following program should prove to be a useful means of easily varying BEEP parameters.

```
100 REMark * sound selection *
110 initialise
120 begin
130 set_up
140 menu
150 selection
160 DEFine PROCedure initialise
170   MODE 8 : WINDOW 512,256,0,0
180   PAPER 7 : INK 2
190   CLS#0 : CLS
200   WINDOW 410,200,50,20
210   DIM p(7),r(3)
220 END DEFine
230 DEFine PROCedure begin
240   CSIZE 3,1 : AT 1,5
250   PRINT"SOUND SELECTION"
260   CSIZE 2,0 : INK 1 : AT 6,0
270   PRINT"The program allows you to set up  the BEEP";
280   PRINT!"parameters in any order."
290   AT 9,0
300   PRINT"All values are initially at zero."
310   AT 11,0
320   PRINT"A range of values may be set for  one"
330   PRINT!"parameter per sequence."
340   STRIP 0 :INK 7 : AT 17,1
350   PRINT"* press SPACE bar to continue *"
360   REPeat wait : IF INKEY$=" "THEN EXIT wait
370 END DEFine
```

```
380 DEFine PROCedure set_up
390   OPEN#6,scr_448x160a28x20
400   PAPER#6,0 : INK#6,6 : CLS#6
410   WINDOW 448,65,28,180
420   PAPER 6 : INK 0 : CLS
430 END DEFine
440 DEFine PROCedure menu
450   CSIZE#6,3,0 : AT#6,0,3
460   PRINT#6,"SELECTION"TO 19,"RANGE"
470   CSIZE#6,2,0 : INK#6,7
480   AT#6,2,0
490   DATA "d","p1","p2","x"
500   DATA "y","wr","fz","rn"
510   FOR parameter = 0 TO 7
520     READ name$
530     PRINT#6,name$; : PRINT#6,TO 3
540     STRIP#6,2
550     PRINT#6,parameter : STRIP#6,0
560   END FOR parameter
570   LINE#6,0,90 TO 207,90
580   LINE#6,25,90 TO 25,30
590   DATA "Play sound","SPACE"
600   DATA "Set range","r"
610   DATA "Clr range","c"
620   DATA "Exit","e"
630   FOR row = 3,5,7,9
640     READ selection$ : AT#6,row,5
650     PRINT#6,selection$;
660     PRINT#6, TO 16 : STRIP#6,2
670     READ action$ :PRINT#6,action$
680     STRIP#6,0
690   END FOR row
700   LINE#6,120,100 TO 120,30
710   DATA "d","-32768/32767"
720   DATA "p1","0/255","p2","0/255"
730   DATA "x","-1/9000","y","-8/7"
740   DATA "wr","0/32767"
750   DATA "fz","0/15","rn","0/15"
760   FOR row = 2 TO 9
770     INK#6,7:AT#6,row,22
780     READ parameter$
790     PRINT#6,parameter$;
800     INK#6,0 : READ range$
810     PRINT#6,TO 25 : STRIP#6,4
820     PRINT#6,range$ : STRIP#6,0
830   END FOR row
840   RESTORE : INK#6,7
850   LINE#6,0,30 TO 207,30
860   AT#6,12,4
870   PRINT#6,"After each parameter or range";
880   PRINT#6,"          value press";
890   PRINT#6, TO 18 : STRIP#6,2
900   PRINT#6,"ENTER" : STRIP#6,0
910 END DEFine
```

```
920 DEFine PROCedure selection
930   REPeat check
940     AT 0,0 : PRINT "Selection?";
950     LET k = CODE(INKEY$(-1))
960     SELect ON k
970       ON k = 48 TO 55
980         PRINT !k-48,
990         set_parameter
1000      ON k = 32
1010        PRINT !"PLAY"
1020        play
1030      ON k = 114
1040        PRINT !"RANGE":PAUSE 50
1050        range_select
1060      ON k = 99
1070        PRINT !"CLEAR"
1080        LET r(0) = 0
1090      ON k = 101
1100        PRINT !"END": PAUSE 50
1110        finish
1120      ON k = REMAINDER
1130        error_message
1140      END SELect
1150      display
1160   END REPeat check
1170 END DEFine
1180 DEFine PROCedure set_parameter
1190   STRIP 5
1200   SELect ON k
1210     ON k = 48
1220       PRINT "DURATION"
1230     ON k = 49
1240       PRINT "PITCH 1"
1250     ON k = 50
1260       PRINT "PITCH 2"
1270     ON k = 51
1280       PRINT "GRAD X"
1290     ON k = 52
1300       PRINT "GRAD Y"
1310     ON k = 53
1320       PRINT "WRAP"
1330     ON k = 54
1340       PRINT "FUZZ"
1350     ON k = 55
1360       PRINT "RANDOM"
1370   END SELect
1380   STRIP 6 : AT 1,4
1390   INPUT "Value? "; p(k-48)
1400 END DEFine
1410 DEFine PROCedure display
1420   PAUSE 50 : CLS
1430   STRIP 3 : AT 3,0
1440   IF r(0)= 1 THEN
```

```
1450        FOR value = 0 TO 7
1460          IF value = n THEN
1470            PRINT !"R";
1480          ELSE
1490            PRINT !p(value);
1500          END IF
1510        END FOR value
1520        STRIP 6 : AT 5,2
1530        PRINT "Range:"!r(2)!"to"!r(1)!"step"!r(3)
1540      ELSE
1550        STRIP 3 : AT 3,0
1560        PRINT p(0)!p(1)!p(2)!p(3)!p(4)!p(5)!p(6)!p(7)
1570        STRIP 6
1580      END IF
1590 END DEFine
1600 DEFine PROCedure play
1610   IF r(0) = 1 THEN
1620     FOR value = r(2)TO r(1)STEP r(3)
1630       LET p(n) = value : AT 1,25
1640       PRINT "VALUE:" : AT 1,32
1650       CLS 4 : PRINT value
1660       BEEP p(0),p(1),p(2),p(3),p(4),p(5),p(6),p(7)
1670       PAUSE p(0)/350
1680     END FOR value
1690   ELSE
1700     BEEP p(0),p(1),p(2),p(3),p(4),p(5),p(6),p(7)
1710   END IF
1720 END DEFine
1730 DEFine PROCedure range_select
1740   REPeat test
1750     CLS : AT 1,2
1760     PRINT "Parameter number?";
1770     LET n = INKEY$(-1)
1780     PRINT !n;
1790     IF n>=0 AND n<8 THEN
1800       EXIT test
1810     ELSE
1820       error_message
1830     END IF
1840   END REPeat test
1850   LET r(0) = 1 : PAUSE 50
1860   CLS : AT 1,2
1870   INPUT "Minimum value?"!r(2)
1880   AT 2,2
1890   INPUT "Maximum value?"!r(1)
1900   AT 3,2
1910   INPUT "Step size?"!r(3)
1920   PAUSE 50 : CLS
1930   STRIP 3 : AT 3,0
1940 END DEFine
1950 DEFine PROCedure error_message
1960   FLASH 1
1970   PRINT !"Wrong selection!"
1980   PAUSE 50 : FLASH 0
1990 END DEFine
```

```
2000 DEFine PROCedure finish
2010   INK 2 : CLS : AT 3,3
2020   PRINT "Are you sure?..type 'y' or 'n'"
2030   IF INKEY$(-1)="y" THEN
2040     CLS : AT 3,12
2050     PRINT "BYE!"
2060     PAUSE 100 : initialise
2070     CLOSE#6 : STOP
2080   ELSE
2090     INK 0
2100   END IF
2110 END DEFine
```

APPENDIX 1
RGB PIN CONNECTIONS

Pin	Signal	Specification
1	COMPOSITE MONOCHROME VIDEO	75 ohm 1 volt p-p non-inverting
2	GROUND	
3	PAL	composite PAL *
4	COMPOSITE SYNC	TTL active low
5	VERTICAL SYNC	TTL active high
6	GREEN	TTL active high
7	RED	TTL active high
8	BLUE	TTL active high

*May be suitable for some VCR units

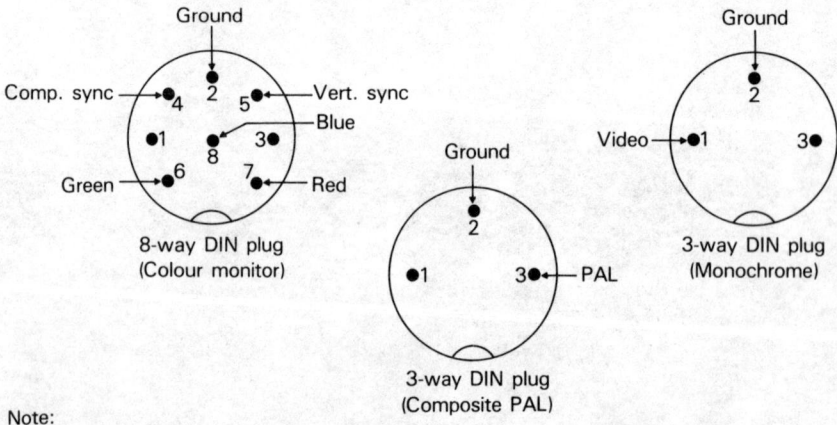

8-way DIN plug
(Colour monitor)

3-way DIN plug
(Composite PAL)

3-way DIN plug
(Monochrome)

Note:
(1) Plugs labelled as when viewed from **rear**.
(2) Some plugs may not have pin numbers labelled. Use physical locations as above.

APPENDIX 2
BINARY NUMBERS AND ALL THAT

INTRODUCTION

In this Appendix you will find sufficient information concerning the binary number system and the exclusive-OR logical function to enable you to create the single-value stipple colour codes discussed in Chapter 2.

BINARY NUMBER SYSTEM

Man must have first learnt to count by using his fingers and thumbs and so a natural number system evolved whereby values from 1 to 10 were used to identify each of the ten digits . . . the **decimal** system.

Computers, however, do not have fingers, but they do have switches – thousands of them – controlling their internal operations. A switch can have two possible conditions, ON or OFF. We can give two values to these conditions such that:

ON = 1
OFF = 0

We can now represent any combination of switch settings as combinations of zeros and ones. For example:

SWITCH:	A	B	C	D	E	F
SETTING:	ON	OFF	OFF	ON	ON	OFF
VALUE:	1	0	0	1	1	0

We have therefore produced a number system where only two values can exist. It is called the **binary** system.

Now, in the decimal system when we write 1243 we really mean:

$1 \times 1000 + 2 \times 100 + 4 \times 10 + 3 \times 1$

Writing it another way:

$1 \times (10 \times 10 \times 10) + 2 \times (10 \times 10) + 4 \times (10) + 3 \times (1)$

The values in brackets are called **weightings**, each being ten times the value of the one to its right. The same principle can be applied to the binary system except that we use 2 instead of 10. So a binary number, for example: 1101 would have the decimal value of:

$1 \times (2 \times 2 \times 2) + 1 \times (2 \times 2) + 0 \times (2) + 1 \times (1)$
i.e.   8   +   4   +   0   +   1
       = 13

You may find this easier to understand if you work it out from right to left.

We do not really need to write down all the 'twos' in this way. First, write the weighting values below the binary number to be converted. Then for every '1' that occurs in the binary number write down its corresponding weighting value. Finally, add up the weighting values to obtain the equivalent decimal number.

For example:

1 0 1 0 1   Binary number to be converted
16 8 4 2 1 weighting
16 + 4 + 1 = 21 in decimal

Note that each weighting is twice the value of the one to its right.

Converting the other way, from decimal to binary, a simple way is by 'inspection'. There are four steps:

1. Write down the weighting values from right to left up to the value which is either equal to or greater than the number being converted.

2. Compare the weighting values with the decimal number starting at the left-hand end.

3. Subtract the weighting value from the number, or remainder if the value is less than or equal to the number or remainder, until a zero remainder is left.

4. Write a '1' where a subtraction occurred.

This example should make it clear:

Convert 106 to binary

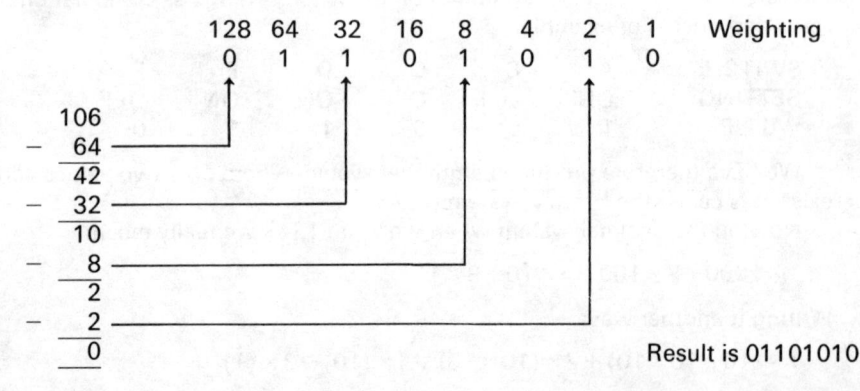

```
                128  64  32  16  8  4  2  1   Weighting
                 0   1   1   0   1  0  1  0
       106
     -  64
       ---
        42
     -  32
       ---
        10
     -   8
       ---
         2
     -   2
       ---
         0
                                    Result is 01101010
```

BITS AND BYTES

You will occasionally see reference to the word **bit**, which is a contraction of **binary digit** (each '1' and '0' in the previous example is a **bit**). If we include the bit number reference in our previous example's binary number we would have:

7	6	5	4	3	2	1	0	Bit number
128	64	32	16	8	4	2	1	Weighting value
0	1	1	0	1	0	1	0	Binary number

The bit with the largest weighting value is called the most significant bit.

The QL works with eight-bit binary words when processing colour codes, the word being called a 'byte'. As you will see if you refer back to Chapter 2, the single-value colour code in binary form actually consists of three separate binary numbers side by side in an eight-bit word. The following table shows the eight colours with their decimal and binary code equivalents.

Colour	Decimal	Binary
Black	0	000
Blue	1	001
Red	2	010
Magenta	3	011
Green	4	100
Cyan	5	101
Yellow	6	110
White	7	111

The stipple codes (0–3) can be represented using only two bits, since the most significant bit is always zero (0 = 00, 1 = 01, 2 = 10, 3 = 11).

EXCLUSIVE-OR

Imagine you have two switches A and B that can either be ON or OFF. There are only four possible combinations in which the switches can exist. Using our earlier one, zero convention, the combinations are:

A	B	Condition
0	0	both off
0	1	either on
1	0	either on
1	1	both on

Supposing our switches were to be connected to a lamp to perform an exclusive-OR function. Then the lamp would only be on if either switch were on. So if both were off or both were on, the lamp would not light. If you have two light switches in your house that control the same light (upstairs/downstairs control of a hall light) they will be wired in this way:

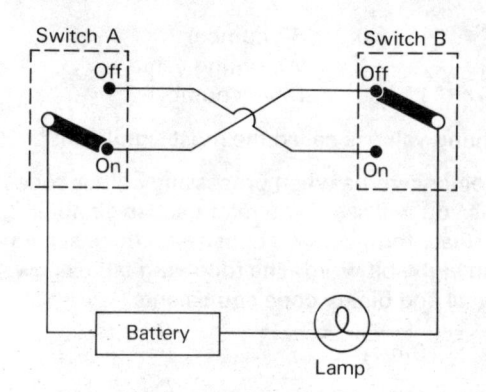

We can represent this action with a logic **truth-table**:

A	B	Exclusive-OR
0	0	0
0	1	1
1	0	1
1	1	0

Every time A and B are unequal in value, the exclusive-OR function will give a '1' result.

If we take two binary numbers and perform an exclusive-OR function, then each pair of bits with the same weighting are treated just like our switches A and B. For example:

Exclusive-OR the binary numbers 010 and 110

Bit value:	2	1	0
First number:	0	1	0
Second number:	1	1	0
Exclusive-OR:	1	0	0

Each column is treated separately, the final result of three bits then being used by the computer.

The first and second numbers' bits for bit 0 and bit 1 are both equal (both ones or both zeros), so the result is zero in the first two columns. The bit 2 pair of bits, however, are opposite – therefore the result is 1 in that column.

Armed with the information in this appendix you should have little trouble converting single-value colour codes to or from binary when required.

APPENDIX 3
COLOUR PALETTE TABLES

It would be impossible to precisely label every colour stipple shade, especially as the final result will depend upon the quality and colour of your monitor. Tables A3.1 and A3.2 show the composite colour codes for all stipple variations in both high- and low-resolution modes. Reference between these tables and the corresponding colour palette program (see Chapter 2) will establish the true colour on your screen.

The two groups of colour shades created by stipple code 0 are indicated thus:

Type 1: main, contrast, stipple
Type 2: contrast, main, stipple

Colour key

Black	B	Green	G
Blue	Bu	Cyan	C
Red	R	Yellow	Y
Magenta	M	White	W

Table A3.1 High resolution

Colour		Stipple code				
Main	Contrast	3	2	1	Type 1	Type 2
B	R	208	144	80	16	18
B	G	224	160	96	32	36
B	W	248	184	120	56	63
R	G	242	178	114	50	52
R	W	234	170	106	42	47
G	W	220	156	92	28	31

Table A3.2 Low resolution

Colour		Stipple code				
Main	Contrast	3	2	1	Type 1	Type 2
B	Bu	200	137	72	8	9
B	R	208	144	80	16	18
B	M	216	152	88	24	27
B	G	224	160	96	32	36
B	C	232	168	104	40	45
B	Y	240	176	112	48	54
B	W	248	184	120	56	63
Bu	R	217	153	89	25	26
Bu	M	209	145	81	17	19
Bu	G	233	169	105	41	44
Bu	C	225	161	97	33	37
Bu	Y	249	185	121	57	62
Bu	W	241	177	113	49	55
R	M	202	138	74	10	11
R	G	242	178	114	50	52
R	C	250	186	122	58	61
R	Y	226	162	98	34	38
R	W	234	170	106	42	47
M	G	251	187	123	59	60
M	C	243	179	115	51	53
M	Y	235	171	107	43	46
M	W	227	163	99	35	39
G	C	204	140	76	12	13
G	Y	217	148	84	20	22
G	W	220	156	92	28	31
C	Y	221	157	93	29	30
C	W	213	149	85	21	23
Y	W	206	142	78	14	15

APPENDIX 4
SINE CURVE GENERATION

To generate a sine-wave curve we used a formula:

POINT x, INT (SIN(x * PI/250) * 150 + 0.5)

The numeric expression is equivalent to the y co-ordinate. This is how the expression is created:
To draw a sine wave we start with the basic formula of:

y = SIN (x)

This defines the value of y for every value of x, so every point on the curve will have the co-ordinates of (x, SIN (x)).
Now, the X-axis range as shown in the figure is:

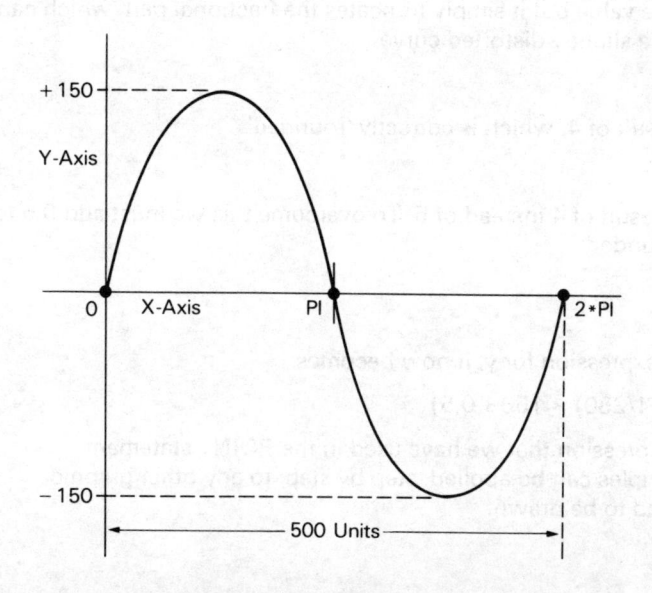

0 TO 2 * PI radians

In our example this axis is 500 units long. Therefore each unit must be equivalent to:

2 * PI/500 radians

This simplifies to:

PI/250 radians

Hence the value, in radians, of any point x on the X-axis must be:

(x * PI/250) radians

Therefore on the curve the y co-ordinate equivalent to each x point is going to be:

y = SIN(x * PI/250)

However, the sine of an angle can give only a value in the range:

−1 TO +1

This means that the resultant value for y could be only one unit positive or negative at its maximum. To enable the curve to fill the screen in the Y-axis we scale up this sine value by multiplying, in this instance, by 150.

y = SIN(x * PI/250) * 150

Now, y will vary between:

−150 TO +150

The values will, though, have fractional parts which must be rounded off to whole (integer) values, since we cannot select part of a pixel. The function INT will 'integerise' the value but it simply truncates the fractional part, which can lead to errors and a slightly distorted curve.

INT (4.2)

This will give a result of 4, which is correctly 'rounded'.

INT (4.9)

This also gives a result of 4 instead of 5. To overcome this we must add 0.5 to the value to be rounded:

4.9 + 0.5 = 5.4
INT (5.4) = 5

Returning to our expression for y, it now becomes:

INT (SIN(x * PI/250) * 150 + 0.5)

This is the final expression that we have used in the POINT statement.
The same principles can be applied, step by step, to any other graphic expression required to be drawn.

SOLUTIONS TO PROBLEMS

The solutions offered, with the exception of those for Chapter 1, are not intended to be unique. There are often several ways in which a program may be written. It is hoped that should you need to refer to those in this section they will help to 'put you back on the rails' towards your own solutions.

CHAPTER 1

1. The QL's memory 'forgets' your program.

2. F2 Function key.

3. Top left-hand window (coloured white at switch_on).

4. 'a' and 'c' are incorrect.

5. 'c' – picture quality is degraded.

6. The one labelled 'RGB'.

7. The smallest single area of illumination that can be displayed on a screen.

8. 512

9. 40

10. You will lose definition and possibly strain your eyes.

CHAPTER 2

1.
```
100 REMark * primary/secondary *
110 MODE 8 : BORDER 10,4
120 FOR colour = 1,2,4,0,3,5,6,7
130    PAPER colour : CLS
140    PAUSE 50
150 END FOR colour
```

The BORDER parameter gives the thickness at the top and bottom. The sides are twice that value.

2.  ```
    100 REMark * split screen *
    110 MODE 8 : PAPER 4 : INK 6 : CLS
    120 FOR down = 1 TO 4 : PRINT
    130 PRINT "      GREEN"
    140 FOR down = 1 TO 5 : PRINT
    150 PAPER 5 : INK 3 : CLS 2
    160 FOR down = 1 TO 5 : PRINT
    170 PRINT "      CYAN"
    ```

3.  ```
    100 REMark * flash/strip/over *
    110 MODE 8 : PAPER 5 : INK 2 : CLS
    120 PRINT "THIS SHOWS";
    130 FLASH 1 : PRINT!"FLASH ";
    140 FLASH 0 : STRIP 0
    150 PRINT"STRIP"; : STRIP 5
    160 PRINT!"AND"; : OVER -1
    170 PRINT!"OVER" : OVER 0
    180 PAUSE 100 : RECOL 1,1,5,3,4,6,6,2
    ```

Note the space left after FLASH at the end of line 130 and the absence of an 'intelligent' space (!) before STRIP on line 150. This prevents the STRIP colour starting from the next character position after the word FLASH. The OVER-1 keyword produces the exclusive-OR colour change to give white ink, but do remember to turn it off (line 170) when you have finished with it!

CHAPTER 3

1.  ```
    100 REMark * random blocks *
    110 WINDOW 460,200,20,20
    120 MODE 8 : PAPER 7 : CLS
    130 REPeat blocks
    140   FOR number = 1 TO 50
    150     LET across = RND(5 TO 435)
    160     LET down = RND(5 TO 175)
    170     LET colour = RND(7)
    180     LET contrast = RND(7)
    190     BLOCK 20,20,across,down,colour,contrast
    200   END FOR number
    210   REPeat wait : IF INKEY$ <>"" THEN EXIT wait
    220   IF KEYROW(1)= 8 THEN EXIT blocks
    230 END REPeat blocks
    ```

The ESC key has been chosen as the one to stop the program. Any other key will repeat the process.
    ```

2.
```
100 REMark * windowed   block *
110 MODE 8 : WINDOW 512,256,0,0
120 PAPER 6 : CLS : CLOSE#2
130 WINDOW 200,100,156,78
140 PAPER 0 : CLS
150 OPEN#5,scr_80x100a356x78
160 PAPER#5,2 : CLS#5
170 BLOCK 50,20,75,40,4
180 BLOCK#5,50,20,15,40,7
190 CLOSE#5 : OPEN#2,scr_
```

Two points here. When reducing the default channel window (#1) in size, it will reveal the channel 2 window (the 'listing' window) behind it. CLOSE # 2 removes the blue window and allows all the yellow background to be seen. We have restored #2 at the end of the program.

When placing blocks within windows remember that their co-ordinates are relative to their respective window, not the whole screen area.

3.
```
100 REMark * scroll & pan *
110 MODE 8 : WINDOW 260,100,110,50
120 PAPER 5 : INK 2 : CLS
130 PRINT "MY NAME HERE"
140 FOR row = 1 TO 90
150   SCROLL 1
160 END FOR row
170 FOR column = 1 TO 130
180   PAN 2
190 END FOR column
```

The direction of the scroll and pan action is the only thing to be aware of here.

CHAPTER 4

1.
```
100 REMark * square move *
110 MODE 4 : WINDOW 400,200,20,20
120 PAPER 7 : INK 4 : CLS
130 FOR factor = 180,300
140   SCALE factor,0,0
150   LINE 20,40 TO 140,40 TO 140,160 TO 20,160 TO 20,40
160   PAUSE 100
170 END FOR factor
180 LET scale_change = 300/180
190 SCALE factor,-80*(scale_change-1),-100*(scale_change-1)
200 LINE 20,40 TO 140,40 TO 140,160 TO 20,160 TO 20,40
```

The example emphasises the need to draw the square after each scale-change operation. Also note that on leaving the loop the variable 'factor' still has the value of 300.

2.  ```
    100 REMark * big H *
    110 MODE 8 : WINDOW 350,220,20,20
    120 PAPER 1 : INK 7 : CLS
    130 SCALE 299,0,0
    140 LINE 25,20 TO 25,266
    150 LINE 325,20 TO 325,266
    160 LET colour = 2
    170 FOR bar = 25 TO 300 STEP 25
    180   FOR segment = 0 TO 24
    190     INK colour
    200     POINT bar+segment,143
    210   END FOR segment
    220   LET colour = colour ^^ 5
    230 END FOR bar
    ```

    Lines 180 to 210 display each group of 25 pixels. The change of colour has been achieved by using a bit-wise exclusive OR operation between the current colour value and 5. This operation exclusive-ORs the binary values. Hence:

    2 (010) XOR 5 (101) = 7 (111)
    7 (111) XOR 5 (101) = 2 (101)

3.  ```
    100 REMark * cosine wave *
    110 MODE 4 : WINDOW 490,220,10,10
    120 PAPER 4 : INK 2 : CLS
    130 SCALE 300,-245,-150
    140 LINE -245,0 TO 245,0
    150 LINE 0,-150 TO 0,150
    160 FOR x = -245 TO 245
    170   POINT x,INT(COS(x*PI/245)*150+.5)
    180 END FOR x
    ```

    The graphics origin offset at line 130 allows all points to be plotted with respect to (0, 0) at the centre of the window. The cosine formula is very similar to that produced for the sine curve in Appendix 4, except that the x-axis range is 245 units for PI radians.

4.  ```
    100 REMark * arc petals *
    110 MODE 8 : WINDOW 260,200,125,20
    120 PAPER 5 : INK 4 : CLS
    130 SCALE 200,0,0
    140 LINE 0,0 TO 190,200
    150 LINE 0,200 TO 190,0
    160 ARC 95,100 TO 0,0,PI/6 TO 95,100,PI/6
    170 ARC TO 0,200,PI/6 TO 95,100,PI/6
    180 ARC TO 190,200,PI/6 TO 95,100,PI/6
    190 ARC TO 190,0,PI/6 TO 95,100,PI/6
    ```

    Care is needed to ensure each arc is drawn in the right direction to produce the curve on the correct side of the line. The number of units in the x-axis, required to be known for the LINE and ARC statements, was obtained from the standard formula derived earlier in Chapter 4.
    ```

5.  ```
    100 REMark * circle/ellipse *
    110 PAPER 4 :INK 2 : CLS
    120 ELLIPSE 75,50,20,1.5,0;75,50,20;75,50,30
    ```

    The outer circle has a radius equal to half the major axis of the ellipse. The latter being eccentricity * 2 * height.

6.  ```
    100 REMark * around disc *
    110 MODE 8 : WINDOW 465,200,15,15
    120 PAPER 0 : INK 2 : CLS
    130 FILL 1 : CIRCLE 75,50,30 : FILL 0
    140 REPeat around
    150   LINE 75,50 : INK 7
    160   LET angle = RAD(RND(360))
    170   FILL 1
    180   CIRCLE_R 40*COS(angle),40*SIN(angle),10
    190   FILL 0 : INK 6
    200   LINE TO 75,50
    210   PAUSE 15 : INK 0 : FILL 1
    220   CIRCLE_R 40*COS(angle),40*SIN(angle),10 : FILL 0
    230 END REPeat around
    ```

    The LINE statement at line 150 is used to place the cursor at the centre of the red disc each time around the loop. It has been used solely to demonstrate use of the more compact relative CIRCLE statement at line 180. With the cursor then positioned at the centre of the smaller circle, the LINE statement at line 200 needs to have only the return point defined. Line 220 can also use a relative CIRCLE statement, since the cursor is back at the centre again.

CHAPTER 5

1.  ```
    100 REMark * name move *
    110 MODE 8 : WINDOW 420,200,45,20
    120 PAPER 0 : INK 2 : CLS
    130 AT 0,14
    140 PRINT "MY NAME" : INK 6
    150 PAUSE 50
    160 FOR down = 1 TO 95
    170   IF down = 50 THEN CIRCLE 77,50,30
    180   CURSOR 168,down
    190   PRINT "MY NAME"
    200 END FOR down
    ```

    Line 170 waits for the text to move within the circle's circumference before drawing the circle – otherwise attempting to move the text over the drawn circle would remove part of the circle. Using OVER 1 would not help, since although it would not erase the circle it would create a yellow shadow effect for the text.
    ```

2.
```
100 REMark * ladder numbers *
110 MODE 8 : WINDOW 465,200,15,15
120 PAPER 0 : INK 7 : CLS : CSIZE 3,1
130 LINE 20,20 TO 150,20
140 LINE 20,40 TO 150,40
150 FOR rung = 0 TO 6
160    LET x_start = 25+rung*20
170    LINE x_start,20 TO x_start,40
180    CURSOR x_start,20,20,-30
190    IF rung <>6 THEN PRINT rung+1
200 END FOR rung
```

The offset values (20, −30) at line 180 can be found by trial and error, but they can also be calculated using these values:

In X-axis: 465 pixels = 170 units
  so 20 units = 55 pixels = distance between rungs.
In Y-axis: 200 pixels = 100 units
  so 20 units = 40 pixels = distance between sides.

CHAPTER 6

1.
```
PAPER 0 : CLS : INK 7
PENDOWN
POINT 75,50
TURNTO 45
MOVE 50
PENUP
MOVE -100
PENDOWN
MOVE 50
TURN 90
MOVE 50
PENUP
MOVE -100
PENDOWN
MOVE 50
PENUP
```

The drawing sequence begins and ends with the cursor at the centre of the screen. The use of PENUP/DOWN commands prevented overprinting, which would have given a more ragged line.

2.
```
100 REMark * rectangle *
110 DEFine PROCedure rectangle (x_start,y_start)
120 PENDOWN
130 POINT x_start,y_start
140 LET angle = 0
150 FOR sides = 26,15,26,15
160    TURNTO angle
170    MOVE sides
```

```
180        LET angle = angle+90
190     END FOR sides
200     PENUP
210 END DEFine
```

Calling the procedure in direct command mode will draw a rectangle in the current INK colour at any specified position.

3.
```
300 REMark * tri-rectangles *
310 MODE 8 : WINDOW 512,256,0,0
320 PAPER 0 : CLS
330 FOR layers = 5 TO 1 STEP -1
340   LET y_start = 10+(5-layers)*15
350   FOR bricks = 0 TO layers-1
360     LET x_start = 10+(5-layers)*13+bricks*26
370     INK RND(1 TO 7) : FILL 1
380     rectangle x_start,y_start
390     FILL 0
400   END FOR bricks
410 END FOR layers
```

Line 340 establishes the starting value for *y* for each layer, while line 360 defines the *x* starting value for each brick of each layer. The program could, of course, have been more easily written by using the BLOCK keyword and dispensing with the rectangle procedure, but it was, after all, a 'turtle' exercise.

CHAPTER 7

1. Axis 1 change: [F3] [E] [L] [F4] $\times 12$

2. SHIFT & TABULATE to move crosswire back to cell 1.

3. Enter new labels: Type SUN [TABULATE]

   Repeat for MON to SAT then: [ENTER]

4. Restore to full size: [V] [ENTER] [ENTER]

5. Edit main title: [E] [T]

   Move crosswires to 'Title': [ENTER]

   Delete 'Title': [CTRL] [↑]

   Type: INVOICES [ENTER]

   Move crosswires to centre 'INVOICES' on 'WED' cell: [ENTER]

6. Edit Axis 1: [E] [A] [H]

   Delete 'Axis 1': [CTRL] [↑]

   Type: DAY [ENTER]

   Move crosswires to centre 'DAY' below 'WED' cell: [ENTER]

7. Edit Axis 2: [E] [A] [V]
   Delete 'Axis 2': [CTRL] [↑]
   Type: QUANTITY [ENTER]
   Move crosswires to centre 'QUANTITY' at '5' label: [ENTER]
8. Enter quantities: [ESC]

   1 5 [ENTER]

   Repeat for 230 to 52
9. Restore to full size: [F3] [V] [ENTER] [ENTER]

The figure below shows the completed graph.

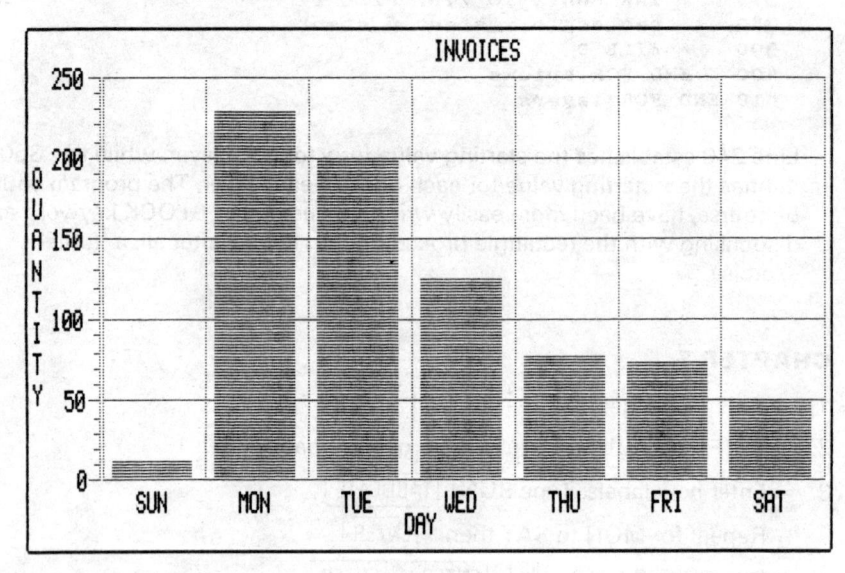

INDEX

arc
  angle range 75
  position 74
  size 78
ARC 72
ARC_R 90
At 108
axis 178
  choice 179
  major 84
  minor 84

BACKUP 187
bandwidth 5, 7
bar 172
  choice 173
  design 173
  graph 137, 167
BAUD rate 190
BEEP 192, 193
  parameters 194
  repetition 195
BEEPING 192, 193
BLOCK 42
BORDER 20
border thickness 173

cell
  deletion 155
  insertion 150
  quantity 155
CHANGE 172
channel 12, 34
  number 34
character 7
  block graphics, 113
  design grid 113
  generation 112
  movement 111
  pixel graphics 117
  positioning 103
  size 101
chromatic scale 198

CIRCLE 80
CIRCLE_R 90
CLOSE 36
CLS 18
colour
  principles 15
  selection 17
COMMANDS 145
concert pitch 197
CONFIG_BAS 191
CONsole 36
control area 143
co-ordinates
  absolute 54
  cartesian 53
  graphics 52
  pixel 31
  polar 82
  relative 54, 87
crosswire
  control 148
  horizontal 148
  vertical 148
crosswires 147
crotchet duration 200
CSIZE 101
CURSOR 103
cursor 9
curves 71

data entry mode 141
default
  microdrive 185
  screen 10
DELETE 187
delete key 150
demodulator 4
design
  implementation 172
  storage 174
device selection 191
direction control 122
display limitation 166

duration 194
  negative values 196

EASEL
  back-up 139
  BOOT program 191
  colour 138
  loading 140
  resolution 138, 141
EDIT 153
editing 152
  axes 155
  key 156
ellipse
  eccentricity 84
  height 84
  rotation 84
ELLIPSE 84
ELLIPSE_R 90
equation 151
ESCAPE 145
exit 156
EXPORT 187
exporting graph data 188

F1 8, 9, 11
F2 8, 11
false line colours 178
figure centring 63
file
  name 184
  protection 186
FILES 186
FILL 91
FLASH 26
flat 198
format
  selection 171
  types 167–70
formatting 139
formula application 159
frequency 196
fuzz 194, 203

GPRINT_PRT 189
grad_x 194, 201
grad_y 194, 201
graph
  colour 166
  design 166
  expansion 148
  formats 167
  paper 178
  storage 184
  transfer 184
graphics origin 58

HELP 143
HIGHLIGHT 180, 183

IMPORT 187
INK 19
input line 146
INTGX132_PRT 190

JX80_PRT 190

KILL 156

label editing 154
line 174
  choice 175
  design 175
  editor 152
  example 175
  graph 137, 167
  numbers 13
  thickness 175
LINE 54
LINE_R 89
LOAD 186
logical file 35
LOGO 121

main display 142, 147
microdrive rules 2, 11
middle C 198
MODE 4 7, 16
MODE 8 7, 16
mode selection 17
modulator 4
monitor 3, 5, 11
  mode 9
MOVE 123
multi-beep 204
multiple
  bar design 174
  graphs 158
musical scale 197

name limitations 161
NEWDATA 161
number 149
  deletion 150
  source 162

octave 198
OLDDATA 160
OPEN 36
put of memory error 158
OVER 28
overprinting 111

PAN 49
PAPER 18
PENDOWN 122
PENUP 122
permanent copy 189
pie chart 137, 167, 170, 181
  creation 181
  editing 183
  HIGHLIGHT 183
  segment option 182
pitch 196
pitch_1 194, 201
pitch_2 194, 201
pixel 6
  graphics 32
  size 7
point 55
POINT 65
POINT_R 88
primary colours 15
PRINT 189
print driver 189
printing 189
PRINT TO 110
program interruption 1
PROMPTS 144

QL sound 192
quadrant 61
QUIT 156

RAD 73
radian 73
random 194, 203
RECOL 30, 38
RENAME 161
reset 1
resolution 3, 6
  formula 68
  low 69
  maximum 68
rests 199

RGB socket 6

SAVE 185
  method 185
scale 53, 57
  factor 57
  graphics 53
  pixel relationship 105
SCReen 36
screen
  dump 191
  formats 8
SCROLL 46
sector 140
segment 180
semi-tone 198
sharp 198
sinewave 71, 164
sound
  channel 193
  selection program 193, 205
status area 146
stave 198
stipple 21, 29
STRIP 27
subtended angle 73

text 150
  editing 153
  design 179
  movement 151
  styles 179
timing 199
tone 198
transmission rate 190
TURN 123
TURNTO 122
turtle
  circle 128
  graphics 121
  patterns 133
  routines 129
TV mode 10

UHF socket 5
UNDER 110

VIEW 159, 171

window
  creation 33
  identification 12
WINDOW 39
wrap 194, 202

ZAP 156